822.409
M35r

96136

DATE DUE			
Dec 2 '76			
Apr 25 '80			

Restoration Serious Drama

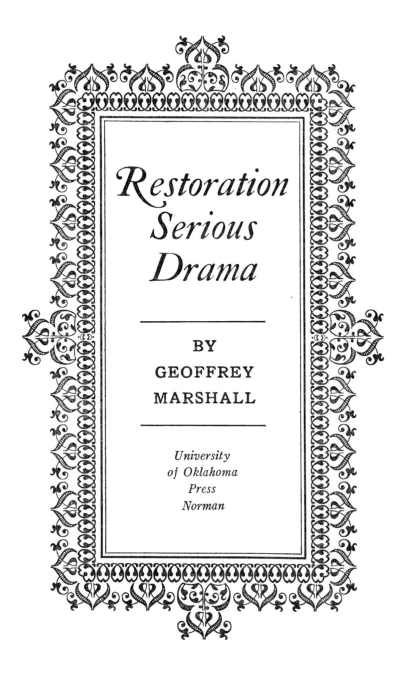

Restoration Serious Drama

BY

GEOFFREY
MARSHALL

*University
of Oklahoma
Press
Norman*

Library of Congress Cataloging in Publication Data

Marshall, Geoffrey, 1938–
  Restoration serious drama.

  Includes bibliographical references.
  1. English drama—Restoration, 1660–1700—History and criticism.
I. Title.
PR691.M37   822'.4'09   74–15901
ISBN 0–8061–1259–X

This book is dedicated to my parents

Ray A. Marshall
and
Mary E. Marshall

who never said a discouraging word

Preface

A key statement for the study which follows appears in John Dryden's "Of Heroic Plays: An Essay" (1672): "It is very clear to all who understand poetry that serious plays ought not to imitate conversation too nearly."[1] To begin with, I have borrowed the term *serious* to indicate that I wish to consider a variety of plays having in common the fact that laughter and amusement are not their primary aims. The plays under study are sometimes tragedies and sometimes historical plays, tragicomedies, or other hybrid genres. I hope that the term *serious* will serve to circumvent questions of definition of genre.

I have been fascinated by the logic of Dryden's assertion about the nature of poetic language and the implications of that logic for critical response to the serious drama of the Restoration. Dryden, I think, is able to write with such conviction that conversation and poetry are not the same because the difference between them is, for him, a matter of conventional wisdom.

Poetry and colloquial discursive prose are as dissimilar as hands and feet; they are relatable, but obviously different.

It seems to me, moreover, that most literary historians have read the serious drama of the Restoration without understanding that for Dryden and his contemporaries certain conventions were natural, necessary, and beyond reasonable dispute. These conventions, in turn, shaped the way in which the playwrights of the era conveyed their ideas and their emotions concerning those things which have touched artists of all ages—love, fear, mutability, political power, despair, hope. . . . Restoration playwrights wrote as they did, I believe, in part because it was "very clear to all who understand poetry" that this was the way to write.

On the other hand, the literary historians of this century have read the plays and found them failures precisely because "it is very clear to all who understand poetry" in our age that this is *not* the way to write poetic drama. Furthermore, we have tended to assume that the failure to write in the way we believe serious drama should be written is a failure of character, of understanding, of historical sensitivity, of verbal creativity, of perception, of common sense. We look back on Restoration drama with the same historical arrogance and vanity as the critic who looks at Egyptian bas-relief and wonders what those artists might have achieved if they had only understood perspective.

My assumption is that the men of the Restoration were in no significant way less sensitive to life than we are. If their serious drama seems flawed to us, then the "flaws" must be the result of the way in which they made their plays, not the result of a failure in them as men. In fact, it is probably more illuminating not to think of the plays as flawed at all, but as different—exhibiting different conventions of art. I hope that what follows is in the spirit of the history of science, which does not chide the Greeks for their failure to understand about gases, or in the spirit of cultural anthropology, which does not, when it is being practiced properly, find one puberty ritual preferable to, or less sophisticated than, another.

I find most literary history of the Restoration to be patronizing, impatient, and judgmental, and I am curious about why we find these plays so unpleasant. I would like to say immediately that I would not enjoy—except for historical curiosity's sake—seeing any number of these plays performed. Why would the generation which produced *The Man of Mode* have produced *The Empress of Morocco*, a play which Eugene Waith has described as "an exciting tale of villainous intrigues and true love between comic-strip characters, whose only claim to heroism is the violence of their ambitions and desires"?[2] How could Dryden write both *Mac Flecknoe* and *Tyrannick Love?* How is it we are able to read *Religio Laici* with pleasure and not Otway's *The Orphan?*

Part of the answer may lie in Northrop Frye's observation that we are sensitive to the overornate, just as earlier periods, like the Restoration, were sensitive to the "low."[3] But the Restoration satirists, such as Butler, for example, seem as sensitive to bombast as we are. It may be that we find the serious plays an unsatisfactory handling of questions of public power, as Thomas R. Edwards has suggested: " 'Serious' drama . . . deal[s] with public greatness either by abstracting it entirely from credible human worlds, as in the Heroick Play of Dryden's theatre, or by banishing it from the stage altogether in favor of 'domestic' tragic actions, as in Lillo or Rowe."[4] And yet the Earl of Clarendon's history of the Civil War seems a mature confrontation with some aspects of public greatness. What, then, is the matter with the drama?

My argument is that there is nothing wrong with the *matter* of the serious drama. The substance of these plays involves themes which have affected most generations. The plays exhibit the anguish which comes from the loss of peace within a man or a nation. They exhibit the intensity, the futility, the momentary victories in the battles of the reason and the will against the energies of appetite and the power of our passions. What makes these plays seem alien to us is the *manner* in which this subject matter is treated, and the chasm which exists between their standards of decorum and our own.

The first chapter offers an argument that these plays are serious in the sense that they explore important human questions with dignity and intelligence. The second chapter examines some of the ways in which this serious exploration was realized, especially the propensity of the age for situations of explicit choice. The third chapter defines manners and decorum and argues that these concepts appropriately define the theoretical conventions shaping all drama in the era. The fourth chapter is devoted to the diction of the plays, the aspect which we find now so repellent, or tedious, or exasperating and which they found the fitting medium. The fifth chapter explores three related topics: the relationship between comedy and tragedy in the Restoration, which I believe was close; the appearance, effects, and meaning of sentimentalism and sensibility; and, at the end of the century, the emerging signs of a crisis in aesthetics, a crisis over the definition of comedy and of tragedy, a crisis which I believe has not yet been resolved.

The arguments which follow are assertive and discursive rather than explicatory. The examples chosen are typically familiar rather than remote because Restoration serious drama is not readily available to most of us. The nineteenth-century editions are performance texts and are untrustworthy; modern editions are excellent, but there are too few of them; and the originals are the treasures of only a few libraries. Therefore, while the number and scope of examples and citations are, I hope, representative, the study does not rely upon fleeting references to plays which exist in unique copies in the Bodleian.

The chapters do not contain extensive explications. Instead, the focus is on the nature of the conventions from which the plays emerge, and which they in turn embody. There are many more pages devoted to discussion of context than to the revelation of theme in specific passages or specific plays. On the other hand, I hope there is something other than a review of scholarship here. I think much of our study of Restoration serious drama begins from a wrong set of assumptions, assumptions which are established and carried by literary history and other forms of literary scholarship. When I discuss that scholarship, it is never with the intention of anthologizing, but always with the intention of pointing toward a new perspective for future study.

In some ways this study is old-fashioned, at least in the sense that it seems to me now, when it is complete, to have come, however imperfectly, out of the spirit described by Alfred North Whitehead in *Science and the Modern World* (1925): "Faith in reason is the trust that the ultimate natures of things lie together in a harmony which excludes mere arbitrariness. It is the faith that at the base of things we shall not find mere arbitrary mystery."[5]

GEOFFREY MARSHALL

Norman, Oklahoma
May, 1974

Acknowledgments

I have some particular debts of gratitude which I would like to repay here. Several years ago I was granted a summer research fellowship by the University of Oklahoma Alumni Development Fund which enabled me to do months of uninterrupted reading. More recently I received support from the University's Faculty Research Committee which made possible bibliographic and other research at the Henry E. Huntington Library. I cannot mention the Huntington Library without expressing my appreciation of the courtesy and skillful professional help which the staff accorded me and accords everyone who comes to make use of the collection. It was an extraordinary pleasure for me to work there. Finally, I wish to acknowledge the patience and care with which the manuscript was prepared (and often saved from my careless errors) by Mrs. Teri Brackin.

G. M.

Contents

Editions of Plays Cited

Addison, Joseph.
Cato. London, J. Tonson, 1713

Banks, John.
The Innocent Usurper; or, The Death of the Lady Jane Gray. London, R. Bentley, 1694.
The Island Queens; or, The Death of Mary, Queen of Scotland. London, R. Bentley, 1684.
The Unhappy Favourite; or, The Earl of Essex. London, Richard Bentley and Mary Magnes, 1682.

Behn, Aphra.
Abdelazer; or, The Moor's Revenge. London, J. Magnes and R. Bentley, 1677.

Buckingham, George Villiers, second Duke of.
The Rehearsal. London, Thomas Dring, 1672.

Caryll, John.
The English Princess; or, The Death of Richard the III. London, Thomas Dring, 1667.

Congreve, William.
> *The Way of the World* (1700). Ed. by Kathleen M. Lynch. Lincoln, University of Nebraska Press, 1965.

Crowne, John.
> *The Destruction of Jerusalem by Titus Vespasian*. London, James Magnes and Richard Bentley, 1677.
>
> *Juliana; or, The Princess of Poland*. London, William Cademan, 1671.
>
> *The Misery of Civil-War*. London, R. Bentley and M. Magnes, 1680.

Davenant, William.
> *The Seige of Rhodes*. London, Henry Herringman, 1656.

Dryden, John.
> *All for Love; or, The World Well Lost*. London, Henry Herringman, 1678.
>
> *Amboyna*. London, Henry Herringman, 1673.
>
> *Aureng-Zebe*. London, Henry Herringman, 1676.
>
> *Cleomenes, The Spartan Heroe*. London, Jacob Tonson, 1692.
>
> *The Conquest of Granada by the Spaniards*. London, H. Herringman, 1672.
>
> *Don Sebastian, King of Portugal*. London, Jo. Hindmarsh, 1690.
>
> *The Duke of Guise* (with Nathaniel Lee). London, R. Bentley and J. Tonson, 1683.
>
> *The Indian Emperour* (1667). Ed. by John Loftis. Vol. IX of the California Edition of *The Works of John Dryden*. Berkeley, University of California Press, 1956–.
>
> *The Indian Queen* (1665). Ed. by John Harrington Smith and Dougald MacMillan. Vol. VIII of the California Edition.
>
> *Secret Love, or The Maiden Queen* (1668). Ed. by John Loftis. Vol. IX of the California Edition.
>
> *The Spanish Fryar; or, The Double Discovery*. London, Richard and Jacob Tonson, 1681.
>
> *Troilus and Cressida; or, Truth Found Too Late*. London, Jacob Tonson, 1679.
>
> *Tyrannick Love; or, The Royal Martyr* (1670). Ed. by Maximillian E. Novak. Vol. X of the California Edition.

Etherege, George.
> *The Man of Mode* (1676). Ed. by W. B. Carnochan. Lincoln, University of Nebraska Press, 1966.

Fielding, Henry.
   Tom Thumb. London, J. Roberts, 1730.
Gay, John.
   The Beggar's Opera (1728). Ed. by Edgar V. Roberts. Lincoln,
   University of Nebraska Press, 1969.
Lee, Nathaniel.
   The Works of Nathaniel Lee. Ed. by Thomas B. Stroup and Arthur
   L. Cooke. 2 vols. New Brunswick, New Jersey, Scarecrow Press,
   1954–55.
   Lucius Junius Brutus (1681). Vol. II.
   The Rival Queens, or The Death of Alexander the Great (1677).
   Vol. I.
   Sophonisba, or Hannibal's Overthrow (1676). Vol. I.
   Theodosius: or, The Force of Love (1680). Vol. II.
Lillo, George.
   The London Merchant (1731). Ed. by William H. McBurney. Lin-
   coln, University of Nebraska Press, 1965.
Orrery, Roger Boyle, first Earl of.
   The Dramatic Works of Roger Boyle, Earl of Orrery. Ed. by Wil-
   liam Smith Clark. 2 vols. Cambridge, Massachusetts, Harvard
   University Press, 1937.
   The Tragedy of Mustapha, The Son of Solyman the Magnificent
   (1668). Vol. I.
Otway, Thomas.
   The Works of Thomas Otway. Ed. by J. C. Ghosh. 2 vols. Oxford,
   Clarendon Press, 1932.
   Alcibiades (1675). Vol. I.
   Don Carlos, Prince of Spain (1676). Vol. I.
   The History and Fall of Caius Marius (1680). Vol. I.
   The Orphan: or, The Unhappy-Marriage (1680). Vol. II.
   Venice Preserv'd, or, A Plot Discover'd (1682). Vol. II.
Ravenscroft, Edward.
   King Edgar and Alfreda. London, M. Turner, 1677.
Rowe, Nicholas.
   The Fair Penitent. London, Jacob Tonson, 1703.
   Tamerlane. London, Jacob Tonson, 1702.
Settle, Elkanah.
   Cambyses, King of Persia. London, William Cademan, 1671.
   The Empress of Morocco. London, William Cademan, 1673.

The Female Prelate; Being the History of the Life and Death of Pope Joan. London, William Cademan, 1680.

Ibrahim, The Illustrious Bassa. London, W. Cademan, 1677.

Southerne, Thomas.

The Fatal Marriage; or, The Innocent Adultery. London, Jacob Tonson, 1694.

The Fate of Capua. London, Benjamin Tooke, 1700.

The Loyal Brother; or, The Persian Prince. London, William Cademan, 1682.

Oroonoko. London, H. Playford, B. Tooke and S. Buckley, 1696.

Steele, Richard.

The Conscious Lovers (1723). Ed. by Shirley Strum Kenny. Lincoln, University of Nebraska Press, 1968.

Wycherley, William.

The Plain Dealer (1677). Ed. by Leo Hughes. Lincoln, University of Nebraska Press, 1967.

NOTE: Inverted letters, wrong fonts, and other obvious compositor's errors have been silently corrected. All act, scene, and line references (or, if lines are unnumbered, page references) are made parenthetically in the text.

Restoration Serious Drama

1

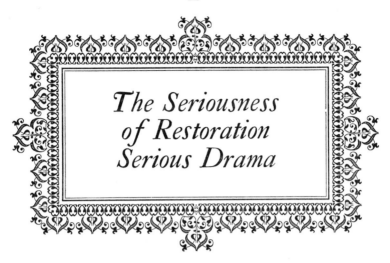

*The Seriousness
of Restoration
Serious Drama*

I

Restoration drama is often bombastic, arrogant, tedious, prolix, and unconvincing. Its settings are remote in place and time and its characters remote from modern standards of psychological verisimilitude. The characterization is formulaic, and the dialogue is at times Renaissance schoolbook dialectics and at other times paroxysms of exclamation, self-pity, and denunciation. The plots are implausible, the themes difficult, and the possibilities for production in the twentieth century not worth discussing. And yet at the same time the Restoration produced thirty or forty years of great comedy. Some of the same men who wrote the tragedies wrote important literary criticism, memorable lyric and satiric poetry, and, sometimes, comedies.

As historians, we could explain the incredible features of Restoration serious drama as matters of taste, about which there is no disputing. Taste is obviously an important component in the literature of any era. We could, and we do, explain the nature of this drama as frankly escapist—as drama meant to per-

3

form an emotional catharsis, not Aristotelian, but Elizabethan
—that is, as plays that were simply pills to purge melancholy.
We could, and we do, explain the nature of this drama as pro-
jection and wish-fulfillment. The Restoration audience, this explanation suggests, surrounded by court chicanery and pettiness,
went to the theater to be reminded of heroism and tragic grandeur. They could, as it were, be heroic for three hours without
fear of obligation to reality. As they left the Duke's Company
performance, they could reassume their worldly wisdom and yet
know, deep inside them, that they understood heroism and ap-
plauded it and would, indeed, even perform it if these were only
different times.

And yet these explanations must leave nagging doubts in us
because it does not seem plausible that men who showed such
acerbic taste in one another's public and private performance,
men who understood their fellow men as well as Pepys, Dryden,
Rochester, Hobbes, and Clarendon obviously did, would create,
accept, and praise a literature so empty of meaning. This was
an era when men were aware of the difference between rhetoric
and logic (either from Ramistic schooling or from the new science, or from experience) and for that reason alone the historian
must be dissatisfied with a description that shows them swathed
in bombast and liking it.

I am curious, as others have been, about why Dryden, for
instance, was able to create Almanzor, Achitophel, and Don
Sebastian all in one creative lifetime. If we are right in thinking
that the court of Charles II was intensely political, that it was a
place of lying, conniving, deceit, disguise, and dread, then how
could the courtiers accept the patent unreality of the courts
described in heroic drama? There is one important and obvious
answer to such a question: that is, the Restoration audience defined their serious drama in such a way as to include the unrealistic, the remote, and the bombastic. They did not merely
accept these features in an evening's entertainment—they demanded them. After all, today's politician might willingly sus-
pend disbelief in order to enjoy a portrayal of the workings of
Washington or London or Moscow which he knew to be untrue

4

to the facts, exaggerated, and romanticized. We all accept the implausible in the cause of amusement.

But the doctrine of the willing suspension of disbelief cannot explain why intelligent men would passionately defend the unreasonable in terms of its rational content. Dryden and Rymer and Hobbes and Dennis did not argue that Restoration serious drama was entertaining and should therefore be accepted. They argued that it was serious. They argued that it was morally profound, morally useful, morally important. They took it seriously and assumed that the audience did so as well. To return to today's politician for a moment—if he were to leave a motion-picture theater after having spent ninety minutes enthralled by the colorful spectacle of international intrigue as described in Hollywood, and were to say, "The spy film is, next to the epic, the most important form of art," *then* we would have a contemporary parallel to the place of serious drama in the Restoration. Restoration men of the world and men of letters argued that heroic drama and tragedy, as practiced in their time, were important and substantial in moral and aesthetic terms.

In contemporary literary history the phenomenon of Restoration serious drama has been defined in three ways: affectively (as escapism), formally (by exploring the genres of tragedy and heroic drama as they were then defined), and inductively (typically, and very often recently, this method is applied to a single author's canon). These three types of definition are not discrete. If the Restoration, for example, understood tragedy to encompass escapism as one of its effects, then presumably a study of Dryden's tragedies would reveal plot, character, and settings which could be understood in terms of escapism. The present study will not attempt to replace these three definitions—although I think the escapist discussions are of little value to a student of this drama—but will add to them. What I will suggest about the intentions of the dramatists and the conventions of art which they explicitly and implicitly followed does not depend upon disproving theories advanced in earlier studies.

5

The three ways of defining Restoration serious drama will be surveyed briefly here in order to create a frame of reference. This survey is not intended to set up straw men, and the argument that follows would be valid or invalid without it. The survey may, on the other hand, point up the need for other arguments and explanations.

The majority view of the literary historians of this century has been that Restoration serious drama is escapist. "The heroic play," Allardyce Nicoll has said, "is like a Tale of a Land of No-where." The tragedy is "the true child of the enervation that had come over England. The age was debilitated: it was distinctly unheroic: and yet it was not so cynical as to throw over entirely the inculcation of heroism."[1] Lewis N. Chase argues, "There is not a single instance of human nature being either the inspiration or the source of heroic character."[2] Moody E. Prior observes, "The dramatist in search of the stuff out of which to mould the heroic figure ended up with an extravagant artifice."[3] John Harold Wilson says, "No matter what the play was, it took a bored and cynical audience into the realm of make-believe."[4] And, Wilson has added more recently, the heroic drama is a product of "the Walter Mitty syndrome—everyman's yearning for heroism."[5] Lastly, Anne Righter has stated this view clearly. The tragedies produced between 1660 and 1685 are, she says, "essentially frivolous": "the furious gestures of the heroes, the rant and the declarations of passion are literary and hollow. Behind them, as behind the painted gardens and palaces of the scenery, there was nothing at all." "Faced with the real issues of the age," Restoration tragedy "retreated in confusion to a land of rhetorical make-believe."[6]

These critics trace the escapism in the plays to various sources, but all seem to agree that there is something essentially trivial about the plays. Interestingly, this conclusion parallels an older view of Restoration comedy first developed by Charles Lamb and more recently restated by F. W. Bateson. In this traditional view, the protagonists of Restoration comedy are "not the habitants of this earth, but of an aerial, fantastic fairyland."[7] Lamb offered this suggestion as a corrective to the even older view of the comedy which has been expressed by such men as Jeremy Collier, Thomas Babington Macaulay, and Allardyce Nicoll. In this older tradition, Restoration comedy only too steadily held the mirror up to nature and accurately reflected the dissolute, debauched, immoral grotesquerie of the court of Charles II.

The old Scylla of Lamb and Charybdis of Macaulay have been navigated by recent students of Restoration comedy, and few critics today would accept either view.[8] Restoration comedy, it now seems, was serious; at least it was serious in the sense that it concerned issues which have been taken seriously in almost all ages. Restoration serious plays have not received a similar re-evaluation.

The view that Restoration serious plays were escapist is based in part on history. Dorimant, in Sir George Etherege's *The Man of Mode* (1676), may have been modeled on the Earl of Rochester. At least Dorimant and Rochester have much in common, and Charles and his circle would have known Dorimant's type intimately.[9] Even those Witwouds who were not accomplished lovers and poets and dressers and dancers would have liked to be thought as urbane and as easy as Dorimant. If accused of having been the model for Dorimant, many a man might have subtly acknowledged that, while he did not actually pose for the portrait, he did think the playwright took just a little of him for the characterization. But when we turn to *The Conquest of Granada*, or *Venice Preserv'd*, or *The Mourning Bride*, contemporary models are hard to find. The histories of drama and drama's patrons are not full of stories of men who may have been the model for hero X or tragic protagonist Y. Almanzor may owe something to Achilles, but he owes very little to General Monck. Later, in the late 1680's perhaps, John Churchill might have provided the model for a martial figure; but partisan politics was strong and Churchill was a political man, which partially limited his appeal as a literary model.

Setting, too, seems to substantiate the escapist claims. Restoration comedy takes place, mostly, in London. To be more exact, it takes place at locations which can be identified precisely (like St. James's Park) and are familiar to most urbane Englishmen. But the serious plays take place in Rome, Moorish Spain, Greece, Poland, Alexandria, and other remote and romantic locations. The serious plays take place in never-never lands, while the comedies occur around the corner.

The plots of the serious plays are nearly impossible to summarize, but many of them, as John Harold Wilson has said, are "limited to a narrow range of subjects: chiefly love, ambition, revenge, villainy, and war." Wilson's summary may sound ironic, but he apparently does not intend it to be. These subjects are "narrow," not in their potential for treatment, but in the realities of Restoration dramatic conventions. Play after play involves a royal family, a siege, a captive prince or princess. The audience "had not the slightest interest," Wilson says, "in realistic treatments of political or social injustice, corruption and immorality in government, the grinding poverty of the lower classes, or the problems of farmers, merchants, craftsmen, and Quakers."[10] I believe that Wilson is wrong about injustice and corruption, and that he could give us no very long list of plays on the remaining subjects from any era. But it is true that the serious drama of the Restoration was unimaginative in plotting and that the stock situations are predictable and wearying after a while.

Most striking of all the "proofs" of the escapist theory is undoubtedly the diction of the plays. Obviously, unquestionably, no real man or woman ever spoke like this:

> No, proud Triumpher o're my falling state,
> Thou shalt not stay to fill thee with my Fate:
> Go to the Conquest which your wiles may boast,
> And tell the world you left Statira lost.
> Go seize my faithless Alexander's hand,
> Both hand and heart were once at my command:
> Grasp his lov'd neck, dye on his fragrant breast,
> Love him like me, which cannot be exprest,
> He must be happy, and you more then blest.
> (Nathaniel Lee, *The Rival Queens*, III. 199–207)

I chose that passage by opening a play by Lee at random, and the drama of 1660 to 1700 abounds with similar passages of intense and carefully patterned poetry. The plays at times drone with speeches all at the same pitch of earnest intensity or of anguish and recrimination. Moreover, the level of diction appears to have been deliberately chosen. Dryden, in an oft-cited passage, has Neander say that tragedy does imitate nature, "but 'tis nature wrought up to an higher pitch. The plot, the characters, the wit, the passions, the descriptions, are all exalted above the level of common converse, as high as the imagination of the poet can carry them. . . ."[11] (I have left out the remaining phrase of this sentence because it does not often get quoted, and when it does it is treated lightly. Neander says, ". . . as high as the imagination of the poet can carry them with proportion to verisimility." I will discuss verisimilitude at length later.)

In fact, Dryden has seemed the best apologist for the escapist position, and much of his earlier literary criticism seems ample theoretical warrant for the practice of the age: "An heroic poet is not tied to a bare representation of what is true, or exceeding probable: but . . . he may let himself loose to visionary objects, and to the representation of such things as depending not on sense, and therefore not to be comprehended by knowledge, may give him a freer scope for imagination."[12] In the heroic drama, at least, Dryden seems to sanction the poet who rides Pegasus bareback and without reins, thereby filling us, the audience, with gaping admiration.

The view which I have perhaps unfairly called escapist is defended most soberly by Lewis N. Chase, whose valuable study of heroic drama was first published in 1903: "With all its faults, [the heroic drama] was a wholesome antidote to the shameless affronts to taste and morals for which contemporary comedy is notorious. It insisted upon decency and decorum of language, it encouraged many of the virtues, such as generosity and bravery, and consistently kept aloof from the sordid cares of everyday life."[13] In this view, the unrealistic qualities of the drama are its strength: they are signs of moral intensity in an age of moral slackness.

Formal or generic criticism of the serious drama includes

9

books like that by Chase cited above, Cecil V. Deane's *Dramatic Theory and the Rhymed Heroic Play*, Clarence C. Green's *The Neo-Classic Theory of Tragedy*, and, the best study of the subject, Eric Rothstein's *Restoration Tragedy*. The studies which preceded Rothstein's have searched the milieu of Restoration drama and its traditions in order to discover the intentions and conventions of the form. They have traced the French influence (in romance, in drama, and on the personality and the court of Charles), the English tradition in dramatic forms and in acting, and the classical and Renaissance theoretical heritage.

Perhaps the most famous contribution of the formal critics has been the suggestion that Restoration serious drama consists of plays on the theme of love versus honor.[14] Here, again, Dryden is cited as the theoretician. "An heroic play," Dryden wrote, "ought to be an imitation, in little, of an heroic poem; and, consequently, . . . Love and Valour ought to be the subject of it."[15] Love and honor are not the sole themes, according to these historians, especially not in unrhymed tragedy after 1680, when domestic and pathetic themes and situations begin to appear. Nevertheless, these twins, love and honor, are spoken of as definitive in nearly every handbook and history of English literature.[16]

The "conflict of love and honor," as a definition of a genre, has the defect that any highly generalized summary has: that is, it serves no useful purpose when coming to grips with a specific play. One could as easily, and as correctly, say that Restoration serious drama concerns the themes of appearance versus reality, or public versus private, or inner versus outer, or good versus evil. Each of these conflicts is present in every play, and therefore these conflicts cannot differentiate play A from play B. "Love" means what in these definitions? Does it include lust? Adultery? Incest? Friendship? What is "honor"? Is it the discharge of all socially acceptable responsibilities? All obligations upon the protagonist of which we approve? Or do we count all obligations, even patently evil ones, such as the oriental custom of doing away with one's brothers—and rivals—upon

10

the death of the pasha (see *Aureng-Zebe*)? If love is defined so as to encompass any affection which wishes well for its object, and honor is defined as social and moral responsibility, then *Oedipus Rex* and *Hamlet* and *Death of a Salesman* all involve conflicts of love and honor.

The impossibility of defining love and honor so as to include the diversity of plays written between 1660 and 1700 and yet exclude all the other serious plays ever written is evident repeatedly. Chase writes: "In all but one of Orrery's heroic plays, friendship is a form of honor, and they are entirely concerned with the conflict between love and friendship, the friends being rivals in love." And, summarizing for all of these plays he says: "By honor was meant all that was not love, and no matter under what name this went, whether war, ambition, reason, or friendship, it was considered as a form of honor; its mission was only to act as a foil for the display of love; and only in this comprehensive sense . . . were love and honor the subjects of the heroic play."[17] In opposition to this summary is the evident rejoinder that in this "comprehensive sense" of love and honor nearly all plays show the conflict. Notice that "all plays" includes comedies, some of which certainly play love against honor. For ancient examples, we can recall Roman comedies in which the young man falls in love with a girl he mistakenly believes to be married or a prostitute.

The theme of love versus honor has not been the only defining characteristic of these plays, according to the early formalist critics. These critics have been much more helpful, and much more convincing, with their careful historical study of French and classical models for the plays, and with their patient reading of classical and Renaissance literary criticism in search of a theoretical framework for the Restoration.[18]

Careful reading of the theoretical background has produced several of the real contributions made by Eric Rothstein toward understanding these plays. He has shown two general theories of the purpose of tragedy to have been simultaneously present in the late seventeenth century: the fabulist and the affective. The fabulist theory argued that the fable of a tragedy was the

11

key to tragedy's ability to instruct. That tragedy should instruct was assumed as a given, as it had been at least as far back as Horace's formulation in the *Art of Poetry* (*Epistle to the Pisos*) that the function of art was to delight and instruct. The affective theory had its source in Aristotle and argued that the moral function of tragedy was served by a purgation of the emotions ("catharsis"). Rothstein lucidly shows the growing strength of affective theories and the changing understanding of exactly how emotions were involved in effecting moral change.[19]

Rothstein also reveals the sources and the theory (which lagged behind the practice) of "emotional serial drama," that is, drama which is structured like a string of beads, each bead being a highly emotional vignette. English drama had always seemed to take this shape—the pageants of medieval mysteries are physical analogues of the metaphoric beads just mentioned —and theoretical justification for what the English knew and loved in practice was eagerly sought. Rothstein describes many of the effects of such serial drama, and his descriptions will be used occasionally throughout this study.

I have mentioned three critical approaches to Restoration serious drama: the affective, the formal, and the inductive. *Inductive* is perhaps not so distinctive a term as it should be because Rothstein, for example, and many other critics so far mentioned proceed inductively. Despite the use of inductive methods, however, formalist critics focus upon theme or form. The critics I am labeling "inductive" proceed with explicatory analysis of the plays, often treating each play independently and allowing generalizations to grow out of accumulated evidence. There have been a number of perceptive studies of Dryden's plays: Selma Assir Zebouni, *Dryden*; Arthur C. Kirsch, *Dryden's Heroic Drama*; Bruce Alvin King, *Dryden's Major Plays*; Anne T. Barbeau, *The Intellectual Design of Dryden's Heroic Plays*. These books and others like them are not easily summarized, but they have tended to find the plays fragmented and "serial" (Rothstein's term) in structure, and have tended to reject the love versus honor cliché in favor of alternative dichotomies. Zebouni, for instance, writes: "Dominated by passion, a character is a villain; dominated by reason, he is a hero. Honor or dishonor is the necessary consequence of the presence or absence of reason: this is why it is very often difficult to distinguish between these two concepts. Honor being a necessary consequence of reason, the characters use the terms interchangeably."[20]

Arthur C. Kirsch has seen most clearly the complexity of Dryden's vision, and he explores several avenues, several knots in relationships described in these plays. Love and honor appear again, as they must, but with new significance: "In a sense, all the conflicts between love and honor in the play [*The Indian Emperour*] are metaphors for the larger conflict between the individual's obligations to himself and to his society."[21] The clash of public and private which Kirsch sees and shows us is a subtle and a sophisticated thing. Love and honor are still involved, but rather than functioning as the center of the drama, they function as the means, or even as metaphors, through which a more complex and less hackneyed conflict takes place.

Bruce King's book is unique. It owes much to D. W. Jefferson, who originally made the suggestion that Dryden's heroic plays were in some important measure ironic—King does not hesitate to say "comic." The contention is not that the heroic plays are comedies, but rather that they "are a form of satire: that is, the values and sentiments of the characters are often humorous or ironic." The humorous sentiments and ironic imagery tell the audience that the speaker is not to be trusted, that his values are askew, that he is "aberrant and psychologically or morally defective."[22] In this way King takes what has sometimes embarrassed or annoyed critics as bombast and fanciful exaggeration and renders it intentional, functional, and dramatically organic. Montezuma's rant reveals his madness, and we smile at his lack of control and learn thereby to take more control of ourselves. King's idea will be examined later in more detail, but we might note that interpreting the plays according to this theory could do away with the potential for the Aristotelian tragic emotions of pity and fear. If Maximin of *Tyrannick Love* is comic in his tyranny, then we cannot fear for

Catherine, whom he threatens. At least our fear is mitigated, for who fears a comic figure? By the same token, how can we pity the misfortunes of Catherine if they are caused by a man at whom we smile?

If the preceding exaggerates King's claim, and what he intends to suggest is not so much amusement on our part as the quick perception of hyperbole, which in turn reveals emotional stress or even madness, then his argument is badly flawed by polemical exaggeration. He calls Maximin "a comic creation, a foreshadowing of Mac Flecknoe."[23]

King's suggestion of intentional comedy can bring this hurried survey to an end near where it began. The escapist critics and King alike try to deal with the apparent lack of seriousness in Restoration non-comic drama. King finds the grotesque to be intentional; Nicoll and others find it decorous because appropriate to a never-never land.

Suppose, however, that the Restoration playwrights understood that man is not a creature of perfect bifurcation, a yin-yang of passion-reason. Suppose that they realized, in various degrees, of course, that nobody they knew spoke fustian except fools. Suppose they knew that love was not one emotion, but one word desperately pressed into service to cover hundreds of subtly distinct emotions. Suppose they understood that a man's concept of the reality around him was shaped by his role, his place in the scheme of things. And suppose, too, they knew that the world was changing: not only that the understanding of the physical universe was growing at an astronomical rate, but also that the old politics would not work any longer, and that Sir Philip Sidney might have been replaced by the Earl of Rochester as the paradigm courtier, and that divine right was terribly hard to adopt seriously any longer, that money was beginning to push aside land as the token of economic power, that anarchy of all kinds—emotional, intellectual, social, political—was right at the door, right up close to be heard breathing in the night. If we suppose that the playwrights knew these things and more, then how can we understand them to have seriously undertaken

14

such plays as *The Conquest of Granada, Venice Preserv'd*, and *Lucius Junius Brutus*?

We can understand this easily if the plays deal seriously with those issues of the day which every intelligent participant in the life of the times recognized, worried with, talked about, legislated on, and described in every other form of verbal art. And the plays do in fact deal with these issues. They deal with them repeatedly; and while they deal with them in terms of conventions that are for us outmoded, they deal with them in terms which appear in all the documents of the Restoration—sermons, essays, poems, comedies, letters, histories, prologues, billets-doux.

We must first recognize that manner is not the same as matter. That seems obvious enough—we do not judge a book by its cover—but it is not obvious, or has not been made to appear obvious, in studies of Restoration serious plays. For example, take the subject of settings. The Earl of Orrery's *Mustapha* (1668) takes place in Turkey; Elkanah Settle's *The Empress of Morocco* (1673), in Morocco; John Crowne's *The Destruction of Jerusalem* (1677), in Jerusalem; Nathaniel Lee's *Sophonisba* (1676), in Zama, and so on. These settings are certainly exotic if compared with Tottenham Court, and yet what conclusion can be drawn? What makes Jerusalem a never-never land and Colonnus a tragic city? Is Elsinore less exotic than Granada? It is embarrassing to state such truths, but there is no substance in an argument which finds meaning in location. Cities and nations have histories and climates and other qualities which certainly make them appropriate for some sorts of actions rather than others: the English like to understand the Latin nations as steamy with sexual passion and jealousy, and surely the gray winters of the north provide a kind of analogue to an agony very different from the merciless and white desert sun in Albert Camus' stories. But within the limitations of geography and history, a setting is nothing but potential until characters in action fill it with meaning. Thebes is as "real" as it is because of Oedipus—or Sophocles—and not because of its geography.

15

If Granada is "remote" it is because we do not find Almanzor, Almahide, and Boabdelin to be "real."

At the same time, compared with contemporary comedy, the serious plays consistently prefer the remote in time and place. This tends to universalize the action—to free it from ordinary time and place—and so makes possible heroic action.[24] I assume that in every age, including Homer's and Virgil's, men were much as they are now, in potential and in fact. Heroes, therefore, are always rarities, and only in myth do several heroic figures come together in one society. In Northrop Frye's terms, only in literature do we have a high mimetic culture. If the men around us are less than heroic, then the heroes we know must have come to us from literature and from history. Achilles is one of our ancestors. Within my assumption of the universality of low mimetic life, then, the Restoration is little different from Augustan Rome. Virgil and Dryden both look out and back for heroes, and not in and around. The Restoration artists turned to the past for heroes: first, they turned to the past for models, such as Achilles and Aeneas, and, second, they turned to the past as the only verisimilar setting possible for heroism. Elkanah Settle, in the Dedication to *Cambyses, King of Persia* (1671), defended his own practice by saying that "the great Characters, and Subjects of serious Plays, are representations of the past Glories of the World."

Only in the past, or in the remote distance of some dimension, can there be convincing heroes. Contemporary men may serve as partial models; but, so far as we know, the epic and the three categories of myth, romance, and high mimetic are never created by a stenographer, never appear from the actual moment, never appear as autobiography. Dryden, Lee, Otway, and the others knew, as Shakespeare knew, that man can be given elevated stature only by distancing him. Up close, as Swift knew, every blemish is a pothole or a mountain; and we all suspect, somewhat cynically, that we would be disappointed in intimacy with the heroic. As a character in Southerne's *The Fate of Capua* (1700) says, "Your Heroes, I find, are little more than other Men, when you come near to examine 'em" (II, p. 28).

16

There is another assumption operative in my argument, of course, and that is that Restoration writers were intending epic or heroic narratives in their drama. That this is so is evident from their apologetics and from their universal practice.[25] Moreover, this intention is, I believe, the key to much of the what and the why of their practice. When Dryden's characters speak in a manner that is unlike the manner of Mirabell, the difference is significant. Epic heroes do not talk like contemporary lovers, no matter how sophisticated those lovers are. If Almanzor strides into a scene and announces that he will change the tide of the war single-handed, he is stating a fact. He is not boasting. He can do these things. We cannot and Mirabell cannot, but Almanzor can. When we read, "the mighty *Tamerlane* / Comes like the Proxy of enquiring Heav'n, / To Judge, and to Redress" (Rowe, *Tamerlane* [1702], I. i), I believe Rowe intends us to anticipate a hero. We know the name Tamerlane. We may know something of the story already, and the majesty of the announcement is not blemished by a flaw in the heroic claim to Heaven's concern. It is only when we substitute an ordinary man for Tamerlane that such an announcement fails as epic and becomes, instead, burlesque:

> All humane things are subject to decay,
> And, when Fate summons, Monarchs must obey:
> This *Fleckno* found, who, like *Augustus*, young
> Was call'd to Empire, and had govern'd long.[26]
>
> (Mac Flecknoe, ll. 1–4)

> This Day, O Mr. *Doodle*! is a Day
> Indeed,—a Day we never saw before.
> The mighty *Thomas Thumb* victorious comes;
> Millions of Giants crowd his Chariot Wheels.
>
> (Fielding, Tom Thumb, I. i. 6–9)

In the burlesque announcements of the heroes Fleckno and Thumb, their names provide the clue to comedy. In Dryden's poem especially, the context is either serious or, at times, ambiguous. The opening lines take their comic significance from the name Fleckno, and not from any doubts we might have about the moral generalization that fate can touch even monarchs.

I will try to say more about epic intentions as my argument develops. I assume that the Restoration dramatists understood serious drama (heroic drama, tragedy, and serious tragicomedy) as related to the epic and as involving heroes and heroic conventions. They assumed that the hero was a man different from other men in degree, not in kind. A hero was more intelligent, stronger, more ferocious, quicker to anger and to love, and more passionate than the rest of mankind. They assumed also that heroic superiority justifies boasting, arrogance, and apparent fustian and makes those attributes verisimilar. If we accept Almanzor as a hero, then his boast is not a boast; it is a statement or a promise. It is a decorous announcement of will.

The reverse of my assumption forms an important corollary about epic intention: that is, if we do *not* accept these figures as heroes, then the plays are failures, and very often burlesques. To illustrate this point, we might look at Muly Labas, the son of the Emperor of Morocco, who is in chains at the opening of Elkanah Settle's *The Empress of Morocco*. Despite his imprisonment, he asserts that he is spiritually free:

> My Soul mounts higher, and Fates Pow'r disdains,
> And makes me reign a Monarch in my Chains.

(I, p. 1)

In a speech like this, everything depends on a nice balance of parts. The constituent elements are the poetry, the speaker (his ethos and his appearance), the meaning of the statement, and the setting. I believe most of us will accept the meaning; the speech is a restatement of the conventional notion that a man's spirit may be free although his flesh is not. The poetry is conventional heroic couplet aphorism—a familiar metaphor (soul as eagle or falcon) and familiar abstractions (soul, fate, power, monarch, chains). The setting is not described, but we can imagine the tableau of an obviously royal figure, chained hand and foot. We can also imagine his person—young, strong, attractive. But if any of the four constituents (poetry, ethos,

18

meaning, setting) fails badly, the scene is weakened or destroyed.

Suppose, for instance, that in person Muly Labas were tiny, like Tom Thumb. Then the speech would be obviously comic. Labas could not rule as monarch of anything. Or suppose the setting were such that Muly Labas were dwarfed by massive stone walls and he chained tight against them, in rags, with a dim rift of light coming from a small barred opening above. If the situation looks impossible, then Muly Labas' speech is ironic, perhaps even foolish and comic.

The poetry of the statement is not memorable, but it is familiar within the conventions of the age and might, given a larger context, be part of a moving and intelligent statement of spiritual strength. Certainly the remark is not lyrical, but then neither is the occasion. As beautiful as is Lovelace's "To Althea, From Prison," it is not a dramatic statement, and it would seem effeminate and excessively melodic in the mouth of a man placed before us in real chains:

> Stone walls do not a prison make,
> Nor iron bars a cage;
> Minds innocent and quiet take
> That for an hermitage;
> If I have freedom in my love,
> And in my soul am free,
> Angels alone that soar above
> Enjoy such liberty.

Muly Labas might sing this if music were a part of the play, but otherwise the lyric would be inappropriate.[27] The speaker (his ethos) has not been established at this point in the play and does not yet enter our judgment as fully as he will later in other contexts. We can only judge appearance, and that, presumably, allows us to grant him majesty. But if we knew him well and thought him a coward, we would interpret his facile bravado about soaring spirit as so much whistling to keep up his courage.

The four constituents—ethos, setting, poetry, and meaning—are always present in evaluation and, if given their rhetorical

19

names, will be recognized as elements traceable through rhetorical theory in an unbroken line from Aristotle. In the chapters on diction and decorum the Restoration conventions will be explored further—but to return now to the corollary of the epic intention mentioned earlier. If we do not accept the epic nature of the elements, then the epic intentions become pretensions, and I believe that is what happened historically in our evaluation of Restoration serious drama. We no longer accept the heroic conventions employed at the end of the seventeenth century, and the plays which employ them either bore us or amuse us. We cannot take them seriously.

I do not wish to argue for the reacceptance of the heroic conventions of the Restoration. Literary conventions are fashions, and, like all fashions, once dead they are nearly impossible to resurrect. To be sure, there are sporadic revitalizations of fashions in clothing or furnishings or music, but these are usually brief and almost always involve genuine revision of the original fashions. The new fashions are only *like* the old ones. It is the likeness—and the difference—that interests me: the nature and the substance of Restoration heroic conventions as compared with conventions of other genres and other eras.

The division between convention and substance introduces a familiar critical disagreement. That the two are only partially separable seems obvious to me. An heroic figure treated unheroically may remain heroic no matter what happens to him; but the difficult question is, how would we know? We have no sources of data save the treatment itself. We cannot look into his soul. By the same token, experience makes perfectly clear that identical substances may be expressed in many ways, and that the ways are not necessarily obvious or clear outgrowths of the substance described. In other words, as art historians like E. H. Gombrich have shown, perception and description are matters of convention: "There is no neutral naturalism. The artist, no less than the writer, needs a vocabulary before he can embark on a 'copy' of reality."[28] The "vocabulary"—the body of convention—of the Restoration is different from ours, and thus no matter how skillfully a Restoration playwright "presents" reality to us, we remain to a large extent illiterate or blind to it.

The Restoration artist, like the artist of any era, perceived according to patterns. He understood reality in terms of a vocabulary of concepts, images, ideas, values, and matrices of space and time. Our patterns in the twentieth century are different, and reading a Restoration serious play is much like reading in a foreign language. There is more at stake here than the old saw about the necessity to approximate the meaning as it was apprehended by the contemporary audience. There is a point beyond which our historical reconstruction cannot go—an area of "feel" in an era that is inexpressible because unexpressed. A Restoration playwright did not have to express some patterns, for his audience already possessed them. In this sense, some patterns are often thought but never expressed.

The Restoration world picture affected every element of a play—style, ethos, substance, invention—and gave, I think, a seriousness to the plays which we can in part re-create, or better, re-perceive, but never fully. Nor, as far as that goes, are we under obligation to perceive as others have perceived. We are, though, under some obligation if we wish to understand history and to understand art as a product of time. We are obliged to recognize that patterns of perception—that is, perceptions themselves—change. What I see is not what Dryden saw. I care about what he saw because change is not in its nature progressive or ameliorative. I do not see better than Dryden, just differently.

The escapist critics, and most historians of Restoration drama, have understood the difference between the Restoration and the present in terms of perceptual and artistic progress. They have written about the past as though history recorded a fixed order of nature and an ever more perceptive mankind. Only if we assume that man is always accumulating understanding and wisdom can we condescend to the past. The picture of Restoration dramatists and audiences naively indulging themselves in mindless fantasies of a heroism they knew to be false is a picture drawn by prideful historians who see our ancestors as children in the long process of maturation, which fortunately has come to completion in the twentieth century.

If this seems to deny self-indulgence and fantasy in the Restoration, it is not meant to. Surely much of the appeal of heroic and tragic drama has always been spectacle and the opportunity to be taken out of and beyond oneself. The intrigue, the murders, and the sex in Restoration serious drama gave energy to lives which all too often were merely perplexing, threatening, and vaguely erotic. But it is not the entertainment value of these plays that has been overlooked. It is their seriousness that has.

One last general comment before looking at that seriousness. The artist has what Gombrich calls the "problem of abbreviation and information."[29] That is, the artist must decide how much information he wants to convey and how many and what clues he must give in order to convey that information. What can be left to the imagination? *What* here means not only what facts but also what arrangement of facts, what conclusions, what assessments, what responses. *What* means the full range of imaginative-cognitive-affective responses and interactions.

Anne Killigrew's portrait of King James II is usefully reproduced, though not in color, in the third volume of the California edition of *The Works of John Dryden*. We see in the painting a man of indeterminate age (twenty-four? forty-five? sixty?) in a periwig and a deep-cuffed brocade coat of knee length, buttoned negligently and worn with a puffed white blouse that appears luxuriously at the neck and wrist. Crossing his chest from the left shoulder he wears a sash suspending an order, barely visible, but obviously the Garter, for he wears the badge below the left knee. The hilt of a sword projects from behind his left hand, which holds what appear to be gloves. He is wearing boots, ornamented at the ankle and heel. To his right is a staircase leading upward off the painting; the newel is decorated by a classical figure in bas-relief and topped by a sculptured urn. At his left, on the ground, is an embossed shield with armorial bearings. The background is a misty prospect of vague distance, clouds, and water. In the poem "To the Pious Memory of the

Accomplisht Young Lady Mrs Anne Killigrew," Dryden describes the painting this way:

> ... with bold Erected Look
> Our Martial King the Sight with Reverence strook:
> For not content t' express his Outward Part,
> Her hand call'd out the Image of his Heart,
> His Warlike Mind, his Soul devoid of Fear,
> His High-designing Thoughts, were figur'd there,
> As when, by Magick, Ghosts are made appear.

(Ll. 127–33)

The relationship of the poem and the painting is complicated by the occasional nature of the poem and the conventions of elegiac praise. Dryden clearly wishes to reveal Anne as a type of the perfect artist, whose conceptions are realized without any of the clumsy errors forced on most artists by the intervention of the flesh between conception and realization. The inner nature of her subject is figured as if "by Magick." But what in the painting justifies Dryden's verbal paraphrase?

James may be said to have a "bold Erected Look," but nearly all the rest of the description is interpretive within conventions not easily available to us. Few of us would recognize anything martial about the painting, or high design in the thoughts, or courage. The conventions of portrait art have changed to some extent, and the "problem of abbreviation and information" is solved differently now. We need other clues to see martial qualities, courage, and nobility. Although Anne is described in the poem as a type of artistic perfection, we recognize the irony in our difficulty understanding her painting and Dryden's poem. Dryden's praise may be excessive in terms of the young woman who was Anne Killigrew, but the woman of the poem is symbolic, and much of the praise goes to artistic perfection symbolically represented. Dryden is, in this poem, exaggerating Anne the smallpox victim, but he is serious about Anne the symbol. We recognize the clues in the poem much more quickly than we do those in the painting.

The playwright has a parallel difficulty in choosing the clues that will convey to us the information he wishes conveyed. The audience to *Death of a Salesman* recognizes instantly the anachronism of the windshield which Willy says he put down on his trip.[30] But we do not always recognize similar revelatory clues in Restoration drama. The conventions of decorum seem silly to us, and not subtle or revealing. Love at first sight is a juvenile cliché, not the necessary consequence of the meeting of two heroic souls. Anguished indecision over choices between love and duty seem at best prolonged, and at worst stupid, to us because we have settled that issue and chosen love. Or so our convention has it. In an age of interchangeable functionaries in government, the prince who debates his duty and his love is a wonderful, romantic anachronism, and we treasure him like a museum piece, to be shown and admired by all. We all loved our Duke of Windsor, but the Restoration was in search of *admiration*, and that is another matter altogether.

II

The Restoration maintained a traditional psychology inherited from the Renaissance and modified it in very particular ways with the materialism of Thomas Hobbes and the dualism of René Descartes. The traditional psychology credited man with three internal mechanisms which affected his behavior: reason, passion (or appetite), and will. Reason was variously defined, but typically it was the faculty of thought, of calculation, of logic, of contemplation, of decision-making. A healthy reason is often figuratively described as possessing clarity of sight. As a result of clear sight, a healthy reason sees distinctly; and because it can make distinctions, it is also able to draw accurate conclusions. The operations of the reason are mathematical, or, more specifically, patterned very like the operations of geometry.

The passions, or man's appetites, are directed toward objects and are not entirely under man's control. That is, some appetites, such as hunger, sex, and fear, seem to operate instantly and instinctively. Although they can be brought under control by a healthy reason, their initial response to a stimulus is instinctive and immediate. The passions, then, are an obvious link between man and the other earthly creatures, whose lives are entirely instinctual. The word *passion* has suffered a constriction in its popular meaning since the seventeenth century. We now think of the term primarily as referring to love or lust. Only adverbially or as an adjective does the term convey other emotions such as anger or envy—and even then the term is often used redundantly, as in "a passionate rage." For the seventeenth century, contrariwise, *passion* was a generic term for all of man's emotions. Each emotion has an object—envy of a neighbor, greed for gold, lust for the neighbor's wife—but the moral value of a passion depended, for the seventeenth century, on the object and, in another way, on whether or not the passion led to action. In the first instance, everyone knew the Biblical archetype: "Whosoever looketh on a woman to lust after her hath committed adultery with her already in his heart" (Matt. 5:28). But they knew also that only in ultimate judgment would the heart of a man be open for inspection, and therefore mundane life would have to be judged according to the second criterion— action. Adultery of the heart was a matter between man and God. Adultery of the flesh was a matter between man and man: between man and state, man and church, man and society, man and law. A political version of this distinction occurs as Lady Jane Gray defends herself and friends from the charge of treason in Banks's *The Innocent Usurper* (1694):

> As to th' Offence, the Treason of the mind,
> We still persist, and plead our Innocence.
> But to the Fact on which the Law takes hold,
> We say w' are Guilty.[31]

(IV, p. 41)

Passions are man's motive force; they are his source of energy. Reason is man's compass, as it were, his means of establishing direction and of imposing order.[32] But, in one of the Restoration's most commonly used metaphors, neither the wind in the sails (passion) nor the rudder (reason) is alone sufficient to direct the ship which is man. A man without reason is a ship without a rudder; and, in an equally common extension of the metaphor, he is in the midst of a storm, a hurricane of feelings, and is driven erratically, aimlessly. The man without passion is becalmed; he could steer if he had motion, but he has none. Georges de Scudéry, speaking in 1654 of the protagonist of his play *Alaric*, epitomizes the argument that passion is not only natural but necessary to the good man: "Not that I have formed him like the Stoic sage who is more the statue of a man than a man; on the contrary, as Achilles, Ulysses, and Aeneas experienced love, I have given him a taste of it, following their example; for, after all, virtue does not consist in not having passions but in having them and mastering them."[33]

The will is often described as the agency of choice, the agency which acts to bring reason and passion together into purposeful action. Action without purpose is possible and, in fact, common, but purposeful action demands the will. The exact nature of the will is not clear, and yet there seems to have been little trouble in most men's minds about it. Few plays question the exact way in which the will acts to bring reason to bear on passion; they simply assume that it does. Descartes faced a similar problem in attempting to bridge the apparently complete chasm between matter (*res extensa*) and mind (*res cogitans*).[34] His solution, the pineal gland, did not seem useful to Restoration dramatists, who focused instead on the will, or, just as often, left unexplained the nature of the agency of interaction between passion and reason.

A summary of the relationships between reason, passion, and will is available in Archbishop Richard Hooker's *Laws of Ecclesiastical Polity* (1594):

> The object of Appetite is whatsoever sensible good may be wished for; the object of Will is that good which Reason doth lead us to seek. Affections, as joy, and grief, and fear, and anger, with such like, being as it were the sundry fashions and forms of Appetite, can neither rise at the conceit of a thing indifferent, nor yet choose but rise at the sight of some things. Wherefore it is not altogether in our power, whether we will be stirred with af-

26

fections or no: whereas actions which issue from the disposition of the Will are in the power thereof to be performed or stayed.[35]

The Hobbesian physiology and psychology brought mind and matter, reason and passion, together by identifying them, and by finding them both of the same substance—matter—and differing only in arrangement and motion. Hobbes's thoroughgoing materialism incisively defined *reason* as addition and subtraction, *appetite* as a kind of magnetism between man and object (sense and sensed), and *will* as a fiction.[36] The clarity of Hobbes's arguments and their implications were profoundly unsettling to the late seventeenth century. Given his premises, his conclusions seemed inevitable, and yet they were in part so distasteful that Hobbesian ideas were quickly associated with ruthless political and personal self-seeking of any kind. Hobbes plays in Restoration literature a role like that played by Machiavelli in the Renaissance. A Hobbesian is a villain or a rake and is characterized by a misuse of his reason to justify his appetites.

All three of the terms so crucial to the period are imprecisely used, and their exact significance must be determined in almost every instance from the context. Yet some assumptions and meanings are consistent. One agreed assumption is that the passions are not all evil. Greed, gluttony, and the other five are the seven deadly sins still; but ambition, love, courage, ingenuousness, benevolence, charity, and others are either positive or neutral until given a context. Passion, until further defined, is not man's antagonist. The traditional dichotomy of passion and reason implies that passion must be overcome by reason, but that is not the case. Passions must be directed by the will, which is led by reason, but some passions are essential to coherent and healthy human life. David R. Hauser has argued convincingly for the applicability of Cartesian voluntarism, or something like it, in much Restoration serious drama:

> According to this system, all virtue is the result of proper ordering and control of the passions by a reasoned use of the will, all evil a failure to channel the passions. Thus the strength of an

27

individual soul depends on the strength of the will. A corollary theory, found in Dryden and elsewhere, was that the nobler an individual, the greater the passions. Consequently, a hero in heroic drama gains his exalted position not by great deeds and noble birth alone, but also through great self-control, a necessary premise to heroic action.[37]

Another consistent assumption is that reason is helpless before passion if the two conflict. Reason has no energy. It can point to the right and the wrong, but it cannot move a man so much as an inch toward either. Only passions move man, and therefore the perceptions of reason can only be realized, can only be made a part of action, if reason has some emotion on its side or is given energy by will. A man may see the truth clearly and yet act falsely, and countless emotional moments in the drama attest to this. In *The Conquest of Granada*, Abdalla is tempted to revolution and the overthrow of his brother to gain the throne. The arguments offered in favor of revolution are clearly false. To obtain his love, however, he must revolt. Abdalla says:

> To sharp ey'd reason this would seem untrue;
> But reason, I through Love's false Optiques view.
>
> (II, p. 20)

There is a cliché, but a significant one, in the image of sharp-eyed reason and blinding love. Later Abdalla reaffirms with impetuous vigor his willful distortion of reality: "I'le love; be blind, be cousen'd till I dye" (III, p. 24).

From whatever perspective one approaches the struggles of passion, will, and reason in the late seventeenth and early eighteenth centuries, voluntarism, which emphasizes will as the primary moral agent, seems to describe the moral disposition of the serious drama.[38] J. W. Johnson, in *The Formation of English Neo-Classical Thought*, finds the tragic sense missing from the three "Hellenist" views prominent in the eighteenth century—Platonism, Epicureanism, and Stoicism. "All three insisted that man's emotional nature be suppressed and his passions be subordinated to his reason and will."[39] Johnson's summary may be misleading in that it suggests that passions were to be repressed or excised according to these philosophies, but that is not accurate except for an extreme stoicism. I would rather stress the idea that almost every major philosophic position in the era 1660 to 1750 emphasized the proper subordination of passion to will and reason. None argued for a passionless existence.

John Dennis, in *The Advancement and Reformation of Modern Poetry* (1701) has a splendid summary of the prevailing view as I understand it. What he says is eclectic in its philosophic heritage and perhaps not true to experience. Nevertheless, it is a view widely held and often reflected in the drama:

> The Passions are either natural and congenial to the Soul, or accidental: These first are those which are pleasing to it, as Love, Joy, Desire, and with these the first Man was created; for Man was created Happy; but without these Passions there can be no Happiness. The accidental Passions, as Anger, Envy, Indignation, and Desire of Revenge, are those with which Man at the first was not created, for they all include Misery, and he was created Happy. They were all the Result of the Fall, which brought Woe to the Race of Men. Man is indeed capable of restraining these last, because they all of them include Misery, and he retaining a vehement Desire of Happiness, tho' join'd to an Impotence of attaining it, is by that very Desire, capacitated to struggle with apparent Misery. But it must needs be a hard Contention when we pretend to moderate the first, because there is something within us, that secretly tells us, they are necessary to our Happiness; and the Conflict must needs be violent, when we strive against our own Happiness. Besides, they are as natural to the Soul as Reasoning, and the Result of that; and a Reasonable Creature can no more be without Admiration, Love and Desire, than it can be without Thinking, or without the Appetites of Sense; and a Man can no more suppress the one by Philosophy, than the other. He can no more take away Love and Desire by Reasoning, than he can satisfy Hunger and Thirst with a Syllogism.[40]

This passage will lead Dennis to a defense of emotion in poetry as a moral tool, but the long passage is of interest here as it

speaks confidently of the human emotional makeup. Dennis believed, and I think most of his contemporaries believed, that the
real struggles, the violent and agonizing ones, were between
passions, and not between reason and passion.

Reason has so long been designated the *summum bonum* of
the Restoration and eighteenth century that it is difficult to see
just what the period understood reason to be, or what relationship, if any, it bore to virtue. Dryden's description of reason's
role and function, in the opening lines of *Religio Laici*, is, I
believe, a definition that was generally acceptable to his contemporaries. In this poem Dryden contrasts reason and religion
(revelation) as moon and sun. Reason, like the moon,

> Was lent, not to *assure* our *doubtfull* way,
> But *guide* us upward to a *better Day*.
>
> (Ll. 6–7)

Reason is a guide, but not an assurance. The only assurance
comes from revelation, from the supernatural, from beyond and
outside of man:

> And as those nightly Tapers disappear
> When Day's bright Lord ascends our Hemisphere;
> So pale grows *Reason* at *Religions* sight;
> So *dyes*, and so *dissolves* in *Supernatural Light*.
>
> (Ll. 8–11)

The context here is explicitly theological, but I am not aware of
any major document in the period which would give reason a
more conclusive or absolute role. At the same time, the path
which Dryden describes here is a path "upward" to heaven.
Religio Laici is concerned with eschatological matters, and the
typical Restoration serious play is not. Restoration plays are
concerned with the path through *this* life, a horizontal path
which is dark enough, and for which man has no surer guide
than his reason, as "doubtfull" as reason is.

Restoration serious dramas have frustrated us by their apparent clarity. They seem lucid about the nature of the problems which torture the characters, and yet the characters seem

30

helpless to resolve their difficulties. Too many characters seem able to see their dilemma and yet are unwilling to act.[41] Wylie Sypher has expressed the seemingly mechanical nature of the dramatic problems: "Characters in Corneille, Dryden, and Otway do not experience the will as a felt impulse but rather as a need to comply with a formula of 'love' and 'honor' which makes passion and duty a ritual performed by an elite." If, in fact, a formula or formulae were involved, then moral problems could be solved in the same sense that a geometric problem can be solved. Sypher puts the proposition: "The dramatic problem is reduced to one question: What is the correct attitude or posture, and what is the condition under which one assumes that attitude?"[42] As spectators to formulaic problems like those described by Sypher, we are naturally frustrated by any failure to act according to formula. That is, if we can see a solution to the dramatic problem and we find no reason to believe that the characters cannot see it also, then we grow frustrated and angry with their inaction. The dramatic inaction under those circumstances is charged to recalcitrance, stupidity, cowardice, or inept dramatic craftsmanship. When a rational solution is before us, only the weak fail to act. At least that is so in plays.

This seems an accurate description of dramatic response to clear-cut choice. But is that the sort of choice which is typically offered to the protagonist of a Restoration play? Abdalla, in the lines about sharp-eyed reason quoted above, knows rationally what is right and yet acts according to his appetites. But Abdalla is a weakling and we are to understand him so. He is testimony to the evil effects of unchecked passion and weakness of will. Almanzor, the protagonist of the play, has no such clear choices between the rational and the passionate. Neither does Antony in *All for Love*, nor Jaffeir in *Venice Preserv'd*, nor Queen Elizabeth in Banks's *The Unhappy Favourite*, nor Abdelazer in Behn's *Abdelazer*, nor Mustapha in Orrery's *Mustapha*. There are other plays in which the solution is clear and is held at arm's length either by unconvincing indecision or by improbable intrigue and misfortune. But in many plays the protagonists are forced to choose, not among postures—which

31

would be the case if a rigid code defined all human situations and the proper responses to them—but among goods or among evils. Antony, for example, must choose between such alternatives as Rome and Alexandria, duty and love, empire and mistress, strength and pleasure, calculation and spontaneity. The choices are not simple and not clear. Reason does not discern a single path through this thicket, and passion is of no help because it never looks where it is going.

There is, in the Restoration insistence upon reason, a tone of desperation. "The Age of Reason" is no longer accepted as a descriptive title for the period 1660 to 1800 on many grounds, but one is the late recognition on our part that in an age which actually lives by reason, reason is not the topic of sermons, periodical essays, and poems. The authors of the Restoration and eighteenth century wrote about reason, held it up to their contemporaries for admiration and even worship, precisely because these writers felt that their contemporaries were not living according to reason. Swift's grudging acknowledgment that, though men were certainly not rational creatures, they might perhaps be capable of reason (*rationis capax*) is only the clearest statement of a motif which runs through the whole Christian tradition—and, more specifically, through most of English thought for a century or so following the Civil War. All around them the men of the Restoration saw madness, fanaticism, fantasy, and distortions of reason. Everywhere—in the established church or the proscribed chapel, in the court, in the theater, in government at every level—men were living by inner light, inspiration, "interest," fixations, neuroses, appearances, impulses. And the spectacle of this madness was terrifying. Priest, poet, and politician united in calling for reason. With near unison they pleaded for common sense, for harmony, peace, stability, logic —reason.

Some version or another of the doctrine explained to Adam by the angel Michael was probably shared by most Englishmen of the time. "Know withal," Michael says:

> Since thy original lapse, true Liberty

32

Is lost, which always with right Reason dwells
Twinn'd, and from her hath no dividual being:
Reason in man obscur'd, or not obey'd,
Immediately inordinate desires
And upstart Passions catch the Government
From Reason, and to servitude reduce
Man till then free.[43]

(XII. 82–90)

In the prelapsarian condition man was a creature in whom right reason was nature. For him, to see was to understand and to act rightly. And in this condition man had true liberty, the liberty of being free from law, limitation, or restriction. With the fall, however, man lost the "innocence of the eye"[44] and no longer had reason and liberty "twinn'd" in his nature. After the fall man was a mixed thing, part angel and part beast, part reason and part appetite. To the extent that postlapsarian man allows his appetites to rule him, he is in "servitude."

The myth of the fall provides a picture of man as possessed of a dream of true liberty, a memory, as it were, of life under right reason. Man, in the fallen state, is simultaneously possessed of a reality made up of the world, the flesh, and the devil. The life of reason is an ideal life, a perfect life. Living in accordance with reason, therefore, is as unlikely as living in accordance with any other ideal. Regaining right reason is like regaining Eden, and the prospect as remote.

There is nothing very erudite about this summary of the fall and its effect. I intend it only as an indication of what the Restoration dramatist might have expected his audience to know about the subject. Surely they were a mixed group intellectually, though for the most part they were socially homogeneous and shared a very similar education. But their understanding of theological doctrine need not have been profound to contain some notion of the mixed nature of man and his problematic aptitude for reason.

Going an important step further, we should notice that living according to right reason, in the terms established so far, would be an heroic act. Only the greatest of men can accomplish this feat. Only a man of heroic will can overcome his appetites and live as man was first made to live. Only the hero can reintegrate or reorder his parts; he alone can put his "inordinate desires" back in order. And when a man fails to put things in their proper places, he is being human in the postlapsarian manner. In the drama, we witness heroes struggle to reorder themselves, and their vigor encourages us; their courage fills us with admiration.

In still another perspective, living according to reason or living with will superior to appetite is an ethical imperative. Like other ethical imperatives—the Decalogue, for example—the command "Live ye by your reason" is more easily affirmed than accomplished. Dryden is very clear about this distinction. In an often quoted passage prefatory to *All for Love*, Dryden writes: "The chief persons represented were famous patterns of unlawful love. . . . The crimes of love which they both committed were not occasioned by any necessity, or fatal ignorance, but were wholly voluntary; since our passions are, or ought to be, within our power."[45] "Or ought to be" is the telling expression. By qualifying his statement in this way, Dryden recognizes the facile oversimplification of "our passions are within our power." They simply are not. In my experience and in yours and in everyman's, it is evident that our passions are not wholly within our power.

If this is the condition of man in 1660, what can he do? We know what he ought to do—our literature of vision, of revelation, of law, of art is full of ethical admonition. But what can he do? This is one of the pervasive questions of Restoration serious literature, drama included. The answers vary and often slide away from the question of *can* into the question of *ought*. But the plays do have a common assumption: they assume that individual morality is the key. They assume that every man must make himself right before the world will be right. They believe that character, that ethos, is everything that counts. They are therefore distinguished from writers who find the answer to the morally good life in terms of any of the following: revelation, institutions, material things, social structures, economic systems, polymorphous perversities, technology.

Every reader of Restoration plays in our century must be struck with their institutional naiveté. The plays never present moral problems which seem to stem in any way from the framework of society. An evil kingdom is often shown, but the evil is always the result of the king or his advisors. It is never the result of the monarchical system, class division, land-based economy, or unfair division of labor. The suffering which we watch is individual suffering stemming from individual and unique causes. Certain familiar blemishes of the human character are present—ambition, lust, greed, envy—but these blemishes are to be controlled, *ought* to be controlled, by the individual, not by the state.

Perhaps this emphasis upon character is only another way of saying that the plays are a reflection of an aristocratic culture. At least that is the conclusion Alexis de Tocqueville might draw:

> Historians who write in aristocratic ages are inclined to refer all occurrences to the particular will and character of certain individuals; and they are apt to attribute the most important revolutions to slight accidents....
>
> Historians who live in democratic ages exhibit precisely opposite characteristics. Most of them attribute hardly any influence to the individual over the destiny of the race, or to citizens over the fate of a people; but, on the other hand, they assign great general causes to all petty incidents.[46]

Whether or not Tocqueville's observation is valid for historians, I think that it is applicable to poets. The literature of the Restoration is a literature of the exploits of individual men. There are signs that the aristocratic view is changing, or even being destroyed by a new view that sees events occurring because of forces rather than men. But, on the whole, it is men, and not institutions or forces, that count in the literature of the Restoration.

The dramatist who perceives the human condition as a matter of individual ethos has a strong tradition to help him create his art. He has the Christian tradition's emphasis on individual moral responsibility. He has the Renaissance humanist tradition of pride in individual accomplishment. He has countless great works of art of the past which show heroic individual struggle (for example, *Oedipus, Hamlet,* and La Calprenède's *Cléopâtre,* all very influential in the Restoration) ; [47] and also historians, such as Plutarch, Cicero, Dio Cassius, and Lucan, who show great men in action. And the evidence from the Restoration is overwhelming: historians saw the events of the past and events around them as the work of individuals and chance and providence. This predisposition is evident in the diaries of Pepys and Evelyn and in Clarendon's *History of the Rebellion and Civil Wars in England,* which was written during the Restoration and probably completed in 1670, though not published until 1702–1704. [48]

The dramatist who perceives the human condition in another way is less sure of what constitutes decorum. He is in new territory and needs new conventions. [49] As Ruth Nevo has pointed out, in *The Dial of Virtue,* one of the first events to bring into conflict what Tocqueville calls aristocratic and democratic views was the Civil War, and one of the first individuals was Oliver Cromwell. [50] Clarendon describes the Civil War as precipitated by men—Henry Vane, Cromwell, and others. Republican historians, on the other hand, see forces at work and Cromwell "elected" to office. We see the clash of conventions in Dryden's *Heroique Stanzas to the Glorious Memory of Cromwell* when compared to *Astraea Redux* or *Threnodia Augustalis,* in which King Charles is the central figure. When describing Charles, Dryden has the whole weight of royal panegyrical convention behind him. He has all the formulae and figures of noble lineage, history, rank, and pathetic fallacy at hand. But Cromwell has no noble lineage; his family has no history, no rank; and no star appeared at his birth. [51] Dryden employs a familiar figure with special poignancy when Cromwell is involved:

> How shall I then begin, or where conclude
> To draw a *Fame* so truly *Circular*?
> For in a round what order can be shew'd,

36

Where all the parts so *equall perfect* are?
His *Grandeur* he deriv'd from Heav'n alone,
For he was great e're Fortune made him so.

(Ll. 17–22)

Cromwell is either a self-made man or a Heaven-made man. If he is the first, then he is ambitious, and ambition is a villainous characteristic. If he is the second, then his career and actions are providential and providence is easily managed within the epideictic conventions.

The difficulties of describing men without lineage or special history begin to appear in serious drama with new force in the Restoration, and Jaffeir of *Venice Preserv'd* is a good example. Jaffeir is a citizen. He is related by marriage to a senator but is not himself involved closely with the establishment, or even, later, with the conspirators. Venice has been preserved in Otway's play, but not Jaffeir. Part of his anguish is a very modern pain—what can an individual do to change the state when the change may itself be as bad as the state, or worse?

Jaffeir and Cromwell are exceptions in the Restoration. They are prefigurative of political realities soon to be acknowledged throughout the western world, and they are, to a lesser extent, signs of a political reality to some degree present at the moment; but the art of the moment is not ready for the new political reality. There are no conventions for the new world and the new philosophies. Dryden, Lee, Otway, Banks, and the others could define *epic* and *tragedy* with relative ease; the significant fact is that these definitions did not include people like Jaffeir and Cromwell. We must note the important additional, and ironic, fact that the definitions of *comedy* which the Restoration held, would accommodate Jaffeir and Cromwell. The new age and the new philosophies demanded new forms of art, and the Restoration only began to experiment with these new forms. (These matters will be discussed at greater length in Chapter 5.)

If, on the whole, the question What can I do? must be answered in individual terms, and if, in addition, every individual is a fallible mixture of reason, appetite, and will, then the only plausible answer to the question is, I can struggle, endure, and

37

hope. Plays which explore this matter further tend to describe or suggest means to struggle and endure. The most frequently suggested means are: wisdom, courage, stoicism, Christian faith, fulfillment of moral obligations to others, and obedience to decorum.

These half dozen are obviously means to endure but are perhaps less obviously means of struggle. They are more evidently means of struggle when the antagonist is understood to be within the self and primarily identified with appetite and passion. Stoicism, for example, helps one to patience with adversity and is also a way of struggling against the natural impulse to indulge one's whims. Seeing stoicism as a means of struggle calls for some recognition that the Stoic doctrine does not advocate annihilating the emotions, or as Swift put it, "cutting off our Feet when we want Shoes."[52] The stoic figure does appear impassive to outward pressures, but he maintains this facade of outward control by means of a fierce inner struggle. Addison's *Cato* (1713) provides an excellent example of this. Cato is a man unmoved by the tempests around him and a towering figure in the eyes of his contemporaries. Yet when we see him alone, we see his inner debates and uncertainties; we see him debate until he exclaims, "I'm weary of Conjectures" (V, p. 56). It is only after debate that he can assert, "Let Guilt or Fear / Disturb Man's Rest: *Cato* knows neither of 'em, / Indifferent in his Choice to sleep or die" (V, p. 57).

Each of the methods has the same double face: each is a means to achieve inner and outer calm, but these ends can be achieved only at the cost of struggle, usually with inner opponents. Decorum (the subject of Chapter 3) is the doctrine that "nothing is truly fine but what is *fit*."[53] It is a doctrine more easily stated than realized, but it clearly calls for choice, for discretion, for restraint. At the same time, it describes an active life in which the golden mean between extremes, not mediocrity, is sought.

The recommended methods are not mutually exclusive. The Christian life is a decorous life, a wise and courageous life. In some ways it is similar to the stoic one and certainly full of moral obligation. The recommended methods are ubiquitous in the Restoration, partly because they fit well together and partly because an atheist who is a stoic may live beside a Christian without conflict, and the absence of conflict is to be desired above almost all other things.

Before looking at some evidence that the plays do advocate these methods, in common with other serious literature of the period, it would help to expand on one of the methods and thereby illustrate its broad nature and flexibility. The central document for the method I have called moral obligation is Cicero's *De Officiis*.[54] It was part of every schoolboy's education and its universal validity seemed beyond question. Cicero, writing to his son, describes the nature of moral obligation and its basis in human character. Reason, he writes, distinguishes man from the other creatures, and its unique function is the perception of truth (I. 4. 11, 13). Moreover, "it is clear that reason should govern, and the appetites should be subject to it" (I. 28. 101). For the leader and man of distinction, "all true courage and greatness of spirit is comprised for the most part of two factors: one is a disdain for externals which arises from the conviction that a man should never admire, wish for or seek anything that is not honourable or decent, or be a slave to another man, to his own impulses or to the caprices of fortune." The other source of courage and true greatness is the doing of deeds which are "not only great and good in themselves, but also particularly difficult, wearisome and dangerous to life itself." While such deeds will bring one glory, it is a disdain for externals that "contains the seeds of true greatness" (I. 20. 66–67).

Cicero has a long discussion of decorum and summarizes by saying: "This 'decorum' of which I have been speaking can be seen in all our deeds, words, and in physical movement and bearing. It is apparent in three ways: in natural beauty, in the due order of parts, and in outward embellishment suited to the appropriate function" (I. 35. 126).

He defines virtue differently in different contexts, but the constituent elements are usually the same: *wisdom,* or the perception of truth in action, character, motive, and consequence;

self-control, or the keeping of the more violent emotions ($\pi\acute{a}\theta\eta$) in check; *public spirit,* or the treatment of others with reason and understanding (II. 5. 18).

Thus Cicero clearly links several methods for a moral life—courage, wisdom, self-control, decorum, and acceptance of moral obligation—the same methods suggested in Restoration drama. Only Christianity is missing, and that option was not available to Cicero. His passages mentioning respect for the gods, we might note, made even this apparent weakness less evident to a Christian audience.

We turn now to the plays and their advocacy of these methods. Courage as a means to deal with life is an idea with its roots remote in the past. The courageous man in Restoration drama is typically martial in his role, and his courage is evidenced by his deeds. Sometimes the figure is a queen, and her courage seems all the more amazing because of her sex. The Hungarian Queen in Orrery's *Mustapha* states flatly:

> Death may, but fear shall never cast me down:
> Who yields, does ne're deserve to wear a Crown.

> (I. ii. 101–102)

This queen is bolstered in her resolve by her office and, we learn elsewhere, by her Christian faith. Office and belief do not create character, but they can reinforce it.

Character, by the same token, is often revealed, at least in potential, by acts of courage. A number of Restoration protagonists are introduced as men of innate courage, courage which is untraceable—for the moment at least—to family or social rank or office. Thus Montezuma is described in the opening lines of Dryden's *The Indian Queen* (1665) by the Ynca, the ruler:

> Thrice have the *Mexicans* before us fled,
> Their Armies broke, their Prince in Triumph led;
> Both to thy valour, brave young man, we owe;
> Ask thy Reward.

Almanzor, of *The Conquest of Granada,* is another heroic figure whose past is vague but whose deeds bespeak a natural leader. We are told, before we see him, that his actions are "more then man" can usually accomplish (I, p. 3). When he does enter, it is at a moment of clash and crisis; he judges the situation quickly and immediately takes action. His spontaneity, his vigor, his authority—all give him stature in our eyes and lend credence to his otherwise arrogant claim to King Boabdelin:

> I brought that Succour which thou oughtst to bring,
> And so, in Nature, am thy Subjects King.
>
> (I, p. 8)

The crucial phrase is "in Nature." Almanzor reveals his kingliness through his courage, much as Havelok the Dane revealed his princely parentage by a glow which appeared in his mouth as he slept, or as other foundlings have shown by some sign or other that they are more than they might otherwise seem.

Office will reinforce character, as in the case of the Hungarian Queen, but office is not sufficient to courage, as witness Boabdelin. And, of course, courage may be possessed by villains, although it is courage defined in a limited way, as boldness, fearlessness, and, ultimately, foolhardiness. Villains do not possess the balanced virtue of courage as defined by Aristotle: "a mean with respect to fear and confidence."[55] Courage is an inner quality and not an action. Courage may be signified by action, but it can exist at moments in which no action takes place. This distinction between inner state and action places the determination of courage by any man other than oneself subject to the ambiguities of appearance and reality. Restoration playwrights often help the audience through ambiguous appearance by means of asides or moral exclamations by the protagonists. Aureng-Zebe enters a dangerous situation with these words:

> Fearless without, because secure within,
> Arm'd with my courage, unconcern'd I see
> This pomp.
>
> (III, p. 37)

Aristotle said, "A courageous man feels and acts according to the merits of each case and as reason guides him."[56] This defi-

41

nition makes courage analogous to decorum and directly linked to reason. Nevertheless, courage is not reason; reason only directs, in the sense of "points the direction," and cannot motivate.

A villain's "courage" is a stock theatrical emotion and is familiar in such varied shapes as the boldness engendered by the miser's monomania (*The Merchant of Venice*), the over-reacher's passion to rule (*Tamburlaine*), the bastard's desperate self-reliance (Edmund in *King Lear*), and the wife's ambition for her spouse (*Macbeth*). Restoration villains, in addition, often owe something to Hobbes and to the dramatic tradition of villainous rant, which can be traced in England back to the Herod of the mystery plays. Crimalhaz, in Settle's *The Empress of Morocco*, speaks for the type not only in the near madness of his speech, but in his claim to natural and historical justification for the evil which is planned:

> ... the more Barb'rous garb our Deeds assume,
> We nearer to our First perfection come.
> Since Nature first made Man wild, savage, strong,
> And his Blood hot, then when the world was Young:
> If Infant-times such Rising-valours bore,
> Why should not Riper Ages now do more?
>
> (III. ii, p. 33)

The Empress is a woman of even greater perverse "courage," and her recklessness appears with increasing intensity as the play nears an end and the pressures around her build. The enormity of her crimes is welcomed as a test of her will and the scope of her ambition. "Let single Murthers, Common Hands Suffice: / I Scorn to kill less than whole Families" (V. i, p. 61). Her actions are bold, but they are all "confidence," to use Aristotle's term. There is no reason in what she does, and her courage is therefore without control or direction; she is flawed in the way all men are who act by appetite alone and without reason.

The opposite of courage is of course cowardice, but an alternative to courage exists and Restoration drama describes it in

42

almost every play. This alternative is the pastoral life, the life of retirement and contemplation. Almost universally, however, the pastoral alternative is denied. Retreat from the active life is not denied as a potential way of life; it is denied for these characters in their special circumstances. Restoration figures have already made their choice of life, and they speak of the pastoral alternative wistfully and wishfully. The Duke of Norfolk daydreams of his relationship with Queen Mary under different circumstances:

> Were she so low, the farthest from a Crown,
> Sate on a Bank for Scotland's gawdy Throne,
> Under no Canopy, but some large Oak,
> And for a Scepter, in her hand a Crook;
>
> .   .   .   .
>
> Glad I wou'd be to dress me like a Swain,
> Steal from her Eyes my Pleasure and my Pain,
> Smile when she smiles, or else out weep the Rain.
> Sit by her side, freed from the Chains of Power,
> And never think of Wealth or Honour more.
>
> (Banks, *The Island Queens*, II, p. 16)

The archetype for the choice between the life of action and the life of contemplation is provided by the figure of Hercules at the fork; but, as Cicero points out, few but the son of Jupiter ever have so clear-cut a choice. Restoration *dramatis personae* have chosen at the fork, and other paths are might-have-beens.[57]

The pastoral life is pictured as temperate in climate, loving in intercourse, psychologically peaceful.[58] Inner peace is a major theme in Restoration plays and appears as the most sought after of all human conditions. Inner peace for most characters can come only through self-control, which in turn is the result of Christian faith or, alternatively, of that philosophic temper which I have called, loosely, stoicism. Stoic self-control is exemplified by such obvious figures as Dryden's Cleomenes, a Spartan: "My mind on its own Centre stands unmov'd, / And Stable; as the Fabrick of the World" (I, p. 1). *Cleomenes*

43

(1692) is a play of considerable spectacle in which Cleomenes and his family endure terrible deprivation which ends only in death for them all.

Calm in the face of misfortune is attractive sometimes by way of contrast. Rather than debate the value of a stoical approach to life, Lee, for instance, reveals the superiority of self-control through the spectacle of passionate outburst. Queen Roxana of *The Rival Queens* cries:

> Roxana, and Statira, they are names
> That must for ever jarr: eternal discord,
> Fury, revenge, disdain, and indignation
> Tear my swoln breast, make way for fire and tempest.
> My brain is burst, debate and reason quench'd.[59]
>
> (III. 48–52)

In contrast, Alexander is able to scorn misfortune which is prophesied for him. He is convinced of the rightness and grandeur of his deeds. If he must fall, he must fall: "'Tis great to fall the envy of the stars" (II. 191). The contrast of calm and tempest fills Restoration drama.

Dryden has several plays in which pagan and Christian, rude and civilized, are played off against one another: for example, *The Indian Queen, The Indian Emperour, Tyrannick Love, The Conquest of Granada*. Sometimes in these plays the civilized characters are distinguished by an admirable polish of manner. Montezuma, in *The Indian Queen*, senses this difference between himself and the Mexican prince Acacis. "How gentle all this Princes actions be! / Vertue is calm in him, but rough in me" (II. i. 102–103). A similar contrast exists between the rough Almanzor and the polished Duke of Arcos.

The stoic figure is often open to only one sort of emotional appeal, the appeal to familial emotion—even if the "family" is the state. Arpasia, in Rowe's *Tamerlane*, flies in rage and despair after seeing her beloved strangled. She had prayed for help in this moment from the "great Examples" of her sex: "Chast Virgins, tender Wives, and pious Matrons" (V, p. 64). But their example is not enough. She dies enraged:

44

> Ye Moralists,
> Ye Talkers! What are all your precepts now?
> Patience? Distraction? blast the Tyrant, blast him.

(V, p. 66)

Similarly, in the serious plot of Dryden's *Don Sebastian* (1690), Sebastian is bold in the face of death ("Souls know no Conquerors") until he is reminded of the misfortunes of his people, at which he weeps (I, pp. 12, 13).

Self-control is an essential heroic virtue because it enables the heroic figure to act with purpose. Achilles is a man of rage in the epic, but rage is his weakness, not his strength. Almanzor, whom Dryden associates in part with passionate epic figures like Achilles, learns in the course of the play's action to control himself, to modify his spontaneity along artificial, social lines. He learns that in order to deal with other men he must moderate his passion. The intelligent Abenamar is able to see beneath Almanzor's outbursts a coherent and admirable man. Almanzor has, Abenamar says,

> A Soul too fiery, and too great to guide:
> He moves excentrique, like a wandring star;
> Whose Motion's just; though 'tis not regular.

(V, p. 58)

Eccentric motion—an exciting allusion to developments in current astronomy—has a pattern and can be reduced to a formula, although the formula is more complex than that of the predictable circle. Almanzor is not a good example of hysteria, then, but of self-control of a private kind. That is, he is able to control himself when it suits his internal standard, but he is indifferent to external, public standards, until very late in Part I of the play.

The more common lack of self-control is rooted in passion without will. The sniveling, masochistic senator Antonio, in Otway's *Venice Preserv'd*, is pathological in his sexual aberration, though "never the worse Senator for all that," as he says (III. i. 23–24). His pathology is lack of self-control exemplified at the border of madness. That border is not fixed, and every

45

man fears that he might cross it. Belvidera, in the same play, has been clear sighted and patient throughout, in sharp contrast to her husband and most of the others; and yet she, too, is finally driven to madness, which is described, as it often is in the seventeenth century, as a turmoil of boiling heat—as, in fact, a personal hell:

> How I could bleed, how burn, how drown the waves
> Huzzing and booming round my sinking head,
> Till I descended to the peacefull bottome!
> Oh there's all quiet, here all rage and fury,
> The Air's too thin, and pierces my weak brain,
> I long for thick substantial sleep: Hell, Hell,
> Burst from the Centre, rage and roar aloud,
> If thou art half so hot, so mad as I am.[60]

(V. 355–62)

With self-control, nearly synonymous with sanity, comes a kind of peace, that most sought after of all conditions.

Self-control is associated with wisdom either as a cause or as an effect, but always as a companion. Wisdom comes only in company with inner peace, or, more accurately, can be expressed or exercised only in company with peace. Passion blinds us always, and leads us, like Arnold's ignorant armies, into dark and directionless struggle. The cynical Thersites of Dryden's *Troilus and Cressida* (1679) wishes for a fight between Troilus and Diomede with these words: "Let neither of 'em have cogitation enough, to consider 'tis a whore they fight for" (IV. ii, p. 56). The spectacle of the ignorant blindly flailing the ignorant is the spectacle of the Civil War, according to the opening lines of Samuel Butler's *Hudibras* (1663):

> When *civil* Fury first grew high,
> And men fell out they knew not why;
> When hard words, *Jealousies* and *Fears*,
> Set Folks together by the ears,
> And made them fight, like mad or drunk,
> For Dame *Religion* as for Punk,
> Whose honesty they all durst swear for,
> Though not a man of them knew wherefore.[61]

46

Ignorance (hard words) and passion (jealousy and fear) are linked, the implication is, in this and perhaps every struggle. Wisdom, on the other hand, has nothing organic to do with passion. (We might recall that this dissociation of wisdom and passion is also a sign of wisdom's weakness. Wisdom alone cannot motivate.)

The opposite of wisdom is folly, and folly in Restoration drama typically takes the form of deception or naiveté and is never in any important way linked with witlessness or intellectual deficiency. In the serious plays, as in the comedies, the simple fool is not a threat. The fool or the "natural" lacks intellectual capacity and is not, therefore, capable of craft or guile. The knave, on the other hand, is an intelligent man, though not wise, and is therefore extremely dangerous. His intelligence is in the service of evil and his talents are applied in deception and various forms of self-interested "policy." Dorimant tells Loveit in *The Man of Mode*: "Take heed; fools can dissemble too." Loveit answers: "They may—but not so artificially as you. There is no fear they should deceive us" (V. i. 111–13).

The knave is a man of artifice both because he dissembles and because he is a man of skill and craft. Restoration villains, as villains have been time out of mind, are plotters. Because they are attempting to subvert or outflank nature, they must create artificial situations which will be to their advantage. In many Restoration serious plays this means that the villain attempts to establish circumstances which will lead him to power—power not rightfully, by law or by nature, his. The protagonist, then, must be a man of wisdom in the special sense that he must be ever alert to the false and the unnatural. He must be wise to the ways of knaves.

Such wisdom, such "prudence" Henry Fielding would say, is difficult to come by for several reasons. For one, the protagonist is sometimes naive about his fellow man and about civilization. Almanzor is such a figure, and so is Gabriel Towerson, a protagonist of Dryden's topical potboiler *Amboyna* (1673): "he thinks all honest, 'cause himself is so, and therefore none suspects" (I, p. 5).[62] Such a man sees all men as reflections of himself. He is an ironic figure because his ignorance is a handicap and a weakness in the way of the world, and yet we must be conscious at the same time that naive trust in one's fellow man —what the eighteenth century called "candor"—is clearly preferable, morally, to worldly wisdom and prudence. Richard III, in John Caryll's *The English Princess* (1667), can represent the perceptive villain. He says in an aside:

> . . . watchful prudence cannot trace
> The subtle ways of a dissembling Heart:
> I am well read in that mysterious Art,
> And can discern where all my danger lyes:
> Mines have destroy'd more Towns, than Batteries.
>
> (I. iii, p. 7)

Towerson and Almanzor must learn prudence, and yet we watch their education with mixed feelings. They are sheep in a world of wolves, but what a shame that it is a world of wolves.

The trusting innocent is susceptible to dissimulation, and so, too, is a more sophisticated figure if the dissimulation is in turn sophisticated. The clash of skills in perceiver and perceived is nowhere more apparent than at court. Restoration serious plays frequently allude, often unsubtly, to the slick courtesy and hypocrisy which everyone saw at the court of Charles II. The polished appearances at court made especially difficult the recognition and evaluation of merit. Philocles is praised in Dryden's *Secret Love* (1668) as "so rare a thing as rising vertue, / And merit understood at Court" (I. iii. 7–8). Often men flee the court to escape the hypocrisy and the misevaluation of merit. Acasto, in Otway's *The Orphan* (1680), was a familiar figure to a Restoration audience. He has gone to the country, nursing a just resentment:

> When for what he had born,
> Long, hard, and faithful Toyl, he might have claim'd
> Places in Honour, and employment high; [but]
> A huffing shining flat'ring cringing Coward,
> A Canker-worm of Peace was rais'd above him.
>
> (I. 20–24)

The moral indignation focused on Charles' court had many sources, but one was the revulsion many felt at the intense and relentless hypocrisy which seemed the necessary way of life there. "Good God," Pepys exclaimed, "what an age is this and what a world is this, that a man cannot live without playing the knave and dissimulacion" (September 1, 1661).[63] The perception of true merit is difficult in the best of circumstances, and it is nearly impossible in a milieu of flattery, fashion, and self-interest.

The monarchs of Restoration plays are not always allegorical of the English monarch, but they are always emblematic of monarchy and its nature. The monarch who judges badly and who rewards merit unjustly is a bad monarch, and in the world of rapid reward and punishment which the drama always provides he is a ruined monarch. There is, once again, the presumption that politics is the acts of men, and not the expression of institutions or forces. Therefore the men who make up the court are its essence and not simply its staff. The something, for instance, which is rotten in Denmark is primarily Claudius, and not the state of the Danish judiciary, or its welfare system, or the extent of the franchise. When Oedipus is guilty, all of Thebes suffers. When Boabdelin is the monarch, there is civil war within Granada and enemy armies are camped without. There is, then, terrible irony in Boabdelin's opening words, "Thus, in the Triumphs of soft Peace I reign." When Queen Elizabeth, in Banks's *The Island Queens* (1684), is torn within herself by conflicting loves, all of England is affected. If she misjudges her advisors, she rules badly. Like Lear, every monarch must have the wisdom to judge men aright, or the whole kingdom will suffer.

Wisdom in these plays is primarily a matter of the knowledge of the characters of men, and not a matter of learning. It is worldly wisdom that the plays inculcate, a worldly wisdom which is not only self-serving but also public-serving. It is wisdom that will enable these characters to fill their functions as public figures—as kings or princes or generals—as well as their private functions as fathers or brothers or friends.[64] The theme

49

of worldly wisdom is not novel—*Othello* can be read in part as a parable on it—but it is ubiquitous. The Restoration was a time of plots and disguises and secrecy. Charles dealt secretly with France and publicly with mistresses and cohorts known to be untrustworthy in their professions of good will and conscience. Self-serving men concealed their wishes beneath the language of religion and public welfare.

Dryden and Lee collaborated on an allegorical play, *The Duke of Guise* (1683). This play mirrors the plotting and counterplotting of contemporary England, and the Tory authors portray the play's villains as religious hypocrites helped by the devil, who looks "like one that preaches to the Crowd, / Gospel is in [his] Face, and outward Garb, / And Treason on [his] Tongue" (IV, p. 41). The conflict of appearance and reality had special significance for Restoration audiences. The political world they inhabited had all the elements of one of their plays: the clash of fathers and sons and brothers was present in the relationships of Charles, James, and the Duke of Monmouth; dissimulation and demagoguery were everywhere. The plots of many of the plays are hackneyed, in retrospect, but then they were the stuff of immediacy.

Isaac Barrow, in 1661, gave a sermon entitled "The Pleasantness of Religion."[65] The sermon is in fact about wisdom and is based on the text of Proverbs 3:17: "Her ways *are* ways of pleasantness, and all her paths *are* peace." Barrow defines wisdom pragmatically as "an habitual skill or faculty of judging aright about matters of practice, and chusing according to that right judgment, and conforming the actions to such good choice." Wisdom is thus a means of doing and is more than an intellectual condition. As he explicates his text further, Barrow mentions nearly all of the methods of creating a good life that have been discussed above with relation to Restoration serious drama. Wisdom, for instance, is the parent of self-control: "Wisdom instructs us to examine, compare, and rightly to value the objects that court our affections, and challenge our care; and thereby regulates our passions, and moderates our endeavours, which begets a pleasant serenity and peaceable tranquility of mind." Regulation and moderation are the means, and peace and tranquility the goals.

Wisdom can, and must, lead us to religion, but it does not lead us to sectarianism: "The principal advantage of Wisedom is, its acquainting us with the Nature and reason of true Religion, and affording convictive arguments to persuade to the Practice of it." Further, religion consists "not in a pertinacious adherence to any Sect or party, but in a sincere love of goodness, and dislike of naughtiness, where-ever discovering itself; not in vain ostentations and flourishes of outward performance, but in an inward complexion of mind, exerting itself in works of true Devotion and Charity." Thus the true religion of which Barrow speaks is a faith which exhibits itself in charity, in outward and public action which reflects an inward and spiritual condition—in a word, benevolence.

The denial of sect and party is a focal Restoration theme and one which can be found in all writing of the period, even sectarian writing. The Civil War was still fresh in everyone's mind, and the tension between Whig and Tory, Protestant and Catholic, was a daily reality.

Finally, Barrow argues that wisdom is the source and guide of decorum: "Wisdom distinguishes the circumstances, limits the measures, determines the modes, appoints the fit seasons of action; so preserving *decorum* and order, the parent of peace, and preventing confusion, the mother of iniquity, strife, and disquiet." (my italics). Decorum is a matter of context, and the appreciation of context is a matter of wisdom. A wise man understands his circumstances, their nature and constituent elements. He is—and he uniquely is—able to act with decorum. Barrow does not mention this, but wisdom as he defines it is necessarily connected with morality. It is linked to "love of goodness" and "right judgment" and "good choice." What Barrow does not mention is that a villain is often every bit as perceptive and able to distinguish "the circumstances" as is a good man, and therefore a villain may be a man of great apparent decorum. A villain's behavior is "fit" in the sense that he has consciously chosen the manner best suited to the circumstances

51

and his goals. Put another way, what distinguishes the good man and the evil man is not their decorum. What distinguishes them is their goals.

Nevertheless, it does seem true that wisdom in the sense of skill and facility of judgment is prerequisite to decorum, and decorum is recommended in Restoration drama, as it is in Barrow's sermon, as a means to peace and the prevention of confusion. Solyman, the monarch of Orrery's *Mustapha*, hesitates to war against the Hungarian Queen:

> But now the War does seem too low a thing,
> Against a Mourning Queen, and Infant King;
> *Pyrrhus*, it will unequal seem in me
> To Conquer, and then blush at Victory.

(I. i. 15–18)

Although Solyman's advisors persuade him to proceed, the audience has fixed the inappropriateness and the ugliness of his war. He is a bully and, worse, a weak man because he knows the "inequality" of his actions.

Solyman's concern is with decorum as it applies to his public role. He is worried about the etiquette of warfare or kingship, a superficial concern. Solyman does not mention the fundamental issues of war and peace, love and hate, but is concerned about how things will "seem." One suspects that if there were any way for him to war secretly against Hungary he would do so without hesitation, despite widowed queen and infant son. Yet Solyman does say he would "blush" at such a conquest, and a blush is a sign of conscience. I believe the seventeenth century understood decorum as a pervasive and profound ethical concept, one that touched every aspect of life from the most important to the most trivial, from war to table manners—which Hobbes scornfully, and brilliantly, called a matter of "small morals."[66]

Perhaps the ubiquity of the concept can be seen in the familiar form of the outer man as a reflection of the inner. This notion can be found in Castiglione and his Platonic sources and throughout the Middle Ages.[67] The Restoration accepted a partial correlation of inner and outer, at least for dramatic purposes. Creon, the villain of Dryden's and Lee's *Oedipus* (1679), is crippled and his mind is said to match his back. "Nature herself start[ed] back when [he was] born" (I. i. 142). John Crowne describes England's most famous symbol of the distortions of political ambition, Richard Plantagenet:

> He is a hell at whose foul front appears,
> Ill manners, and ill nature, and ill shape,
> Like a three-headed Dog, that barks at all things
> That dare come near him, specially at beauty.
>
> <div align="right">(<i>The Misery of Civil-War</i>, II, p. 22)</div>

But outer appearance mirrors inner nature in more subtle ways as well. Morat, in *Aureng-Zebe*, is all disorder within, and though he is not physically flawed in the crudely symbolic way of Creon (or Oedipus himself, for that matter), his actions reveal the essential disorder of the inner man. He is said to have a soul "irregularly great," to be a man "wanting temper" and having "unequal pulses" (V, p. 68). Each of these descriptive phrases comes from the vocabulary of decorum, whose positive values incorporate regularity, temperateness, and equality. No man of unequal pulses can act in a way which is fit except by chance and sporadically. He has no control over himself, and control is of the essence. Decorum and self-control seem sides of a coin. Decorum demands self-control but is not limited to it.

Decorum, or fitness, can be a demanding standard which even tortures the basic nature of man. This is seen rather superficially in the numberless laments by monarchs in Restoration drama who find themselves with two natures, or more, to be matched with several patterns of decorum. There is, for instance, a decorum for the lover and another for the queen.

> Shall I, I who am born a Sovereign Queen,
> Be barr'd of that which God and Nature gives
> The meanest Slave, a freedom in my love?
>
> <div align="right">(Queen of Sicily in Dryden's <i>Secret Love</i>, I. iii. 157–59)</div>

When the queen (any queen) takes a lover, the decorous modes of action, the fit things to do, are not at all clear. The Hungarian Queen, in *Mustapha*, exclaims:

Without a Clue I'm in a lab'rynth left:
And where even Hope is of her Eyes bereft.
With Noble *Zanger Mustapha* contends,
They strive as Rivals and they yield as Friends:
I injure one if I the other chuse;
And keeping either I the Sultan lose.
Flying from both I from my refuge run;
And by my staying shall destroy my Son.
Them for their false Religion I eschew,
Though I have found their Virtue ever true.
And when Religion sends my thoughts above,
This Card'nal calls them down and talks of Love.

(III. iii. 547–58)

The speech is more programmatic and extreme than some, but the complexities of the queen's relationships are obvious. What is the decorous way for her to behave?

As desperate as the Hungarian Queen's condition is, there may be a solution. For others there is no solution possible. There is none, for example, for the bastards of Restoration (and earlier) drama. A bastard is a man without a universe. He has no family, no home, no role, no place—in any sense of the word. For him there is no decorum because he is not fit in his nature. This is the agony of Edmund in *King Lear*, and it is the agony, sympathetically portrayed, of the Duke of Monmouth in Dryden's *Absalom and Achitophel*:

... oh that Fate Propitiously Enclind,
Had rais'd my Birth, or had debas'd my Mind;
To my large Soul, not all her Treasure lent,
And then Betray'd it to a mean Descent.
I find, I find my mounting Spirits Bold,
And *David*'s Part disdains my Mothers Mold.
Why am I Scanted by a Niggard Birth?
My Soul Disclaims the Kindred of her Earth:
And made for Empire, Whispers me within;
Desire of Greatness is a Godlike Sin.

(Ll. 363–72)

In the same year that he wrote this poem, Dryden drew another bastard with a nearly identical lament. Torrismond, in *The Spanish Fryar* (1681), cries, "Good Heav'ns, why gave you me a Monarch's Soul, / And crusted it with base Plebian Clay?" (II, p. 20).

The bastard is outside the conventional patterns of life and therefore may act as his desires or will dictates. But that freedom is a frightening freedom—the freedom to do anything—and therefore most illegitimate sons in drama quickly find some basis for action, some principle which justifies purposeful action. In other words, they find a decorum, and that decorum is typically in a libertinism conceived of as "natural," as reflecting the state of nature before man's cowardice and greed created moral law. The bastard such as Edmund, or Otway's Don John in the passage which follows, justifies his action as "fit" according to the essential, the radical nature of man. He recognizes that his actions may be antisocial, but social paradigms for behavior are artificial and false to man's birthright. In *Don Carlos* (1676), Otway presents a representative illegitimate son in the King's brother, Don John. John's soliloquy opening Act II owes much to *King Lear*, but it is in Restoration diction and reflects the argument of many Restoration libertines: [68]

> Why should dull Law rule Nature, who first made
> That Law, by which her self is now betray'd?
> E're Man's Corruptions made him wretched, he
> Was born most noble that was born most free:
> Each of himself was Lord; and, unconfin'd
> Obey'd the dictates of his Godlike mind.
> Law was an Innovation brought in since,
> When Fools began to love Obedience,
> And call'd their slavery Safety and defence.
>
> . . . .
>
> Why should it be A Stain upon my Blood
> Because I came not in the Common Road,
> But Born obscure and so more like a God?

Thus the illegitimate makes himself more truly natural than other men. He is, he argues, closer to man as he was first made and, in fact, in his radical freedom, is even like the gods. What is appropriate for the gods—ambition, trickery, lust—is appropriate for him, and therefore he has a pattern for his behavior.

The audience recognizes in Don John another pattern—the pattern of the overreacher, whose archetype is Satan, who also wanted to act with more freedom and more like a god. The audience in the Restoration would also have recognized the reference to the state of nature as one of the catch phrases associated with Thomas Hobbes and the *Leviathan*. Don John speaks both like a Hobbesian and like a disciple of the devil. In the state of nature described in the *Leviathan*, every man is radically free and driven only by the selfish passions: "for as to have no desire is to be dead, so to have weak passions is dullness; and to have passions indifferently for everything, GIDDINESS and *distraction*." Hobbes, however, was a man of the middle and late seventeenth century, and like most of his peers he found peace to be the supreme good. The state of nature that Hobbes described was not one that he admired (a fact his contemporaries seemed to forget); life in the natural state is, in his memorable phrase, "solitary, poor, nasty, brutish, and short."[69] For no man is this solitary life more stark than for the bastard. His life, significantly, gives dramatic evidence for the power of Hobbes's insight and one more argument for decorum as a crucial necessity in a peaceful and harmonious life.

III

The Hobbesian man (that is, the man Hobbes describes as existing in the state of nature) has no obligations whatsoever to his fellow man: "during the time men live without a common power to keep them all in awe, they are in that condition which is called war, and such a war as is of every man against every man."[70] It is perhaps this conclusion about the uncivilized condition of men that is most disturbing to society. We could, after all, live patiently with the knowledge that we are all driven by lusts of the flesh, or that all men seek power. But to fear that every man is every man's enemy is to live a terrifying, paranoid existence.

Hobbes acknowledged that terror, and he argued that it served as the motive impelling men toward social contract and absolute monarchy. Absolutism was not attractive to Hobbes's contemporaries, and so they attacked the problem of man's selfishness in other ways. They offered, among other alternatives, innate moral sense, divine law produced by revelation, man-made law, and the argument that the monarch controlled his people better when they loved him. These ideas seemed to justify and to encourage moral obligation and the tie of man to man in aid and comfort on a basis other than fear. Of course moral obligation can have its roots in a great many concepts, some very poorly thought out but nevertheless passionately held. The Restoration serious plays rarely explore the basis for moral obligation. Instead they preach it, plead for it, exemplify it, and, in sum, do all they can to bring the audience to a sense of the desperate need for man to be lovingly related to his fellow man.

I include most of the more familiar Restoration positive values under the general heading of moral obligation, since they are means of combating selfishness and effecting the loving tie of man to man. Such values are friendship, generosity, and self-sacrifice, and that undefined set of obligations called duty.[71] Sometimes the source of selflessness is religious injunction. The Cardinal in *Mustapha* says that religion makes it greater to "dye a Martyr than to live a King" (I. ii. 150). Sometimes the responsibilities of office force the denial of self, as Queen Elizabeth laments in *The Unhappy Favourite*:

> Now now support thy Royalty,
> And hold thy Greatness firm; but oh, how heavy
> A Load is State where the Free Mind's disturb'd!

> (II, p. 18)

There is a unique form of tension between the office and the private man when the character is a villain whose pre-eminent power places him, as Hobbes says it must, in the condition of absolute freedom. Morat, in *Aureng-Zebe*, is forging such an absolutism for himself, an absolute power and simultaneously an absolute freedom:

'Tis not with me as with a private Man.
Such may be sway'd by Honour, or by Love;
But Monarchs onely by their int'rest move.

(III, p. 43)

Morat's use of *love* here is curious and revelatory. Like the words *duty* and *honor*, *love* means what the speaker wants it to mean in the context, and it means nothing absolutely. Morat apparently means *love* in this context to imply an emotion which creates a bond between individuals and limits their freedom. Love, thus, must mean or imply obligations and selflessness. It cannot mean simply lust in this context, for Morat is at this moment offering himself as a lover to Indamora. The love which interest denies is the love which takes an individual out of himself and substitutes another's interest in part for his own.

And this is the chief effect of love in Restoration serious drama. Love takes men and women out of themselves. It gives them a new way to see themselves and their relationships to others. The existence of love is most accurately evidenced, for example, by sacrifice. No gesture gives more convincing proof that love is present than a gesture which is obviously without benefit to the gesturer. Lovers, therefore, are omnipresent as contrasts to villains, not simply because love is good and villainy is evil, but because love prompts selflessness and evil is always selfish.

Love teaches moral obligation, or, more accurately and less causally stated, love is the acceptance of moral obligation. This general truth is dramatically revealed countless times and can be seen in something so small as a single line of dialogue. For example, Montezuma has been offered a reward for service to the Ynca, the Peruvian monarch. Montezuma asks for the hand of Orazia, the Ynca's daughter. He is refused and is on the verge of angry revenge when he is reminded of Orazia. *"Orazia!"* Montezuma exclaims, "how that name has charm'd my Sword!" (*The Indian Queen*, I. i. 65). In fiction at least, love has always conquered conquerors, and the point here is simply to recognize that one important manifestation of love's power is that it turns an individual from motives entirely selfish to motives partially

58

selfless. Lust has no such power, and despite the lexical sloppiness of using the word *love* for both lust and the condition of caring for the well-being of another, no audience has trouble distinguishing the two.

Love educates many noble savages—Montezuma, Almanzor, and Phraartes, the Parthian King in Crowne's *The Destruction of Jerusalem* (1677):

> An unknown passion makes my spirit bow;
> Whose insolence I never felt till now.
> I've seen, admir'd, ador'd, yes and enjoy'd,
> Till both my Eyes and Appetite were Cloy'd,
>
> . . . .
>
> But this one Beauty has subdu'd me more,
> Than all the Armies of 'em did before.

(Part I, Act II. ii, p. 18)

The military metaphor here is seductive and may lead us to imagine that this is a reiteration of the courtly love theme of the absolute power of the mistress, and no more. But the Restoration lovers are military and political men, and one of the effects of love is political: that is, the lover-king as a political figure is substantively different from the loveless, though perhaps satiated, monarch. Love modifies behavior, and the behavior of a hero is heroic. Phraartes illustrates the way love can convert a bloody-minded and revengeful soldier into a spiritual and moral force. Phraartes is never converted to Judaism in Crowne's play, but there is more than military prowess and leadership involved when a Roman says of Phraartes that he has become "the very soul of all [the Jews'] souls" (Part II, Act IV).

Almanzor is, as we have seen, by nature a king. He has decisiveness and courage. And his behavior is modified by love. Significantly, his first act of love is to free Almahide, who is his by rules of war. But Almanzor does not possess a sense of how lesser men perceive him until Almahide shows him. She brings him, slowly, to recognize that ordinary men have unheroic vision and that they must be made to see him with eyes like hers (IV, p. 52). She asks him:

59

> Might I not make it as my last request,
> (Since humble carriage sutes a Suppliant best)
> That you would somewhat of your fierceness hide:
> That inborn fire; I do not call it pride.

(IV, p. 51)

Almanzor's first attempt to modify his behavior according to social need is abortive, but the crucial matter is that for *her* he will do this. Love brings him to moral obligation.

Those characters to whom love is less of a struggle—which is to say those of less than heroic stature—are on occasion pictured as vying with one another for the chance to be self-sacrificing. In *The Conquest of Granada* a young couple, Ozmyn and Benzayda, act as diminutive foils to Almanzor and Almahide. There are obstacles to their love and they must frequently choose among unsatisfactory alternative actions. This brings them to an impasse, and us to a curious feature of Restoration love stories. Because love is selfless, and because the more genuine the more selfless, true lovers are often impotent—not sexually, but in terms of nonsexual action. Near the end of *The Conquest of Granada*, Part I, Ozmyn and Benzayda are at such a stalemate. They have nothing but what is most valuable to them, their love. As Ozmyn says,

> Thus, then, secur'd of what we hold most dear,
> (Each others love,) we'll go—I know not where.

(V, p. 56)

As a variation on this theme, noble rivals may both give up their beloved so as not to compete with each other. This happens in *Mustapha* and, with modifications, in Otway's *The Orphan* and in Addison's *Cato*.

Despite the occasional impotence caused by love, the private emotions are of greatest significance when they affect public action, as they do in every play in which the characters are in some way public figures. We see this effect more in heroic plays like *The Indian Queen* than in domestic plays like *Venice Preserv'd*. While love is often the emotion whereby a selfish individual is brought to selflessness, there are plays in which the figures have selflessness in their character and its source is never explained. Nor, unless one assumes that self-interest is the natural condition of man, does it need explanation. Such a selfless character is Philip, in Aphra Behn's *Abdelazer* (1677). He is motivated by the agony of those around him:

> ... when I look
> Upon my Fathers wrongs, my Brothers wounds,
> My Mothers infamy, *Spain*'s misery,
> I am all fire.

(IV, p. 46)

An analogous moment occurs in Dryden's *Don Sebastian* when Sebastian's stoicism breaks down at the mention of the anguish of his people (I, p. 13).

At the end of the seventeenth century, partly in response to Hobbesian psychology, the notion began to appear that self-sacrifice could be self-satisfying and that a man could best serve himself by serving others.[72] Rowe's Tamerlane expresses the pleasure of doing good:

> Great Minds (like Heav'n) are pleas'd in doing good,
> Tho' the ungrateful Subjects of their Favours
> Are barren in return.

(II. ii, p. 23)

More commonly, Restoration plays emphasize sacrifice as concomitant with moral obligation, and contrast sacrifice with selfishness.

The power of Christianity to reinforce one's turning outward from the self is, the plays say, an important means to a peaceful life. Dryden's *Tyrannick Love* offers the benefits of Christianity in two ways: through the example of St. Catherine and through the warning of Maximin, the anti-Christian tyrant. Dryden took pleasure in the contemplation of religious ideas, and several of his plays contain debates or discussions of theological matters.[73] In *Tyrannick Love* Maximin's ranting and lust contrast with Catherine's calm selflessness. We note, for example, that Catherine is self-controlled: "See where she comes with that high Air and meen, / Which marks, in bonds, the greatness of a Queen"

61

(II. i. 159–60). Her dignity is a reflection of an inner condition, as is Maximin's rage. Her inner calm has two supports: it is secured by faith and it is secured by reason. That reason is once again involved is not surprising, but its relationship to faith is important. Catherine defends the Christian position to Maximin's philosophers:

> ... where our Reason with our Faith does go,
> We're both above enlightned, and below.
> But Reason with your fond Religion fights.

(II. i. 169–70)

Catherine's position can be paralleled elsewhere in Dryden's writings, for example, in *Religio Laici*, twelve years later, as well as in contemporary sermons. Robert South, in "An Account of the Nature and Measures of Conscience" (1691), speaks of the *"Light of Reason"* as a "Ray of Divinity darted into the Soul. *It is the Candle of the Lord* (as *Solomon* calls it) and God never lights us up a *Candle* either to *put it out*, or to *sleep by*."[74] The wise Marquis of Halifax, in *The Lady's New-Year's Gift: or, Advice to a Daughter* (1688) says: "*Religion* is exalted *Reason*, refin'd and sifted from the grosser parts of it: It dwelleth in the upper Region of the *Mind*, where there are fewest *Clouds* or *Mists* to darken or offend it."[75] My point here is that in the Restoration a pervasive and, for all practical purposes, unquestioned assumption existed that religion and reason were intimately related. The relationship varied in particulars from sect to sect and from writer to writer, as above, but all agreed there was one.

Some of the vigor with which these authors supported the cause of religion and reason was prompted by a desire to discredit enthusiasm, that religious intensity which was associated with the Puritans and with hypocritical Roman Catholic priests.[76] The religious fanatic, dogmatically certain of the truth of his beliefs, passionate in the forms of his worship, willing (and this is his worst fault) to provoke schism to advance his cause, is a figure of contempt in the Restoration and is treated sometimes as a source of comedy or farce and sometimes as an unqualified evil. Those who made up the establishment were not of one mind regarding the nature of religion, but they were agreed that schism, enthusiasm, and elaborate external show had nothing to do with it. A true faith could provide the greatest of blessings, a peaceful mind. As Halifax wrote to his daughter, "A devout *Mind* hath the Priviledge of being free from *Passions*, as some Climates are free from all venomous kind of Creatures."[77]

Christianity and Christian figures appear symbolically in Restoration plays. They appear symbolically in the sense that a simple identification of them as Christian is sufficient to prompt in the audience a complex of responses and associations, as do all symbols. Christianity need not be argued out or proven to the audience. It needs only to be tested, tempted, threatened, manipulated, and finally shown triumphant, for its values to serve dramatic and didactic functions. A Christian figure is in some ways analogous to an orphan, or a child, or a helpless virgin, or any of the other stock figures of pity. The Christian is at a disadvantage in this world of trials and tribulations; and though he may triumph ultimately, in this world or the next, it is the struggle he has with the world that forms the drama.

In William Davenant's *Seige of Rhodes* (1656), the Christian citizens of Rhodes under Alphonso are being attacked by Turks led by Solyman the Magnificent. In this moment of duress the Christians exhibit unusual courage and endurance. Alphonso's wife, Ianthe, is captured, and her story awes Solyman:

> O wond'rous vertue of a Christian Wife!
> Advent'ring lifes support and then her Life
> To save her ruin'd Lord!
>
> (Solyman's second entry, p. 11)

The Christian figure is at a disadvantage when dealing with pagans for the reason that he is constrained by values and moral obligations not operative for the enemy. Yet the Christian can sometimes overcome an enemy by the force of his example, and nothing prevents him from attempting to persuade or convert the enemy. Isabella is a Christian in Elkanah Settle's *Ibrahim*,

The Illustrious Bassa (1677), and much of her role consists of arguments with another Solyman. Her arguments are not explicitly Christian, but they are moral, and her constant danger in the presence of the powerful heathen is vivified by her symbolic embodiment of the faith.

The facile and stereotyped tableau of the Christian princess threatened by the monstrous heathen warrior may conceal an important assumption present in all serious plays involving Christian figures in the Restoration. The assumption is that Christianity is heroic. To be fully Christian, to imitate Christ, requires more than any man can accomplish, and those who come closest are so extraordinary and so unlike the rest of us that we call them saints. Their place in the Christian story is analogous to the place of Aeneas, Achilles, Priam, Odysseus, and the other leaders of the Greek and Roman epics. Christianity, like the other methods of coping with life which are under discussion in this chapter, is an ideal, a method which, if it could be perfectly employed, could produce a peaceful life. But it is hard to be a Christian. And it is hard to be a stoic, and morally responsible, and courageous, and wise, and decorous. Surely part of our distaste for Restoration drama stems from our failure to recognize, and the playwrights' failure to articulate clearly, the difference between a means and the utilization of that means.

These two failures—ours and theirs—are oversimplified as just stated because neither has been completely uncomprehending. But the diction of these plays and their propensity to emotional tableaux, presented in series like a string of beads, suggest that all a man needs is X. Get X and in the getting you will get Y, seems too often an acceptable reduction of the "moral" of these plays. What the Restoration playwrights may have understood and articulated sufficiently for their contemporaries, but insufficiently for us, is the difficulty of realizing an ideal. In both the heroic drama and the domestic plays, the characters are able to recognize means to temporal peace, or at least means to endurance. But no matter how complete this recognition, even

64

the most heroic of these figures, excepting St. Catherine, stagger and fall on the path toward the goal.

All Restoration serious plays concern themselves seriously, I think, with one predominant issue—the issue of peace. It is possible that many plays in other eras do, as well, but exclusivity is not the present issue. The search for peace links the drama with all of the significant literature of the Restoration, including the comedies, and it links the drama with the most crucial of the era's political and social concerns. Some ages focus on prosperity, some on expansion, some on foreign policy, some on internecine conflicts or foreign war. The Restoration focused on stability, harmony, and peace. The term is not often used to my knowledge, but the era had as a primary ideal the Greek concept *sophrosyne*—moderation, prudence, harmony. The Restoration focus was worldly and even secular. The Christian figures discussed above, one remembers, do not attempt to convert the audience to a faith, but to show the advantages of a Christian way of life. The assumption is that the audience is already nominally Christian. The enemies of the Restoration are the psychological weaknesses in us all.

There is an important dialogue between St. Catherine and Maximin in *Tyrannick Love* which can bring this issue into focus. Maximin professes love for Catherine and defends it— despite his present marriage to another woman—as a matter which is beyond his control:

> If to new persons I my Love apply,
> The Stars and Nature are in fault, not I:
> My Loves are like my old Praetorian Bands,
> Whose Arbitrary pow'r their Prince commands:
> I can no more make passion come or go,
> Than you can bid your *Nilus* ebb or flow.

(IV. i. 370–75)

Catherine observes that only "Kings who rule their own desires" are godlike (l. 383), to which Maximin replies, "How can I help those faults which Nature made?" (l. 392). Catherine answers:

Your mind should first the remedy begin;
You seek without, the Cure that is within.

(IV. i. 396–97)

Catherine does not deny that Maximin's weakness is his from nature. She argues only that there cannot be an external cure for an internal weakness. The only weapons against passion are reason and will and "good" passions like love. Catherine may state these truths with a kind of clarity which may seem smug in context, and is clearly so out of context, but she is, after all, a saint. Her strength is as the strength of ten, but, even so, she is sorely tried.

The Restoration image of man, in outline, is not very different from the image of man in the Renaissance, with perhaps one significant difference—the Restoration man is a secular creature. He may have intimate ties with the divine or the macrocosmic or the metaphysical, but the plays make little of that. They focus instead on his worldly anguish and the possibilities, such as they are, for his worldly redemption, salvation, and peace. The Restoration image is of a creature made of two parts —mind and matter. The vocabulary for these parts is varied, but the dichotomy remains fairly constant. Mind, most writers suggest, is the key to his power, not his strength, and his passions link him to the creatures and to all of nature. His mind is a potential source of order; his matter is spontaneous and a source of energy. His mind might direct the otherwise Brownian motions of his body.

Moreover, and this too is familiar, the matter in man—his passions, his flesh, his perceptions, his pains—is imaged as orderly or in place when an individual is healthy, and disorderly and chaotic when he is ill. The images are mechanical in the sense that the terms for health suggest the arrangement of parts, and not the organic or chemical bonding of particles into a new whole. The important vocabulary includes such terms as *balance*, *harmony*, *peace*, *order*, *proportion*, and their contrasts, *disorder*, *disease*, *tempest*, *bent*, *ugly*, and so on. Man is spoken of as though he were an engine which could be tuned. A healthy

66

man is seen to be a man of internal and external decorum—a man in whom all was in place, in whom everything fit. Passion is dis-ease. Passion is indecorous in the sense that it strains or destroys the finely balanced proportions which make up decorum and order.

The Renaissance theory of the humours was still alive in literary surroundings, despite the new science, and we find the disorder of passion described in very old-fashioned terms in Dryden's *The Indian Emperour*:

> These heats and cold still in our breasts make War,
> Agues and Feavers all our passions are.
>
> (II. i. 108–109)

War is then metaphorically appropriate as a means to show passions in action—wars international, civil, interpersonal, psychological. In a play like *The Conquest of Granada* all four types of war take place, and all four are related. Boabdelin's weakness, his indecisiveness, and his self-indulgence have created the external war, permitted the internal strife, created an enemy of his strongest ally, Almanzor, and tortured him with the anguish which must come to those unsettled in their will. The healthy man—or couple, or state, or world—is at peace. The unhealthy is a chaos of undirected energy controlled by nothing but chance:

> Our passions,—fear and anger, love and hate,—
> Mere senseless engines that are moved by fate;
> Like ships on stormy seas, without a guide,
> Tossed by the winds, and driven by the tide.
>
> (*Don Sebastian*, III. iii. 467)

In the passage above, "senseless engines" reveals once again the notion that the passions move us but do not direct us. Direction must be given by the individual from some other source than his passions. The person who can give direction to his life is heroic because the struggle is so unequal between the driving power and the ordering will. The passions have as allies the heart, the glands, sexuality, sensuality, the five senses, the

67

stomach, the bowels—apparently every part of man. The will has only logic and rhetoric as weapons and love as an occasional source of power. Love is only occasionally helpful because, like all passions, it cannot be wholly manipulated, no matter how rationally useful it might be if it were under the control of reason or will. I believe every Restoration dramatist would echo Hamlet's standards for a good and valuable man, standards expressed with intense conviction and warmth to Horatio, the only man Hamlet has ever found to possess these qualities:

> ... blest are those
> Whose blood and judgement are so well commeddled,
> That they are not a pipe for fortune's finger
> To sound what stop she please. Give me that man
> That is not passion's slave, and I will wear him
> In my heart's core, ay, in my heart of heart,
> As I do thee.[78]

(III. ii. 73–79)

There may seem a contradiction between the struggle of mind to bring matter under control—a struggle which is described in all of the monuments of late seventeenth-century writing (Descartes, Milton, Dryden, Locke)—and the cry of the Restoration villain to have as much power as is necessary to indulge an unchecked will. The marvelous Lyndaraxa, a Hobbesian villainess in *The Conquest of Granada*, exclaims:

> Yes; I avowe th' ambition of my Soul,
> To be that one, to live without controul.

(II, p. 17)

Ishmael, in Thomas Southerne's *The Loyal Brother* (1682), avows:

> Virtue avaunt! to villages be gone:
> But haunt the luxury of Courts no more:
> Much less aspiring Statesmens nobler thoughts.
> Ambition is our Idol, on whose Wings
> Great minds are carried only to extreams;
> To be sublimely great, or to be nothing.

(I, pp. 12–13)

And the Queen Mother, in Settle's *The Empress of Morocco*, cries, "My Will's my King, my Pleasures are my Gods" (IV. iii. 52). But the Queen Mother's cry reveals the truth of the matter; *will* is the word she uses and the word sometimes employed by others, but what is meant is not the faculty of reasoned or thoughtful choice. Instead, she uses *will* to mean what Hobbes says it means: *"the last appetite in deliberating."* And Hobbes defines deliberation as "the whole sum of desires, aversions, hopes, and fears continued till the thing be either done or thought impossible."[79] Therefore, the Queen Mother means, "I wish to do what I *feel* like doing." It is obvious that this is also the meaning for Ishmael and for Lyndaraxa and for the others who proclaim absolute power as their goal in order to indulge an absolute will. We note, too, that typical of such exclamations is the selfishness revealed in them. The goal of absolute power is possible only to one—such as God, the King, or the Leviathan—and not to two. It is *"my* Pleasures are *my* Gods." And, as Lyndaraxa says, it is "To be that one, to live without controul":

> And that's another happiness to me
> To be so happy as but one can be.

> (II, p. 17)

Passions are private, finally, although they all have objects on which they focus. With the partial exception of love, the indulgence of passion is thus always solipsistic.

The collective and public version of self-indulgence is factionalism. Internal division in England has been a dramatic topic since the Wars of the Roses, but the Restoration emphasis has two particular sources: the Civil War and the Whig-Tory division over the question of succession. *Faction* is a Restoration obscenity. Whig and Tory alike used the term with contempt, even though the Tories felt the word was exclusively their sword to wield, since they were supporting the established and traditional procedures and the Whigs were guilty of novelty and of undermining the foundations.

The dramas of the late 1670's and early 1680's are full of

veiled or blatant allusions to current political division and unrest. Dryden even converts the epic circumstances of *Troilus and Cressida* (1679) to relevance. Ulysses, as the play opens, argues that Troy would have been taken long since,

> but for our disorders:
> The observance due to rule has been neglected.
>
> .   .   .   .
>
> O when Supremacy of Kings is shaken,
> What can succeed[?]
>
> (I. i, p. 2)

The terrible and ambiguous political milieu of Venice in *Venice Preserv'd* (1682) makes the play scarcely partisan, but there is no gainsaying the threat of Pierre's defiant curse of the Senate when he is captured:

> Curst be your Senate: Curst your Constitution:
> The Curse of growing factions and division
> Still vex your Councils, shake your publick safety,
> And make the Robes of Government, you wear,
> Hatefull to you, as these base Chains to me.
>
> (IV. 262–66)

Faction is an evil to any party; faction divides and division vexes, with the result that public safety is threatened. The evil individual seeks political power for himself; a faction in these plays is simply a gathering of like-minded men of self-interest, whose power and intelligence individually are too little to be effective, and so they band together. A faction is a villain made up of many men.

IV

It seems to me, then, that there is no intelligent way to support the contention that Restoration serious drama is not serious. The plays deal, even single-mindedly, with the major epistemological issue of the age: the relationship of mind and matter. They deal with the major political issues of the age: faction,

70

the nature of monarchy, the place of the individual in government. They deal with moral values. The plays grapple thematically with dozens of issues and contrasts that have been identified as crucial throughout literary history: appearance and reality, public and private obligation, lust and love, the perception of true merit, the absolute need for communication among men, the pastoral vision, war, incest, the socialization of the individual, the clash of roles, the quest for psychological equilibrium. The plays portray anguish and repose in families, in couples, and in nations. They portray heroes and villains and ambiguous men and women. They espouse moral criteria long tested and long approved. Don Sebastian, for example, is praised for being the man Cicero would have us all be, "Brave, pious, generous, great, and liberal" (I, p. 4).

The playwrights had no ideological guild, and the preceding pages have not argued for uniformity or identity of themes in the plays. The intelligence and sophistication of Otway and Dryden are not matched by all of their contemporaries. The poetic skill of some is vastly superior to that of others. The argument in these pages is not that the plays are of a piece, but that they consider seriously the important issues of their day and that they have, moreover, certain values and assumptions which seem to be shared. They share, for example, the notions that man is of dual essence (mind and matter); that passions or desires are the motive force in man and that will can give direction to that force; and they universally agree that peace is what all men seek. As Hobbes has said, "the first and fundamental law of nature . . . is *to seek peace and follow it.*"[80] This quest for peace undergirds many plays, whether they emphasize the quest for the "quiet of [the] minde" (*Troilus and Cressida*, III. ii, p. 40), or the quest for political stability nationally (*The Duke of Guise*) or internationally (*The Destruction of Jerusalem*).

If I am right in asserting that they treat serious themes seriously, what then can be said about the hollowness and falsity which so many of us have perceived in reading, or on rare occasions seeing, these plays? The answer is obvious, but not easy:

we do not *take* the plays seriously. The Restoration audience took them seriously but we cannot. There were, certainly, contemporary burlesques of these plays—there are in every era, and they are directed toward every major art form. The distinction between the Restoration response and our response is not often discussed, but it is not the *matter* of Restoration drama that we reject—it is the *manner*. Even given all the pressures of twentieth-century anomie and skepticism, few of us are violently opposed to, or forced to laughter by, such values as are described by the epithets brave, pious, generous, great, and liberal. We may, however, be embarrassed to hear the list read aloud or to witness someone actually applying the list to another individual. The list is too smug, too abstract, too confident, too neat. It is a Boy Scout pledge, and not a picture. It is not descriptive; it is prescriptive.

To give one brief example of the abrasive grind of matter and manner, we might look at the entrance of Almanzor for the first time. He enters on a scene of confrontation between the two internal factions in Granada. Almanzor knows neither group and yet has no hesitation about entering the conflict or about which side to take. His first words are:

> I cannot stay to ask which cause is best;
> But this is so to me because opprest.
> *(Goes to the Abencerrages)*
>
> (I, p. 5)

I think what we object to in this couplet is, not the values which it expresses, but the act of expression itself. If Almanzor entered the scene and took the action indicated by the stage direction, we would feel no discomfort. Many of us still feel that the underdog calls for our support. But our conventions for expressing this value have radically altered. Our convention, our decorum, calls for action in the place of words, for the deed and not the diction. Our protagonists should act as Hemingway would have them act—boldly, courageously, *silently*. Dryden's hero is a rhetorical man in an age when rhetoric had no pejorative connotations. Dryden's protagonists—and all protagonists in the Restoration—are men of consciously shaped speech, men who articulate their feelings more rapidly than they show them in gesture. Dryden's hero has his ancestors in the Greek and Roman epic, where heroes did great deeds and talked about them. They also talked about whether they should do them, what their friends thought they should do, and whether, after they had done or not done the deeds, the doing or not doing was a good thing.

The remaining chapters will explore the *manner* of Restoration drama, both as a means to understanding more clearly why we respond as we do and as a means to answering the historical question of what it is the Restoration playwrights did. The preceding paragraph gives only one suggestion, but its ramifications are complex. We recognize that, in Sir Richard Steele's phrase, we are dealing with "conscious lovers." Restoration characters *know* what they do and what they believe, and what one knows, one can express. After all, it is fundamental to the Restoration concept of how a man deals with life that he bring to bear his reason and his will on feelings which spontaneously lash through him. People knew what happened when they let their emotions free. They saw only too much willingness to be spontaneous, natural, and enthusiastic. They felt what was needed then was control, moderation, ease, peace. Our time may, on the other hand, have seen too much rationality, too much conscious articulation of motive, and too little reality of action and feeling. We distrust words now, and we tend to ask such questions as, Can a man be better than his actions?

And there is another drastic question involved here. If drama, by definition, means play, action, movement, and gesture, if it means showing rather than telling, are not the Restoration plays very close to not being drama at all? Are not the serious plays, with their propensity to narration, straining the limits of the form which they purportedly represent? Because the spectacle of the plays asks only a passive response from the audience, Restoration serious drama seems better suited to listening than to watching, and listening seems a limited way to deal with drama. We are uncomfortable with this, as we would be with a

73

symphony in which there was no music but only the spectacle of the musicians handling their instruments, or, in fact, as we are uneasy in the presence of pantomime. Pantomime is an authentic art form, we all agree, but is it drama? Can there be a silent play?

Assuming, then, that Restoration serious plays deal seriously with serious matters, what is the manner of their dealing?

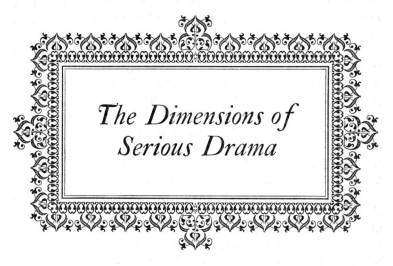

2

The Dimensions of Serious Drama

I. Explicit Choice

In the burlesque play *The Rehearsal* (1672) the central burlesque moment occurs when the king of the play-within-the-play, Volscius, indecisively attempts to put on his boots:[1]

My Legs, the Emblem of my various thought,
Shew to what sad distraction I am brought.
Sometimes, with stubborn Honour, like this Boot,
My mind is guarded, and resolv'd to do't:
Sometimes, again, that very mind, by Love
Disarmed, like this other leg does prove.
Shall I to Honour or to Love give way?
Go on, cryes Honour; tender Love says, nay:
Honour, aloud, commands, pluck both boots on;
But softer Love does whisper, put on none.

. . . .

(*Exit with one Boot on, and the other off.*)
(III, p. 30)

King Volscius seems emblematic of many Restoration heroes,

75

torn between reason and passion, awkwardly but interminably debating their choices and ultimately hopping away, hobbled by problems which lack substance.

Volscius is emblematic not just for us but for Dryden's contemporaries as well. *The Rehearsal* was apparently first written in 1664, long before the fashion for heroic drama reached its peak. Buckingham and his friends saw the crude dichotomies as a potential burlesque practically from the moment they were first employed on stage. They found the spectacle of the soliloquizing, divided hero to be inappropriate for heroic drama and therefore suitable for burlesque. They evidently felt that the true hero did not debate which boot to pull on, or, without the metaphor, which motive to obey, but pulled on his boots (made the kind of quick and certain judgment illustrated by Almanzor) and got about his business. Volscius seems comic for several reasons: his action is trivial and beneath serious consideration; his indecisiveness is weakness in a hero; his concern for the "softer" emotion of love is indecorous in a hero or public figure; his intellectual sloppiness, revealed by the marvelous mixed metaphors, is unheroic.

Burlesque is created by disproportion. For example, burlesque places a monarch in an unmonarchical situation, perhaps in the mundane situation of putting on his boots, and simultaneously puts in his mouth the language of serious human concern, language dealing with the resolution of conflicting demands of love, honor, reason, and passion. From the time of Aristotle at least, the tragic protagonist has been described as a divided character. He is a good man, Aristotle said, with a flaw. This mixed nature, in effect, fragments him. His mixed nature means that he will have to make choices because only the pure— pure evil, pure good, pure greed, and so on—are without doubt. Significantly, only the villain and the saint know what action to take when in situations with good on the one hand and evil on the other. If the choices are not so clear, then even the villain and the saint have difficulty making a choice. They, too, must hesitate and weigh alternatives.

Robert Heilman, in *Tragedy and Melodrama: Versions of*

Experience, and in an earlier essay, has argued persuasively for the critical place of choice in tragedy. He argues that characters like Hamlet are divided and "incorporate the dividedness of a humanity whose values, because they naturally elude the confines of formal logic, create an apparently insoluble situation." Heilman distinguishes most division as incorporating choices involving imperatives and impulses:

> I have used the term *imperative* to denote the obligation of general validity, the discipline of self that cannot be rejected without penalty, whether it is felt as divine law or moral law or civil law, or, in a less codified but no less prescriptive way, as tradition or duty or honor. Imperative reflects a communal conscience. By *impulse* I refer to the force that originates in or is rooted in or identified with the individual personality and is of an almost biological sort.[2]

Some characters are divided by impulses, some by imperatives, some by the tension between imperative and impulse. Whatever the situation, division implies choice, and choice implies consciousness. A character without consciousness is torn apart by his circumstances or his psyche or both. He can only provide us with an example which seems to illustrate the law that two bodies cannot occupy the same space at the same time. He is pushed and pulled as an object and is not himself the actor. A conscious figure, on the other hand, is active and aware of choice.

Volscius, I would suggest, is comic not because he is unsure whether to follow passion or reason. He is comic because he mixes choosing boots and choosing ideals. The choice of ideals is not comic; the metaphor for the choice is. So, too, in Restoration serious drama the repeated choice situations may reveal awareness on the part of the playwright and his protagonists of the divided nature of self and the divisions which exist between self and not-self, between self and the universe around it. What vitiates this awareness is that too many plays describe choices which seem oversimplified, repetitive, stereotypically conceived, and arranged according to formula rather than according to character and situation. Restoration serious plays fail, not because they present choice, but because they fail to convince us that the objects of the choice have greater significance than Volscius' boots.

Why are the choice situations so pervasive in Restoration drama? Probably because the playwrights and audiences understood that tension is essential to drama and that tension is created when an object or subject is divided in impulse and imperative. Dryden's definition of drama suggests, as Anne Barbeau has pointed out, that the tension of conceptual contrasts is at the heart of things. A play ought to be, Lisideius says, "a just and lively image of human nature, representing its passions and humours, and the changes of fortune to which it is subject, for the delight and instruction of mankind."[3] A play is to be both just and lively; it is to delight and instruct; it is to represent character and circumstances of character. It would seem obvious that there must be alternatives or movement for there to be liveliness, passion, or change.

Also in the essay *Of Dramatic Poesy*, Eugenius suggests that audiences "watch the movements of [the characters'] minds, as much as the changes of their fortunes. For the imaging of the first is properly the work of a poet; the latter he borrows of the historian."[4] Dryden certainly illustrates this movement of the mind frequently, searching out and exploiting what Arthur Kirsch has called "dialectical dilemmas, situations in which a character must either choose or strike a balance between conflicting alternatives."[5] In such situations Dryden's characters and those of his contemporaries often lament the necessity for choice or seek to avoid choice through images of the pastoral alternative to the active life. Their speeches at such moments are, in Alfred Harbage's phrase, "sighs of ethical perplexity."[6] If the essence of drama is the representation of characters in tension, characters whose minds are in motion, then the propensity to situations of choice is easily understood.

There is another impulse which promotes situations of choice, an impulse which exemplifies, perhaps, the desire to instruct as well as delight and the desire to obey the decorums of contemporary poetry. Dichotomies are a means to make situations in-

78

telligible which are otherwise muddy with complexity. Dichotomies or apparent dichotomies lay out before us, at once clearly
and dramatically (with tension), the division within or between
characters. Over and over again in Restoration drama, we watch
characters confront X and Y. B. J. Pendlebury has, in fact, expressed a complaint stemming from the repetitiousness and
lucidity of the crisis situations which fill these plays: "The
working of the springs of emotion is too clearly revealed in Dryden's plays. His characters are too logical and consistent; like
those of Racine, they are specimens acting under experimental
conditions, which would never obtain outside the laboratory of
the dramatist's brain."[7] Pendlebury no doubt has in mind such
speeches as this, by Montezuma, in *The Indian Queen*:

> Oh, Tyrant Love: how cruel are thy laws!
> I forfeit Friendship, or betray thy Cause.
>
> (IV. ii. 37–38)

Certainly the issue is clearly stated in Montezuma's speech:
love's laws demand X, friendship's demand Y. The word *laws*,
moreover, suggests the abstractly lucid situation of choice which
Pendlebury rejects as suitable only for the laboratory. In life
such "laws" are never to be found. I will argue later that the
choice is not at all clear, here or in many other places where the
superficial lucidity of the vocabulary conceals a more profound
complexity. *Love* and *friendship*, in Montezuma's speech, have
multiple referents.

Dichotomies make choices clear; they express dividedness in
pairs and so reduce a choice which may involve several alternatives to a choice between two. Dichotomies also produce dialectical dilemmas for the pleasure of debate itself. Every educated
man in England grew up with debate, knew its rules and knew
some of the most famous examples of debate from ancient history and classical literature. As Lewis N. Chase recognized, a
distinguishing trait of Restoration drama is a liking for discussion for its own sake.[8] The plays show characters struggling to
resolve their dilemmas in arguments whose form was familiar
and to an extent specialized. Dialectic is, after all, a form of

79

combat and, like all forms of combat, can easily be supported as a spectator sport. This seems true no matter what kind of debate is involved; it is true whether the debate is intellectual or emotional.

Between 1660 and 1700 there was a shift of sorts from debates that were intellectual to those that were emotional, though at no time did either extreme stand alone. Moody Prior has shown that in Otway's *Venice Preserv'd*, for example, the scenes of persuasion and debate "no longer consist of a debate on the issues, of the balancing of intellectually framed positions; they are here in the nature of a direct appeal to intimate feelings, urged in such a way as to make the choice rest with the sentiment which can be appealed to most tellingly."[9]

The dichotomy, then, can function in a number of ways: it can clarify, often at the cost of oversimplifying, the issues; it can create tension, both in the sense of suspense for the audience which awaits resolution and in the sense of tension in the character who is psychologically discomfited by the choice. It can provide the pleasure we all take in witnessing a combat. And, yet, after we list these functions and recognize their presence in any number of plays, we may still be unsatisfied by dramas which are structured upon a series of dialectical dilemmas. Like a pulse, these moments of tension and release become formally repetitive, no matter what the issues that stand at the poles of the dichotomy. The neat division into parts grows overwhelming in its monotony. Sooner or later we will all be driven to imagine King Volscius' boots—division is the thing, let the playwright name the matter.

John Dennis argued profoundly that debate, the articulated resolution of divisions, was psychologically false if it were pictured as a means to resolve human problems. A man, Dennis argued, was not to be convinced by witnessing or taking part in a debate.[10] In his argument for the usefulness of the stage in 1698, Dennis recognized that reason may "make us miserable" and typically keeps us "in a languishing State of Indifference" by keeping before us our imperfections and our impotence. Reason is therefore "an Impediment to our Pleasure, which is our

Happiness: For to be pleas'd, a Man must come out of his ordinary State; Now nothing in this Life can bring him out of it,
but Passion alone, which Reason pretends to combat."[11]

We might answer by saying that although it is no doubt true
that man must be brought to happiness through passion, there
is a pleasure which comes from the witnessing of a drama. Man
is put in a state of passion, or emotion, by witnessing the intellectual and emotional struggles of others. Dennis would grant
this and so find drama useful; but he would also question
whether argument on the stage is verisimilar, and if it is not, he
would ask how it is we take pleasure in watching something
which is false to the image of man. Dennis offers a handsome
summary statement for the Restoration and early eighteenth
century with respect to man's most fundamental distress, its
nature and causes. All men of all eras have agreed, Dennis says,
"that the Misery of Man, proceeded from a perpetual Conflict
that is within him, and from a Discord continually reigning
among the Faculties of the Soul; a cruel War between the Passions and Senses, and the Reason, while the Reason violently
draws one way, and the Passions and the Senses another." And
when man is thus miserable, "he can no more take away Love
and Desire by Reasoning, than he can satisfy Hunger and Thirst
with a Syllogism."[12]

Finally, the argument leads Dennis to a defense of poetry as
the most morally useful of the verbal forms: "For whereas
Philosophy pretends to correct human Passions by human Reason, that is, things that are strong and ungovernable, by something that is feeble and weak; Poetry by the force of the Passion, instructs and reforms the Reason.[13] Sir Philip Sidney said
much the same thing about poetry, and it is not Dennis' novelty
that requires our attention. It is rather the fact that while he recognizes that we are not to be brought to happiness by reason, he
employs the neat dichotomies which are familiar to us from
drama in order to make his point. In other words, Dennis uses
the same vocabulary (*reason, passions, sense*) that the playwrights use and the same clean lines of division between warring
parts. Balance and antithesis mark his sentences as strongly as

they mark the heroic couplets or blank verse of the plays. Dennis says throughout his critical career that passions are the key to moral instruction, to beauty, and to the sublime, and he says this in the blunt abstractions and divisions which so oversimplify human experience.

I would like to suggest that the heart of the matter is the vocabulary which the period employed, the vocabulary which consisted of the Restoration's significant signs. For reasons which lie beyond this discussion, men of the Restoration chose to describe mankind in a vocabulary at once limited and abstract. This phenomenon has long been recognized, and it fills the volumes of discussion of poetic diction. But I want to argue that the vitiated vocabulary for the faculties consists of *signs*. These signs were more significant for the Restoration than they are for us. Nevertheless, the Restoration vocabulary consisted of words which, like all signs, were felt to convey or imitate or echo reality. There is no more reason to assume that a man who describes the human psychology in terms of Reason, Passion, Sense, and Will perceives four discrete powers, or fluids or energy sources—whatever the metaphor—than there is reason to assume that a man who describes the human psychology in terms of Ego, Superego, and Id perceives the three as forming the physical mass of the mind, arranged in horizontal levels, with the Id an ugly and incoherent mass boiling at the bottom. We have changed our vocabulary, and we condescend to former ages that have struggled with terms which we find less scientific, less revealing, less useful than our own. We might recall with more humility the scientists of Brobdingnag who examine Gulliver in an attempt to classify him and finally, when he can be compared to no existing category of creatures, triumphantly determine him to be a *lusus naturae*—a determination, Swift says, "exactly agreeable to the Modern Philosophy of *Europe*: whose Professors, disdaining the old Evasion of *occult Causes*, whereby the Followers of *Aristotle* endeavour in vain to disguise their Ignorance; have invented this wonderful Solution of all Difficulties, to the unspeakable Advancement of human Knowledge."[14] We may, in fact, have made unspeakable advancements, but we can still recognize that the signs of the Restoration might not reveal completely to us the things signified to contemporaries. This is more likely to be true if we can show that the Restoration signified reality in other ways besides the limited vocabulary spoken of so far, or if we can show that the dichotomies are more complex once we examine the signs more carefully. It may appear that I speak of complexity here and elsewhere as though it were a virtue or an aesthetic achievement. I am not sure that it is. But I am emphasizing the existence of complexity beneath apparent simplicity as a response to the more traditional view of the period as limited in vocabulary and therefore limited in perception. The Restoration is more likely to be characterized as psychologically naive than as needlessly complex.

A few choices will show that the apparent dichotomies are complexly significant and do not consist simply of neat divisions into pairs. The choices look and sound like pairs, but they signify more. In *Mustapha*, Mustapha and his friend Zanger are in love with the same woman, the Hungarian Queen. At the same time, Mustapha's father, Solyman the Magnificent, sends Mustapha orders to go on a long and dangerous expedition, hoping in this way to remove what he has been led to believe is a threat to the throne. Mustapha is in a quandary:

> I to my Friend and Brother Rival am;
> She, who did kindle, would put out my flame;
> I from my Fathers anger must remove,
> And that does banish me from her I love;
> If, of these Four, the least a burden be,
> Oh how shall I support the other three?

> (III. i. 35–40)

Mustapha apparently has four choices: friend, father, mistress, banishment. These four can be reduced to two, however, since if he accepts his father's command (does his duty), then he will remove himself from competition with Zanger, his friend, and remove himself from his love. He has, then, a choice between duty and love. Put another way, he has the choice between love and honor in several of his alternatives: he can fulfill the obligations of friendship to Zanger, an honorable course, or he can follow his passions and become Zanger's rival. He can prosecute his love with the Hungarian Queen (which his passion prompts him to do) or obey her commands and suppress his feelings (which the courtesies in the conventions of courtly love demand from a man of honor). He can stay and represent his loyalty to his father through argument (which his pride urges upon him) or he can obey his father (and sovereign) and go forth against the Persians (which might imply that he is guilty of the ambition of which his father implicitly accuses him). Without presenting the alternatives under any other shapes, it seems evident that the choices for Mustapha are not clear; they are only expressed clearly. Perhaps it is even more accurate to say they are expressed tersely and in neatly balanced lines.

Even if we examine a single choice, its nature is evidently complex. Mustapha and Zanger are brothers as well as friends, and their friendship is heroic friendship. They share the intense personal friendship which marks such pairs as Achilles and Patroclus. Earlier in the play we have found them professing this friendship and expressing such claims as, "Friendship's a stronger tye than that of blood" (I. iii. 227). There is dramatic irony in this when we learn of their rivalry, and there is another kind of tension in it from the start because a strong dramatic convention informs us that such professions of faith early in a play imply difficulties later. Given such an heroic friendship, rivalry in love later provides a difficult, perhaps unresolvable test for the young men. When Mustapha reveals his love to Zanger, who has already confessed his, the two know fully their predicament and they search for a way out of it. In a fashion reminiscent of *The Knight's Tale*, they debate the primacy of their love, the relative strengths and weaknesses in their love. But we know, and they come to realize, that there is no solution to rivalry. There is no compromise and no sharing possible. There is only rivalry, the elimination of a rival, or the elimination of rivalry. To continue in rivalry is unacceptable to two men who love one another, and to eliminate one another is unthinkable. On the other hand, self-sacrifice is possible, and both make gestures to withdraw. With echoes of earlier speeches and earlier choices, Mustapha departs in Act V:

> And who would with a Father be in strife?
> Rather than duty lose, I'le lose my life.
> *Zanger*, farewel! I leave, in leaving you,
> The best of Friends and best of Brothers too.

(ii. 81–84)

We can say that Mustapha struggles to reconcile duty and love—after all, he very clearly says exactly that—but given the dramatic context, the summary statement about love versus duty, whether in our mouth or his, seems surely insufficient to the anguish it expresses. I believe accepting as satisfactory the statement that Mustapha must choose between duty and love is as foolish and simplistic as it would be to say that *Oedipus Rex* reduces to a choice for the King of Thebes between duty and love.

In *Aureng-Zebe*, the Emperor expresses an archetypal struggle taking place within himself:

> I feel my Virtue strugling in my Soul,
> But stronger Passion does its pow'r controul.

(III, p. 25)

The Emperor at this moment in the play is his son Aureng-Zebe's rival in love and is taking steps to remove Zebe from potential power in the kingdom. Simultaneously, the Emperor realizes that Aureng-Zebe is loyal and more trustworthy than his other son, Morat. As with many Restoration protagonists, the Emperor knows intellectually the impropriety of his actions, and yet he persists in going ahead. There is visible contrast between knowledge and action.

We might make a number of reflections on the Emperor's epigrammatic summary of the tensions he experiences between virtue and passion. The first is that he is correct. His virtue and passion are in conflict. Second, the statement is reductive. The Emperor is already married and is not free to love another woman or to be his son's rival. Virtue and political pressures both forbid it. In addition, virtue rejects his behavior toward Aureng-Zebe and makes him aware of his unjust favor toward Morat. *Virtue,* then, in the dichotomy virtue-passion, is not single in reference but multiple. I am excluding the probable additional connotations of "manliness" and "heroism" which the word *virtue* etymologically carried, and which were self-evident to any English schoolboy who had gotten as far as the Latin noun *vir,* "man."

We notice also that the Emperor naturally expresses his struggle in a physical metaphor which is so commonplace as to have lost much of its power, but which still, perhaps, conveys the idea of physical analogues to spiritual condition. Virtue *struggles* while stronger passion *controls.* We might compare the figure the Emperor uses to a political situation in which a nation struggles for independence while under the control of a foreign tyrant. The Emperor and his audience might then understand his anxiety in gross terms, that is, as a struggle similar to physical combat and probably subject to physical laws and behavior such as weakness, attack, attrition, siege, or starvation —all familiar metaphors for spiritual combat. But if we hear the vehicle of such figures and ignore the tenor, we lose most of the meaning. The Emperor may also be aware of the "struggle" as a metaphor with physical connotations. I do not wish to distinguish our response from his at the moment. To imagine the Emperor as a container for two small creatures—another possibility—is of course comic. It is distracting to imagine passion with a half-nelson on virtue, and yet these wrestling personifications threaten to appear at any moment when the Emperor says,

> I feel my Virtue strugling in my Soul,
> But stronger Passion does its pow'r controul.

The Restoration, in all its literature, personifies the faculties, and the result is, I think, a judgment on our part that the basic conception of man which gave rise to the personifications is oversimplified and foolish, just as the soul as an arena for diminutive wrestling matches is a trivial expression of human anguish. The Emperor's situation is potentially exciting. The excitement is repressed, however, when the many constituent elements of it are reduced to two and then clumsily and unimaginatively paired off.

Lastly, we can say one other thing about the Emperor's speech: it conceals rather than reveals. Rather than exposing to us the conflicts within him, the couplet, by reason of its diction at least, turns our eyes away. Because we do not wish to see the homunculi grappling in his soul, and perhaps because we fear that if we looked carefully they might really be there—as the Emperor and his contemporaries assure us that they are, again and again—we look away. We hurry past the speech to avoid embarrassment, and so learn less about the nature of his problem than another figure of speech might provide.

This interpretation exaggerates our reaction to one couplet, and yet it might reveal something of an important conflict in our responses to these plays and to other speeches like this one. That is, we recognize simultaneously that the Emperor is correct and that he has failed to understand himself. He is correct in the sense that he accurately uses a reductive vocabulary in describing himself which we all know and also use. He fails to understand himself because nothing he says suggests to us that he is aware that the vocabulary is reductive. We can see that he is being pulled apart by his feelings and his responsibilities, his weaknesses and his strengths. What we see is a man in a stressful situation, a man with important decisions to make and making important decisions. What we hear does not match what we see. Where we go wrong, as twentieth-century audience and critics, is to assume that it is only what we hear that reveals Dryden's understanding of the condition he portrays. To accept the Emperor's couplet as an adequate summary is to imitate him and be correct in that limited way; it is to be reductive, to trivialize, and to conceal a larger truth about the play.

Near the end of Act IV of *Venice Preserv'd*, Jaffeir is distraught as the result of the moral chaos around and within him.

He has betrayed the conspirators to the Senate, has found the Senate to be faithless, and has been denied by his friend Pierre. Jaffeir turns to Belvidera and pleads:

> Take me into thy Armes, and speak the words of peace
> To my divided Soul, that wars within me.

(IV. 405–406)

His soul is divided many ways, but it is superficially accurate to say that he is torn between friendship for Pierre and love for Belvidera. This play has been read carefully by critics who have revealed the complex ambiguity of the moral universe Otway has created.[15] The imagery of the play makes Jaffeir's plea to be taken into her arms suspicious and even sinister in implication. We know, too, that the division of which he speaks can be described in many pairs: Senate/Conspirators; oath to friend/oath to Senate; love of Pierre/love of Belvidera; preservation of Venice/preservation of political corruption; overthrow of corruption/patricide, slaughter, rebellion. Jaffeir's choices are impossible ones, and there is no chance in his world for the peace which he seeks.

His plea to Belvidera contains several familiar elements, his search for peace being one which I have argued is typical of Restoration drama. Jaffeir is a fragmented man and will not find peace until he can be made whole. Like the Emperor in *Aureng-Zebe*, further, Jaffeir speaks of his inward and spiritual condition in physical (and clichéd) terms. His soul "wars" within him, for example, as souls have done since at least the time of Prudentius' *Psychomachia*. But Otway's play cannot successfully be reduced to the familiar dichotomies of passion versus reason or love versus honor. One mark of the genius of this play is the way in which Otway, rather than simply pairing terms, makes a single term carry complexities of meaning. For example, Jaffeir is not divided between friend and mistress; he is divided between friends:

> ... take me, *Belvidera*,
> And lead me to the place where I'm to say
> This bitter Lesson, where I must betray

My truth, my vertue, constancy and friends:
Must I betray my friends?

. . . .

Belv. Hast thou a friend more dear than *Belvidera?*
Jaff. No, th'art my soul it self; wealth, friendship, honour,
All present joys, and earnest of all future,
Are summ'd in thee.

(IV. 72–76, 79–82)

This is a pivotal speech. At this moment Jaffeir decides who is
his dearest friend and, in so doing, arranges and orders his
values. If Belvidera is his dearest friend, then Jaffeir knows
how he must act. Otway has shown Jaffeir trying to determine
good, better, best. He is not trying to determine good and evil.
There is, as Renault says in this play, "nothing pure" here, and
every action in *Venice Preserv'd* seems capable of inversion or
perversion. Every embrace is potentially comforting and affirmative while at the same time it is potentially empty of significance, or even dangerous.

The division of which Jaffeir speaks is a division which mirrors the divisions around him. His soul reflects the macrocosm,
and his most wicked deed, the betrayal of his friends, is his
noblest deed, the preservation of Venice. Belvidera imagines
monuments raised in his honor:

Every Street

Shall be adorn'd with Statues to thy honour,
And at thy feet this great Inscription written,
   Remember him that prop'd the fall of Venice.
  Jaff. Rather, Remember him, who after all
The sacred Bonds of Oaths and holyer Friendship,
In fond compassion to a Womans tears,
Forgot his Manhood, Vertue, truth and Honour,
To sacrifice the Bosom that reliev'd him.

(IV. 10–18)

Which motto will the statue bear? This is not a small question.
It is the most significant question in the play because it is a
version of the question What is the play about? The play, like
the statue, is "in memory of" Jaffeir. It is his monument, and, as

audience, we are expected to see in the monument some significance. We are asked to read the sign (the play) and understand it.

To understand the play as a sign brings us back to the original subject of this chapter: the way in which the matter of Restoration drama is conveyed, the dimensions of this drama. What is the nature of the significant signs in the Restoration, and what sorts of things do they signify? So far, I have argued that the Restoration typically structured moments of stress upon divisions, most typically dichotomies of an abstract kind. Furthermore, these divisions, contrasts, and pairs are signs, and not things signified. Volscius is a fool because he makes his boots signify his faculties, which makes his faculties seem trivial and his problems as unimportant as the question of which boot to pull on first. We, too, are somewhat foolish if we accept the sign for the substance—if we accept as sufficient summary the statement that Jaffeir must choose between friend and friend, or friend and mistress, or friendship and love, or any similar pair. That is how his choices are spoken of; that is not what they are made of.

Before moving on, I want to clarify the implications of what has been said. I have separated manner and matter in these plays in order to make clear that they are two different things. I have not attempted to argue that there is a qualitative significance in this separation. That is, if I am right in asserting that the plays have often been described in terms of their signs rather than their significance, it does not follow that they are superior art if correctly understood. I am not satisfied aesthetically by a speech in which the character says his virtue is at war with his reason. This reductive abstraction has little dramatic power for me, no matter how fully I recognize the complexities which the reductive vocabulary conveys. By concentrating on choices I may have seemed to suggest that the plays have a profundity which, in fact, I think they lack. The existence of choice makes the plays seem appropriate to the structural principles described by Robert Heilman in *Tragedy and Melodrama*, but Heilman makes a telling point in defining pathetic tragedy as "drama in which the structure remains tragic but in which exploitation of feeling takes precedence over the exploration of character in action."[16] As Eric Rothstein and others have illustrated, it is the exploitation of feeling that these plays explicitly sought on moral and aesthetic grounds. They are, then, for me, and perhaps for Professor Heilman, pathetic tragedies and are less significant than those plays which explore character in action. Feelings are a part of human character, but they are not all of it. My chief concern in these pages is to argue that we should not mistake manner for matter. After we have carefully distinguished the two, we may still find the plays ineffective as drama.

The clear-cut choices which so often appear share a quality with those structural devices in Restoration drama which are designed to achieve the two goals of emotional effectiveness and didactic clarity: that is, the choices are *explicit*. Explicitness is a characteristic of the drama in all its features—characterization, diction, setting, gesture, plot. There seems to have been a fundamental, though not theoretical, distrust of gesture and action as significant means of communication. The playwrights were unwilling to allow gesture to stand independently as sufficiently significant in itself or as easily interpreted by the audience. Restoration dramatists tell us what their plays mean— they do not show us. Paradoxically, they seem to be denying the roots of drama in this way. Significant moments often appear as stories rather than scenes.

If we think for a moment of small symbolic actions or gestures or tokens—such as the handkerchief in *Othello*, Lear's madness in the storm, Richard III's withered arm—Restoration drama is a desert of examples. The few that come to mind only illustrate the infrequency of their use. The dagger in *Venice Preserv'd* is one of the few that one thinks of immediately. Restoration drama is static, with almost all heroic action taking place offstage. There are good reasons for this, in part, and they will be discussed below. Even in plays of mistaken identity, in which clues to ambiguous character might be expected, Restoration examples are hard to find. In Southerne's *Fatal Mar-*

riage (1694), a widow, Isabella, is about to marry a man who has been kind and loving to her ever since the death of her husband. At the same time, she has premonitions that the remarriage is wrong. We are told this but given no clues as to why it should be wrong. She seems neurotic, not prescient. When she faints at the appearance of a ring which she has given to her husband, we are surprised, for the ring has never been mentioned—and, furthermore, it never again plays a role. It is not the sign that is significant here; it is Isabella's reaction. The same emotional focus is created when identical rings prove lovers to be brother and sister in Dryden's *Don Sebastian*. The rings have not been mentioned before Act V, when the truth is revealed. We may, as audience, be presumed not to have noticed the rings before, but it is incredible that the couple have not.

There are several traditional dramatic influences which shape heroic drama and work inevitably toward making it narrative and explicit, rather than dramatic and implicit. First is the nature of the epics themselves: speeches, rather than action, make up one-half of the *Iliad* and two-thirds of the *Odyssey*.[17] To be like the epics, therefore, heroic drama would have to have many speeches. Second, heroic action is perhaps impossible to imitate physically. The limits of human prowess and of stage pyrotechnics both constrain heroic action. An heroic actor is required for heroic action, and any failure to portray convincingly an heroic action would produce either comedy or embarrassment. Elder Olson has clearly described this fact of dramatic life: "Things which are credible when imagined are sometimes incredible when seen, and what is credible when seen may be incredible when imagined."[18] A hero might overcome a race of giants, but if he should lead them onstage he would shrink beside them into insignificance. Only Henry Fielding ever had his hero, Tom Thumb, do such an optically ironic thing. Robert Hume, in his study of Dryden's criticism, argues that Dryden was aware of this impasse—the clash of the desire to create heroic drama and the fact that heroic actions cannot convincingly be performed—and that this awareness partly influenced his decision to turn away from drama. Dryden's ultimate dissatisfaction, Hume says, "was largely the result of his realization that spectacle tended more to inhibit the 'heroic' than to add to it."[19]

In addition to the epic tradition and the impossibility of performing heroic deeds, there was yet another influence: the Restoration dramatist was part of a culture which was beginning to make plain speaking a dominant virtue. Hostility to metaphor is expressed by philosophers from Hobbes to Locke. The new scientists and the new sermonizers all stressed plainness, clarity, and lucidity as the hallmarks of good writing. So pervasive was this mood or fashion that the literary artists need not have been influenced directly by any particular individual or segment of the life around them to be aware of the trend.

We ought not, at the same time, assume that plain speaking meant for the Restoration what it means for us. For a delightful instance of the difference, a character in Henry More's *Divine Dialogues* (1668) turns to his companion and, with alliterative relish, exclaims: "I shall doe my best I can to serve you herin, *Philopolis*, and that as briefly and as perspicuously as I can, with all plainness of speech, and without any affectation of Scholastick Scrupulosities, being desirous onely to be understood and to convince."[20] This speech is some distance from Hemingway, surely, and yet the impulse to affirm plainness is self-evident, and that impulse may have added something to the dramatist's inclination toward explicitness. What needs to be said needs to be said plainly and without unnecessary figure or jargon.[21]

Whatever the causes, the plays are explicit, and this explicitness appears in part as a strange self-awareness in the characters. Norman Holland links the self-conscious and analytical dialogue to the new science: "The heroic drama . . . emphasizes a crude but scientific psychology: the characters discuss quite transparently their own reactions to the choices and stimuli presented to them by external reality. They are, *ad nauseam*, 'motivated'."[22] Eugene Waith notes that when characters enter such discussions, they seem to be standing apart from themselves, explaining emotion rather than experiencing it. This examination tends naturally to narrative and therefore may relate to the desire for epic imitation.[23] Moody Prior says of Otway's Jaffeir and Belvidera: "Their sentiments are for the most part expressed not through figurative symbols, but by means of explicit and direct description."[24]

The subject of diction in these plays is taken up in a later chapter, but we should acknowledge at this point that the tendency toward narrative in these plays was noticed and objected to by men of the age. There was no theoretical justification for narrative drama. One need only remember the "lively" in Dryden's definition of the drama. Everyone knew that action was the thing.[25] Nevertheless, the plays are explicit and narrative.

There are four fairly common means of achieving explicitness in the dramatic format which the Restoration dramatists employed. One is the aside. Another is the repeated scene—that is, a scene which is performed before us and later recounted at length by one of the characters. Another is the imagined scene, a moment when one character verbally creates a scene for the imagination of another character (and the audience). The fourth is verbal description of an action taking place before us. Each of these partakes of narrative explicitness, but the impulse which brought them into play was probably the desire to make scenes effective, not to make them explicit. The playwright makes a character's emotional state clear to us so that we may better respond to it.

The aside is a time-honored device and needs no elaborate comment here. It is a revelatory means of displaying the workings of a character's mind. The aside attempts to overcome the resistance of the flesh in the sense that it gets "inside" a character in a way that dialogue and action cannot. To be effective, the aside must tell us something that a character wants to reveal but cannot. For example, it is commonly employed by villains because they are forced by their villainy to conceal their motives and yet they take pride in their achievements. Many asides are therefore boastful:

Oh how I love destruction with a Method
Which none discern, but those that weave the Plot:
Like Silk-worms we are hid in our own Weft,
But we shall burst at last through all the strings;
And when time calls, come forth in a new Form:
Not Insects, to be trod, but Dragons wing'd.

(Cassander in Lee's *The Rival Queens*, II. i. 37–42)

Or this delightful burst of enthusiasm from Pope Joan, in Settle's *The Female Prelate* (1680): "I could hug my self / For my rare Mischiefs. Oh my fertile Brain!" (I. ii, p. 9). Others are cries of anguish which are dangerous to be expressed publicly, but which must have vent:

Heavens! 'tis my Princess;
'Tis she, 'tis she, my guilty soul retires
At th' apparition of that bright Divinity
Which my soul whispers I have now offended.

(Ladislaus in Crowne's *Juliana*, II, p. 20)

Although these two types of aside are psychologically verisimilar in dramatic convention, they are discursive, not dramatic. They tell and do not show.

Less satisfactory as drama, and more indicative of the Restoration unwillingness to allow actions to speak louder than words, are asides in which a physical reaction or emotional excitement is described in words:

Ha!
This unthought Blast has shockt me like an Ague—
It has alarum'd every Sence, and spoyl'd me
Of all the awful courage of a Queen;
But I'le recover.

This aside is from Queen Elizabeth in Banks's *The Unhappy Favourite* (I, p. 11). The Queen tells us what she has felt, but presumably we might have seen her shock, her discomfort, and her struggle to recover herself, either in her facial expressions or in her gestures. No doubt the actress did reveal these emotions through action, and the aside then served as reinforcement, as clarification, and as a means to explicitness. The Restoration theaters were not so large that the actress could not be seen, even though the theaters were unevenly lit. Even with the best lighting, however, the conventions of drama in England certainly gave warrant for the practice of self-descriptive asides. Edgar, for one instance, nearly loses control of his "poor Tom" disguise as he watches Lear suffer:

> My tears begin to take his part so much,
> They'll mar my counterfeiting.
>
> (III. vi. 63–64)

Edgar's aside is analogous to Queen Elizabeth's in that we might assume that the gesture being described was sufficient in itself; but we note that while Shakespeare's theater is much less intimate physically, the aside is much more brief. In either case, the aside is a narrative moment in a dramatic context.

Descriptions of inner states, whether in asides or not, are interludes in action insofar as they say something rather than do something. Moreover, self-description in Restoration drama is almost always accurate; characters do not deceive themselves, although they may try to deceive others. This means that self-description is a reliable clue to a character's ethos, as far as the audience is concerned, and therefore an important dramatic convention. At the same time, this accuracy is another form of explicitness. If accuracy is part of the convention, then explicitness is a natural, though not necessary, corollary. One can recall accurate but allusive speeches, for instance, or accurate and nearly opaque ones. Self-description reveals, and the more revealing the more explicit:

> My Heart confesses her, and leaps for joy,
> To welcome her to her own Empire here.
> I feel her all, in every part of me.
> O! let me press her in my eager Arms,
> Wake her to life, and, with this kindling Kiss,
> Give back that Soul, she only lent to me.
>
> (Oroonoko in Southerne's *Oroonoko*, II. iii, p. 32)

The burning Fever rages in my veins;
But hold my heart, restrain the fury in,
Which heaves me, like the fighting winds for vent.
    (Sunamire in Southerne's *The Loyal Brother*, I, pp. 11–12)

O I am shot, a forked burning Arrow
Sticks cross my shoulders, the sad Venom flies
Like Lightning through my flesh, my bloud, my marrow.
    (Alexander in Lee's *The Rival Queens*, V. 315–17)

Ha!
I feel my Hair grow stiff, my Eye-balls rowl,
This is the only form could shake my Soul.
    (Montezuma in *The Indian Emperour*, II. i. 85–87)

Oh! it has pierc'd me like a poyson'd dart,
Which by degrees infects the blood and heart;
And now it higher mounts, divides my head,
Where like a plague its pointed venoms spread.
My brain ten thousand various tortures turn,
Now Agues chill me, and now Feavers burn.
Oh Rosalinda! false ungrateful Maid,
Am I for loss of glory thus repaid?
    (Hannibal in Lee's *Sophonisba*, III. ii. 21–28)

These examples are all drawn from their contexts and thus cannot serve to reveal very much about their dramatic appropriateness or effect. My intention is only to show that repeated speeches of this sort strike us primarily by their explicitness, and that, though they are thoroughly revealing of a character's inner condition, they allow little for action to reveal. After a speech like Hannibal's, above, actions or gestures which revealed his torment would be to some extent redundant.

There is nothing in the nature of drama as I understand it that makes narration unacceptable or places words and deeds at irrevocable odds. But there is certainly a kind of balance between showing and telling, between deeds and words, which every play creates for itself, and which is measured by every audience against its own standards of the proper balance. Restoration drama often offends our sense of balance by an excess of words. These plays too often tell us what we might as easily be shown or, in fact, have already seen earlier.

The balancing of narration and action is subtle and delicate. Burleigh, in Banks's *The Unhappy Favourite*, has been telling Queen Elizabeth of the triumphant public reception of Essex, when she cuts him off. She admits she had asked him to speak, but

> I saw the on a suddain,
> Settle thy Senses all in eager Postures,
> Thy Lips, thy Speech, and Hands were all prepar'd,
> A joyful Red painted thy envious Cheeks,
> Malitious Flames flasht in a moment from
> Thy Eyes like Lightning from thy O'recharg'd Soul,
> And fir'd thy Breast, which like a hard ramm'd Piece,
> Discharg'd unmannerly upon my face.
>
> (III, pp. 31–32)

This is an indecorous and ugly speech, and it is also a description of something that we, as audience, have apparently already seen. But there is something more here. This may be a moment which exposes Elizabeth's deepest jealousies and discomforts regarding Essex through overresponse to Burleigh's narration. It may be, then, that she is not narrating a scene we have already witnessed, but creating a new one—one which shows us, by contrast with the reality which we saw only moments before, the depth of Elizabeth's feelings. If we have seen Burleigh recount the Essex story calmly and straightforwardly, then Elizabeth's hysteria tells us more about her than him. This is put conditionally because much depends upon our understanding of Burleigh's character. No stage direction tells us how he is to behave as he tells the story.

Elizabeth's speech is an exception to a more general practice of having characters describe and comment upon the behavior of other characters fully exposed to us on stage. The commentator acts, as it were, like a museum guide, pointing out to the audience the significant features of the tableau before them. King Massinissa, in Lee's *Sophonisba*, for example, is swayed

by Sophonisba's beauty, her tears, and her pleas; Menander,
watching the scene, says:

> His sighs flow from him with so strong a Gale,
> As if his soul would through his lips exhale.

(III. iv. 172–73)

In *Lucius Junius Brutus* (1681), Lee has a character consciously and purposefully explicate an action being witnessed by the
audience and the other characters:

> Ah! See, Sir, see, against his will behold
> He does obey, tho he would choose to kneel
> An Age before you; see how he stands and trembles!
> Now, by my hopes of mercy, he's so lost
> His heart's so full, brimful of tenderness,
> The Sence of what you've done has strook him Speechless:
> Nor can he thank you now but with his tears.

(IV. 417–23)

Does the balance between word and deed hold in this scene?
Obviously that cannot be answered without the context, but also
obviously the speaker is shaping response to the tableau he describes, and is not simply recounting the details. He is telling
us, or, more accurately, attempting to persuade us, of the meaning of an event.

Dryden understood that *expression*, in the root sense of "to
press outward," was the prime task of painting and of poetry:
"To express the passions which are seated in the heart by outward signs, is one great precept of the painters, and very difficult to perform. In poetry, the same passions and motions of the
mind are to be expressed; and in this consists the principal difficulty as well as the excellency of that are."[26] The "outward
signs" are of the most interest to the present discussion because
I am arguing that it is in these that the Restoration dramatists
fell short. Even when they gave an outward sign, they would
often add to it an explicit summary comment. Perhaps this is
only a way of saying that the only outward sign of inward condition which the Restoration dramatists trusted was the word.

To illustrate the Restoration distrust of the outward sign, we

99

can contrast two parallel scenes, one in Shakespeare and one in
Otway's *Venice Preserv'd*. Belvidera confronts Jaffeir, before
she knows of the conspiracy, and begs to know what is troubling
him:

> Tell me! be just, and tell me
> Why dwells that busy Cloud upon thy face?
> Why am I made a stranger? why that sigh,
> And I not know the Cause? Why when the World
> Is wrapt in Rest, why chooses then my Love
> To wander up and down in horrid darkness,
> Loathing his bed, and these desiring Arms?
> Why are these Eyes Blood shot, with tedious watching?
> Why starts he now? and looks as if he wisht
> His Fate were finisht? Tell me, ease my fears;
> Least when we next time meet, I want the power
> To search into the sickness of thy Mind,
> But talk as wildly then as thou look'st now.
>
> (III. ii. 82–94)

This speech is modeled upon the confrontation of Portia and
Brutus in *Julius Caesar* (II. i. 234–309). Portia also describes
her husband's gestures, but she is re-creating for him, and creating for us for the first time, a scene which occurred the night
before. When she questions Brutus' present behavior, she does
not describe his gestures. In contrast, Belvidera's speech is like
a prolonged stage direction to Jaffeir. She speaks as though he
were not onstage and as though the audience were unable to
see him.

When action and speech are used together, each has its own
demands and conventions. Whether or not they work well together depends upon the uses to which they are put. We are most
conscious of speech intruding upon action when narrative is
employed to heighten an emotional moment. What is already
emotional is made more so, presumably, by explicit commentary
by one of the characters.

Finally, characters will use narrative rhetorically, presenting
a story for its power to move the listeners. The audience watches
the listener react, and also itself reacts, to the story. In Eric

Rothstein's terms, the "imagined scene" is "primarily psychological and only secondarily pictorial."[27] For example, in Otway's *Caius Marius* (1680), Lavinia has been threatened by her father with banishment. She pleads:

> Will you then quite cast off your poor *Lavinia?*
> And turn me like a Vagrant out of Doors,
> To wander up and down the streets of *Rome,*
> And beg my bread with sorrow? Can I bear
> The proud and hard Revilings of a Slave,
> Fat with his Master's plenty, when I ask
> A little Pity for my pinching Wants?
> Shall I endure the cold, wet, windy Night,
> To seek a shelter under dropping Eves,
> A Porch my Bed, a Threshold for my Pillow,
> Shiv'ring and starv'd for want of warmth and food,
> Swell'd with my Sighs, and almost choak'd with Tears?
>
> (II. 142–53)

Lavinia is imaginatively creating a scene in order to move her father to pity, and, paradoxically, it is her rhetorical control that disturbs us. If she is fearful for her future, her speech should be less artfully made, less precious in its details of dropping eves and pinching wants.[28] At least this is our contemporary decorum of verisimilitude. Otway's intention is clearly to create a highly emotional scene in which audience and father alike are moved to pity. The device used to move us is detailed narration.

Lee's editors have recognized another psychological function of the imagined scene. Lee's tendency to have his characters visualize a scene only hinted at by the context, "and thus to heighten their passions, as well as the feelings of the audience, is a dominant feature of his handling of emotion. Such mental visualization takes place especially when a character is under great stress. It usually arouses the character to such an emotional pitch as to drive him to violent deeds, and thus becomes a sort of subjective device for motivation."[29] In *The Rival Queens,* for instance, Roxana works herself into a rage recalling her "nonage" and the growth of her love for Alexander:

101

But when I heard of Alexander's Conquests,
How with a handfull he had Millions slain,
Spoil'd all the East, their Queens his Captives made,
Yet with what Chastity, and God-like temper
He saw their Beauties, and with pity bow'd;
Methought I hung upon my Father's lips,
And wish'd him tell the wondrous tale again:
Left all my sports, the Woman now return'd,
And sighs uncall'd wou'd from my bosom fly;
And all the night, as my Adraste told me,
In slumbers groan'd and murmur'd, Alexander.

(III. i. 85–95)

This speech continues, and Roxana's anger at Alexander's apparent infidelity grows until she has resolved upon violent revenge.

Sometimes a scene will appear twice in a play, once as action and once recounted as narrative. In *Venice Preserv'd* this doubling occurs several times. We see Pierre rebuff Jaffeir and then hear Jaffeir recount the scene to Belvidera (IV. ii. 168–268, 331–45). In near despair, Jaffeir attempts to stab Belvidera as a final gesture of faith to his friends and the vows he made them. Belvidera later tells her father, Priuli, of the attempted murder, which she embellishes with false detail, and we recognize the double rhetorical effect of narrative speeches. *Within* the play, she attempts to move her father to pity; *without* the play, the audience is also moved to pity, not only by the story but also by the spectacle of her urgent plea for help. Belvidera's rhetorical intensity is evident in her repeated "Think you":

Think you saw what pass'd at our last parting;
Think you beheld him like a raging lion,
Pacing the earth and tearing up his steps,
Fate in his eyes, and roaring with the pain
Of burning fury; think you saw his one hand
Fix't on my throat, while the extended other
Grasp'd a keen threatning dagger.

(V. 94–100)

The lion simile is trite, but Belvidera's desperation is forcing her to exaggerate for effect. The speech is paradigmatic in its structure for all the narrative devices used by Restoration dramatists. In narrative moments these dramatists are, rather desperately, urging us to imagine what they describe. "Think you," they urge us, and then they provide the details, the clues to emotional response, which seem fitting. The intent, it seems to me, is reasonable enough. The intent is to move the audience. It is the method, narration, that strains the dramatic conventions and forces us to listen to the plays rather than to watch them.

II. STATUS AND ROLE

There is a famous, or infamous, scene in Dryden's *All for Love* in which Antony, in company with his advisor Ventidius and his friend Dolabella, is confronted by his wife, Octavia, and his children. Octavia is seeking to bring Antony to an awareness of his obligations to her and to Rome. At her first appearance in this scene, Antony has seemed to act as a stranger to her. She asks, "Who am I?" and Antony responds, "Caesar's sister." But she is also his wife and the mother of his children, and to vividly remind him of this she sends the children to him to "hang upon his arms." The tableau of Antony surrounded by friends and loved ones is accompanied by this dialogue:

> *Vent.* Was ever sight so moving?—Emperor!
> *Dola.* Friend!
> *Octav.*　Husband!
> *Both Child.*　　Father!
> *Ant.*　　　　　　　　I am vanquish'd: take me,
> *Octavia*; take me, Children; share me all.
>
> 　　　　　　　　　　　　　　(III, p. 41)

Earl Miner describes this scene as "a painful, even ridiculous tableau, a morality play of the public world exerting its series of claims upon Antony, but so baldly that it is positively good manners on Antony's part to give in with as little delay as possible."[30]

Miner's reaction is probably our reaction, but the scene exemplifies an important and conscious use in Restoration serious drama of what sociologists call *status* and *role*. In this instance Antony is clearly, "baldly," confronted with a number of his social positions as a man and a leading citizen of Rome. He is capable of fulfilling the requirements of all these positions, even simultaneously. His difficulty is that he cannot be both the emperor and the lethargic vacationer in Alexandria; he cannot be at odds with Caesar and be Dolabella's friend; he cannot be Octavia's husband and Cleopatra's lover; he cannot be a father and desert his family.

Sociologists have borrowed the word *role* from drama and used it to describe the pattern of attitude and behavior that society and the individual associate with any given status.[31] *Status* is an individual's place in any social relationship. As used here, status has no connotation of prestige or rank on a vertical scale of values. For example, all human beings aged thirty-five share the status of that age. Male and female are statuses. Thus every individual carries many complexes of attitude and behavior associated with his statuses. We expect, for example, brothers to behave toward one another in certain ways. When one acquires the status of brother, a complex and relatively inflexible set of restrictions and privileges accompanies the status. The role of brother is positive and affirmative in its emotional and social connotations, as are the terms *brotherhood* and *fraternal* and their cognates. The approval we give to the status of brother is essential to the horror that generations have felt in response to the story of Cain and Abel.

Status and role can be seen to be some of the most effective of society's regulatory devices. Status and role define social intercourse, at least in its broad outlines, and they are embodiments of social norms. A son and a father, for example, know how to behave toward and with one another. Each learns the outlines of his duties and privileges and, in addition, the outlines of the duties and privileges of the other. Each expects certain attitudes and behavior from the other, and these expectations become a system of norms. The normative system embodied in culturally transmitted definitions of status and role is so thoroughgoing that, as one sociologist has said, "No circumstance under which different people come together is totally undefined." By the same token, an individual with a private vision of his status is insane.[32] In John Donne's famous lines, status is linked to coherence and "all relation":

> 'Tis all in pieces, all cohaerence gone;
> All iust supply, and all Relation:
> Prince, Subiect, Father, Sonne, are things forgot,
> For euery man alone thinkes he hath got
> To be a Phoenix.[33]
>
> (*The First Anniuersary. An Anatomy of the World*, ll. 213–17)

Status and role function to order and harmonize society; they provide guidelines for the infinite possibilities of behavior. They may also tend to stultify and rigidify society, but the Restoration playwrights saw primarily the integrative and ordering aspects of the cultural phenomena of role and status.

Role is internal as well as external. Role describes the individual's expectations with regard to his own attitudes and behavior and also describes the expectations of those around him. Status and role are radically important to an individual's concept of self; and just as harmonized roles in society regulate society, so harmonized roles within an individual produce internal harmony, a mental and emotional balance, the peace which is ubiquitously thematic in the Restoration. To see Antony confronted with social obligations when Ventidius calls him *emperor* is only half-correct. Antony is also within himself an emperor. R. J. Kaufmann has seen this aspect of the scene in *All for Love*: "Here . . . is an identity crisis, not in adolescence but at the end. Cleopatra, Ventidius, Octavia, Dolabella—all—*know* him and try to recall him to his true self. Each one has a claim that is morally substantial and theatrically potent."[34]

Antony is a fragmented man who searches for some way to bring himself, his roles, into harmony. He does this, it may be suggested, by accepting one set of statuses and giving up another set, at real cost to himself in emotion as well as power and prestige. As Serapion says at the conclusion of the play, the lovers sit "As they were giving Laws to *half* Mankind!" (V, p. 78; italics mine). Antony has given up the statuses of father, emperor, friend (to Dolabella), and husband, in order to accept the status of lover.

The uses of status and role in the Restoration fall into several basic categories. Conflict of status and role, first of all, is of primary importance as a plot device. Conflict of role or contradiction of status involves apparent or real irreconcilability of attitude and behavior. Can one be both wife and lover? Can one be both prince and man? Role conflict can, in addition, be both public and private.[35] It is important to the public realm—to the state and even to the world—for Antony to decide whether he will be emperor or lover, just as it is important to the state for Jaffeir, in *Venice Preserv'd*, to decide who are his friends, and for Mustapha to decide whether he will be first of all a friend, a lover, a son, or a prince. The public dimension of such role conflict (for example, civil war caused by the rivalry of sons for their father's throne) is inseparable from the private struggle (in this case, to reconcile the roles of son and prince). On the other hand, private struggle is often without a public dimension. One of the marks of domestic drama is that the role conflict pictured there is rarely of importance to the state. The private as well as the public psychological struggles with role and status provide plots, and the struggles take these forms: the character attempts to identify and define his role (traitor? hero? friend?); or to evaluate his roles (is it more important to be a prince or a son?); or to integrate his roles (how can I be both father and lover?). Several of these struggles may take place simultaneously.

The second important use of status and role is as metaphor. The vocabulary of status and role will function in all the ways that metaphor will, though perhaps the most common function seems to be as an emotional shortcut or shorthand. The emotionally tongue-tied character may seem to stutter statuses in an attempt to convey the depth of his feelings:

I'll fly my Father, Brother, Friends for ever,
Forsake the haunts of Men.
(Lee, *Lucius Junius Brutus*, III. iii. 96–97)

My Sister, Cousin, every thing that's dear . . .
(Banks, *The Island Queens*, I, p. 6)

To be a Friend, a Father, Husband to you . . .
(Southerne, *The Fatal Marriage*, II. ii, p. 28)

He who was all to me, Child! Brother! Friend!
(Rowe, *The Fair Penitent*, III, p. 35)

A Sister's Husband cannot be a Brother's Enemy.
(Ravenscroft, *King Edgar and Alfreda*, IV, p. 52)

A Father ought not to out-live his Son.
Hah! Brother? Wife? Stand off! No tyes of Blood
Are by aspiring Monarchs understood.
(Caryll, *The English Princess*, IV. ix, p. 49)

The Father's in my Heart, and Mother's in my Eyes.
(Banks, *The Innocent Usurper*, II, p. 20)

Finally, although outside my concern here, role and status are ready-made sources of comedy, especially burlesque.[36] One thinks first of all of Fielding's *Tom Thumb* with its gross disproportion of physical status and social status.

Dryden uses status and role as metaphor throughout *All for Love*. Since nearly every role is accompanied by richness of values and associations—for example, motherhood—the vocabulary of status and role is naturally metaphoric. Motherhood *is* warmth, tenderness, love, protection, home cooking, and so on. Soldiers *are* bold, strong, masculine, authoritative, fearless. As *All for Love* opens, we see Antony failing to behave as we expect a soldier and an emperor to behave. Antony is described by Ventidius as "shrunk" from the figure he was as a Roman and "cramped" in this "corner of the world." He has been made the "toy" of Cleopatra. Ventidius laments to Alexis, in one of the finest lines of Restoration drama, "I tell thee, Eunuch, she has quite unman'd him" (I, p. 6). Antony's opening words are also in the vocabulary of diminution; he has been cast down from the place he once held. He then physically drops to the ground, saying, "Lie there, thou shadow of an emperor" (p. 7).

In a way, Antony struggles to define himself as the play proceeds. His confusion about himself is evident in early scenes. He is startled to see Ventidius:

> *Ant.* Art thou *Ventidius*?
> *Vent.*   Are you *Antony*?
> I'm liker what I was, than you to him
> I left you last.

(I, p. 8)

Antony, a few lines later, asks, "Who am I?" and Ventidius answers, "My emperor." Ventidius insists on the word *emperor*, forcing Antony to recognize his role. Antony is ashamed to accept the title: "Emperor? Why, that's the stile of Victory" (p. 9). Antony at this moment recognizes himself only as the coward of Actium and suitable only for another "style." "I have lost my Reason," Antony says, "have disgrac'd / The name of Soldier, with inglorious ease" (p. 10). There is a rhetorical figure, *antonomasia*, in which a title is substituted for a name. Dryden and his audience were doubtless conscious of that figure in this speech and others like it. "The name of soldier" shows the explicit use of status and role. To be a soldier, to be called a soldier, requires attitudes and behavior which Antony has failed to embody and perform.

Ventidius says Antony's troops are waiting for him; they "long to call you Chief" (p. 11). But until Antony frees himself from Cleopatra, the troops will not fight. Ventidius asks, "Why should they fight indeed, to make her Conquer, / And make you more a Slave?" (p. 12). Ventidius works Antony into anger, makes him see himself as he once was, and Antony seems transfigured:

> *Ant. Caesar* shall know what 'tis to force a Lover,

108

From all he holds most dear.
Vent.   Methinks you breath
Another Soul: Your looks are more Divine:
You speak a Heroe and you move a God.

(I, p. 14)

The transfiguration to hero is short lived, and probably pre-figuratively doomed in Antony's self-description as the angry *lover.*

The use of status and role in dramatic action is, on one level, obviously necessary: any story involving people will involve their roles. But there is also a critical tradition describing the dramatic effectiveness of tightly knit relationships among the characters. Aristotle advises that the "situations to be looked for by the poet" are those in which "the tragic incident occurs between those who are near or dear to one another—if, for example, a brother kills, or intends to kill, a brother, a son his father, a mother her son, a son his mother, or any deed of the kind is done" (*Poetics*, XIV. 4). Corneille comments on this passage from the *Poetics* in his *Discourse on Tragedy* (1660), including it in his discussion of tragic pity. Corneille describes emotional conflicts of the kind that many Restoration dramatists embodied in the vocabulary of status and role: "The opposition of the feelings of nature to the transports of passion, or to the severity of duty, forms powerful emotions which are received with pleasure by the audience." And further, with more direct bearing on the subject of status and role: "The proximity of blood and the intimacy of love or friendship between the per-secutor and persecuted, the hunter and the hunted, the one who causes suffering and the one who suffers is . . . a great advantage for exciting pity."[37] Similar reflections can be found in the criti-cism of John Dennis.[38]

It should be noted here that, as Aristotle's comment would suggest, the use of status and role is not unique to one time or place. *Oedipus* is radically concerned with role and status, and so is *Hamlet*. What does seem true of Restoration drama, how-ever, is a consciousness of the vocabulary of role and an explicit and sometimes mechanical use of it. While the family is in a sense everything in *Oedipus*, there are no extended passages in which the vocabulary of role is hammered at over and over. In *Hamlet*, Shakespeare also controls the vocabulary of role, and when it is used it comes with shocking emphasis. Gertrude asks Hamlet if he has forgotten her. He replies:

> No, by the rood, not so:
> You are the queen, your husband's brother's wife;
> And—would it were not so!—you are my mother.
>
> (III. iv. 14–16)

Every word is like acid. Hamlet methodically, coldly, details the complex familial relationship. His account is scientific, precise, and uttered with barely contained passion.[39]

Role and status are everywhere in human affairs, but the Restoration playwrights seem occasionally to have seen in this aspect of life a way to describe with precision the complexities of human intercourse and emotion. The tersely accurate description by Hamlet of his mother contrasts with the following prolonged discovery of role from Otway's *Caius Marius* (1680). Lavinia, the wife of Marius Junior, comes upon her father-in-law, whom she has never met, alone and near delirium after he has been banished from Rome. Lavinia finds her name carved in a tree.

> *Lavin.* My *Marius* should not be far hence.
> *Mar. sen.*   What art Thou,
> That dar'st to name that wretched Creature *Marius*?
> *Lavin.* Do not be angry, Sir, what e're thou art;
> I am a poor unhappy Woman, driven
> By Fortune to pursue my banish'd Lord.
> *Mar. sen.* By thy dissembling Tone thou shouldst be Woman,
> And *Roman* too.
> *Lavin.*   Indeed I am.
> *Mar. sen.*   A *Roman*?
> If thou art so, be gone, lest Rage with strength
> Assist my Vengeance, and I rise and kill thee.
> *Lavin.* My Father, is it you?
> *Mar. sen.*   Now thou art Woman;
> For Lies are in thee. I? am I thy Father?

110

I ne'r was yet so curst; none of thy Sex
E're sprung from me. My Offspring all are Males,
The Nobler sort of Beasts entitl'd Men.
   Lavin. I am your Daughter, if your Son's my Lord.
Have you ne'r heard *Lavinia's* name in *Rome*,
That wedded with the Son of *Marius*?
   Mar. sen.   Hah!
Art thou that fond, that kind and doting thing,
That left her Father for a banisht Husband?
Come near——
And let me bless thee, though thy Name's my Foe.

(IV. 314–35)

Caius Marius makes use, in part, of the *Romeo and Juliet* plot. Marius' family and Lavinia's are political rivals, and, in this scene, Marius' blessing marks a complete change in his attitude toward her. He calls having female children a "curse," but Lavinia at this moment has brought him the food and water that he needs. Marius has ruled Rome, but banished he calls himself a "creature." The question "What art Thou?" is thematic to the entire play. It applies to Marius Junior and his unwillingness to forgo Lavinia or become a false son to his father. It applies to Marius. Is he a traitor and tyrant, as Lavinia's father maintains, or is he the ruler best for Rome? And in this scene the question applies to Lavinia, that "thing" that "left her Father for a banisht Husband."

Those Restoration plots that involve the family intensify the effects of the use of status and role. In keeping with the convention that required elevated status for the heroes of tragedy, the protagonists of these plays are typically regal. An additional dimension is created as double roles are produced: a given figure may be both father and king, or son and prince, or mother and queen. Perhaps the most familiar Restoration example of this kind of *dramatis personae* is in Dryden's *Aureng-Zebe*.

To review, *Aureng-Zebe* involves an aging emperor who has four sons, including Aureng-Zebe and Morat. Morat is the Emperor's only son by his present wife, Nourmahal. State law decrees that rule descend to the eldest son and that the other sons

111

be killed to prevent rivalry. When news reaches the sons of the Emperor's impending death, three of them converge on the capital with their forces, anxious to seize power. Aureng-Zebe, who is not the eldest son, comes anxious only to be of service to the Emperor and to preserve peace. Nourmahal wants to obtain the throne for her son. The plot is further complicated by the Emperor's love for Indamora, a captive queen. His rivals in love are his faithful counselor, Arimant, and his sons Aureng-Zebe and Morat. In the latter part of the play, Nourmahal falls passionately in love with Aureng-Zebe. The complexities of relationship here are apparent, and Dryden uses status and role at central moments to make clear the tensions among and within the chief characters.

Politically, the Emperor finds that "The name of Father hateful to him grows, / Which, for one Son, produces him three Foes" (I, p. 3). When the Emperor wishes to justify a command to a son, he explains his power in the vocabulary of role, clearly revealing the doubling effect: "O're him, and his, a right from Heav'n I have: / Subject, and Son, he's doubly born my Slave" (I, p. 6). Emotionally, the Emperor finds himself in a complex conflict of roles. He sends a plea to Indamora, instructing the messenger: "Say, I'm a Father, but a Lover too: / Much to my Son, more to my self I owe" (I, p. 9). His conflict with Aureng-Zebe begins to appear openly as the Emperor attempts to close off his role as father. He calls himself "a wretched King" in response to Aureng-Zebe's affectionate greeting.

> *Aur.* A King! you rob me, Sir, of half my due:
> You have a dearer name, a Father too.
>   *Emp.* I had that name.
>   *Aur.*   What have I said or done,
> That I no longer must be call'd your Son?
> 'Tis in that name, Heav'n knows, I glory more,
> Than that of Prince, or that of Conqueror.[40]

(I, p. 10)

When Aureng-Zebe learns of his father's infatuation with Indamora, at the end of Act I, his own situation is clear to him. He describes his inner tension in terms of role: "I to a Son's and Lover's praise aspire, / And must fulfil the parts which both require." But as long as the Emperor loves Indamora, Aureng-Zebe cannot fulfill both "parts."

Morat, also, can be seen in terms of double roles, but, unlike the others, he aspires to both roles. He tells Indamora:

> My Father, while I please, a King appears;
> His Pow'r is more declining than his Years.
> An Emperor and Lover, but in show:
> But you, in me, have Youth and Fortune too.

(III, pp. 45–46)

Nourmahal finds herself struggling to reconcile her roles as wife and lover. The conflict of wife and lover, in a different context, could easily be the kind of conflict found in comedy. It is the situation of a woman about to make her husband a cuckold. But Nourmahal's lover is, by law at least, her son: "Count this among the Wonders Love has done, / I had forgot he was my Husband's Sone!" Incest is rarely comic material, and Nourmahal's empty logic, as she attempts rationalization of her action, is a reflection of the irreconcilability of the roles she is attempting to maintain. She is "made wretched onely by a name," she argues. "If names have such command on humane Life, / Love sure's a name that's more Divine than Wife" (III, p. 41).

The word *name*, in these plays, is an almost certain signal of the author's use of status and role. And the use of names to indicate status and role can easily develop into thematic or occasional portrayal of the distinction between appearance and reality. A name (rank, status, title) can be assumed and dissembled; the reality cannot. As Indamora tells Morat in rejecting him: "Should I from *Aureng-Zebe* my heart divide, / To love a Monster and a Paricide? / These names your swelling Titles cannot hide" (V, p. 67).

Dryden's use of role in *Aureng-Zebe* is illustrative of the way in which the tensions and conflicts of a plot may be described in terms of role. Status and role function in large measure as ve-

113

hicles for theme, as well as being occasionally thematic in themselves. For example, in *Aureng-Zebe*, Nourmahal's inability to reconcile the roles of mistress and wife is also emblematic of the timeless struggles of reason and passion, love and duty, flesh and spirit. The same ageless struggle is evident in the Emperor's attempt to be king and father and husband and lover. When the Emperor comes to understand his error, he describes it in the familiar Restoration dichotomy: "Why was my Reason made my Passion's slave?" (IV, p. 58). The play also seems an affirmation of private and domestic emotions and responsibilities at the cost, if need be, of public emotions and responsibilities. The Emperor decides finally in favor of his son Aureng-Zebe: "Empire, and Life are now not worth a pray'r: / His love, alone, deserves my dying care" (IV, p. 65).

Nevertheless, in conjunction with these themes is also a theme that is intimately a part of role and status. The play affirms the necessity of familial harmony as a good in itself and as an analogue to the harmony of the state. Eugene Waith has described the final moment of the play—including the union in love and power of Aureng-Zebe and Indamora—as one in which "the compelling image of the hero [the dead Morat] lying at Indamora's feet gives way to tableaux of orderly family relationships."[41] At the conclusion of the play, Nourmahal has died from an inner fire, literally caused by poison, but figuratively caused by the inner and private anomie that is partially the result of role conflict. The Emperor removes himself from power and thus strips himself of many of the roles which he has attempted to maintain. The civil war in the nation is over, and "Brothers no more, by Brothers, shall be slain" (V, p. 78). The play ends with no conflict of roles, no conflict in the family, no conflict in the state.

Although the vocabulary of role and status can carry many themes and meanings, it is in part intimately domestic. Man's most basic relationships are those of the family, and most of his other roles are ascribed rather than acquired. Thus, because of the reality of our cultural organization, the familial roles appear repeatedly. Yet there is danger in this truth for the artist. Concentration on the familial roles of any character narrows his significance, or at least the range of his possible influence. Oedipus is Thebes. His illness is its illness, and his search for the killer—which is also a search for a father, a mother, and a self—is the search of the entire community. But in a play like *Venice Preserv'd*, Otway seems to be moving away from conflicts which are as much public as private and beginning to focus on the private alone.

The most apparent evidence of the domesticity of *Venice Preserv'd* is Jaffeir's status in the state. He is a citizen. He is the son-in-law of a senator, and he is a conspirator; but the former is not aristocratic status, and the latter simply makes him a member of a mob. What happens to Jaffeir at home is tenuously related to the health of the state, but familial and public concerns are not identified with one another as they are in *Hamlet* or in *Lear*.

Friendship is the crucial relationship of *Venice Preserv'd*. Jaffeir's shifting friendships provide a kind of outline of the play. In the first moments, Priuli's cruelty leads Jaffeir to believe that Venice is a place "Where Brothers, Friends, and Fathers, all are false" (I. 253), and Jaffeir finds "better Friends" in the conspirators (II. 132); he renounces them to admit that he has no "friend more dear than Belvidera"; he appears before the Senate with the promise that he "may prove a friend" if they reach agreement with him (IV. 147); he loses Pierre because of his betrayal and is rejected as Pierre's "once lov'd, valu'd friend" (IV. 294). And finally, in response to Pierre's anguished, "Heav'n knows I want a Friend" (V. 429), he stabs Pierre and thus proves himself, ultimately, a "generous friend" (V. 427). These moments are moving, but not monumental. The scale of deeds and significance has shrunk since the Renaissance, although the intensity of feeling has not.

Venice Preserv'd also provides some examples of a use of status and role which is both domestic and sentimental. The family is occasionally referred to for no other purpose than to elicit pity from a character within the play or from the audience. In *All for Love*, Octavia's very conscious use of her children in her attempt to win Antony back to Rome is another such moment.[42] A particularly blatant example of the pitiful reference occurs in Southerne's dramatic adaptation of *Oroonoko*. Oroonoko is urged to throw down his arms and end an insurrection. He is reminded, by a friend, of his pregnant wife and unborn child, and he answers:

> There I feel a Father's Fondness, and a Husband's Love.
> They seize upon my Hart, strain all its strings,
> To pull me to 'em, from my stern resolve.
> Husband, and Father! All the melting Art
> Of Eloquence lives in those softning Names.
> Methinks I see the Babe, with Infant Hands,
> Pleading for Life, and begging to be born.
>
> (IV, ii, p. 62)

Here the value of the vocabulary of status as metaphor is explicitly recognized and proclaimed: "Eloquence lives in those softning Names."

Toward the end of *Venice Preserv'd*, Belvidera seeks aid from her father. Her method of attempting reconciliation seems artificially prolonged. Only a part of the dialogue follows:

> *Belv.* By the kind tender names of child and father,
> Hear my complaints and take me to your love.
> *Priu.* My daughter?
> *Belv.*   Yes, your daughter, by a mother
> Vertuous and noble, faithfull to your honour,
> Obedient to your will, kind to your wishes,
> Dear to your armes; by all the joys she gave you,
> When in her blooming years she was your treasure,
> Look kindly on me; in my face behold
> The lineaments of hers y'have kiss'd so often,
> Pleading the cause of your poor cast-off Child.
>
> (V. 37–46)

Here Otway is not only consciously manipulating role, playing upon the accepted emotional attitudes associated with motherhood, childhood, and young love, but detailing these attitudes as well and prompting laggard response with loaded adjectives.

116

Construction of similar scenes seems a wholly mechanical matter, and the pattern may be duplicated with an almost limitless number of specifics. Mechanical repetitiveness was noticed by contemporaries of the Restoration playwrights, as well as by modern critics. In a wonderful scene in Joseph Arrowsmith's *The Reformation* (1673), the advice is given that a playwright "must always have two Ladies in Love with one man, or two men in Love with one woman; if you make them the Father and the Son, or two Brothers, or two Friends, 'twill do the better. There you know is opportunity for love and honour and Fighting and all that" (IV. i, p. 48). Arrowsmith's satire sounds very much like Aristotle's advice quoted above; and though Arrowsmith seems perfectly justified in his criticism of Restoration drama, his satire seems misplaced if applied to much Greek drama with plots every bit as intimate and domestic as those of the Restoration.

The apparently mechanical use of role, which Arrowsmith is satirizing, contributes to the rigidity and lifelessness of Restoration drama which Wylie Sypher isolates in his accusation that the plays seem debates over attitude in a ritualized, elitist cult.[43] Status and role are ritualized, and debates involving role can be so formalized as to produce scenes in which characters shift and change their relationships with a rhythm and stately pace reminiscent of the minuet. Aureng-Zebe does have to determine the correct attitude or posture—shall he be son, prince, lover, rival? But surely so does Hamlet—shall he be son or prince? The attitudes and behaviors of those roles are not reconcilable.

The problem of deciding upon status is not in and of itself a lifeless and artificial question. It is not simply a matter of the baroque and grandiose social conventions of an elite. And therefore the way in which the problem is described must be in large measure responsible for our reaction to the plays which describe this decision. To say that Shakespeare is a better poet than Dryden is perhaps naive, but it helps to indicate a partial reason for the rigidity of Restoration drama. Sypher, for example, points out that the plays of Beaumont and Fletcher before the Civil

War also exhibit the simplified psychology and extreme dialectical form which he describes as characteristic of Restoration, of "Late Baroque," drama. Sypher's example is *The Maid's Tragedy* (ca. 1611). The example is a helpful one because Thomas Rymer also discusses this play in *The Tragedies of the Last Age* (1678), pointing directly to the matter under discussion—status and role. Rymer objects to the prolonged and unnecessarily explicit scene in *The Maid's Tragedy* in which Amintor tells Melantius that the latter's sister has been the King's mistress: "Some broken speeches, as *your Sister, the King, her honour*, or the like, with now and then a sprinkling of his tears, might have suffic'd, and the Brother should have been left to guess and paraphrase the broad meaning. But *Amintor* harps upon the same string out of time himself."[44]

For Rymer, this scene is marked by a failure of manner, not matter. That a man's new bride has been another man's mistress is the viable stuff of drama, but it is the raw material, and not the finished product. Failures of manner may be the hallmark of the sentimental scenes described earlier. As Belvidera seeks forgiveness from her father—a situation which is at least potentially productive of profoundly felt emotions—we are struck with the artifice in her words. Belvidera is using an acceptable rhetorical device in referring to her mother, but, as Rymer says of Amintor, Belvidera "harps upon the same string out of time." The role of mother carries with it universally felt emotional connotations. These connotations do not need to be made explicit.

In summary, Restoration use of role and status, bolstered by aesthetic approval stemming directly from Aristotle, takes two basic forms in serious drama. The dramatists recognized the psychological fireworks produced by role conflict, and they made that conflict the source of a number of plots. They recognized, in addition, the innately metaphorical quality of the vocabulary of role and status. Their use of this vocabulary is not always marked by the art which hides art, but it always takes account of the multiplicity of connotations which this vocabulary bears. The following lines, all from Otway's plays, seem more me-

118

chanical out of context than in, but they illustrate the way whole stories, whole complexes of idea and emotion, can be conveyed quickly in this language:

> ... my hopes were crost,
> When in your Love I a Brother lost.
>> (*Alcibiades*, II. 15–16)

> *Father!* and *King!* both names bear mighty sence:
> Yet sure there's something too in *Son*, and *Prince*.
>> (*Don Carlos*, IV. 16–17)

> When-e're had I a Friend, that was not *Polydore's*,
> Or *Polydore* a Foe, that was not mine?
>> (*The Orphan*, V. 366–67)

III. DESIGNS OF STRESS

Because of the exotic names and places which are common to this drama, and because of the complex plots, I have found it convenient to use a diagrammatic summary of the relationships. The diagram is simple—in fact, oversimplified—but it acts to reveal something of a play's structure, or lack of it, and provides a mnemonic device which I have found useful when investigating a number of plays. Only three signs are used consistently, although some signs are created on an ad hoc basis for special circumstances. The three basic signs seem fundamentally sufficient and prevent the scheme from becoming so detailed as to be undecipherable. The three commonly used signs are:

$\longrightarrow$ Love (or lust), with the arrow pointing in the direction of the object of the emotion

$-\ -\ -\ -\ -$ Familial relationships by blood

$\vdash\!\!-\!\!-\!\!-\!\!\dashv$ Marriage

On occasion, parallel lines may serve to illustrate friendship:

$$=\!=\!=\!=\!=$$

119

A simple example, then, might look like this:

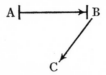

In this diagram, A and B are married, but B does not return A's affection. B, instead, loves C. The relationship is the familiar eternal triangle, spatially represented, with the dynamics somewhat more clearly apparent in a brief form than prose will allow.

Banks's *The Unhappy Favourite* contains a triangle which might look like this:

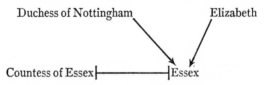

Another triangle occurs in Rowe's *The Fair Penitent:*

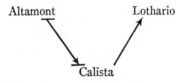

But the relationships in *The Fair Penitent* might also be shown in more detail in this way:

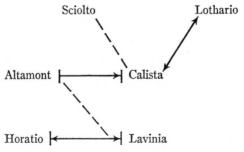

This diagram includes more of the characters, and the triangle is still apparent. It might appear that adding more characters would give a more complete picture of the play, but, in fact, I have found that additional characters make the relationships less apparent because the diagrammatic method employed here cannot reveal, without additional devices, the relative importance of relationships. If the diagram is being used for mnemonic purposes, then a detailed one, like the second for *The Fair Penitent*, can in some ways conceal the core of the play beneath detail. Whose relationship is most important? Are the two blood relationships as significant as the triangle? A few additional notes will, of course, answer these questions. I only wish to illustrate an important weakness of trusting the diagram alone.

In some plays, a single triangle is replaced by two or more interlinked triangles. The result may appear at first to be more complex, but it is sometimes simply more detailed. That is, in plays which involve the protagonist, say, with three women, two of whom are married, the apparent complexity may, if the artist has so managed things, be very clear and informative. Each of the situations may reflect upon the others, and comparison and various forms of "echo" within the plot or imagery of the play are possible. Dryden, for instance, is as interested in comparing Montezuma and Cortez in *The Indian Emperour* as he is in their tangled love affairs. The complex relationships here are mutually illuminating:

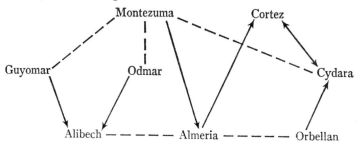

The three characters on the bottom line are siblings and the children of Zempoalla and Traxalla, central figures of *The Indian Queen*. We can see quickly that family may be very important here; and with a little additional information about the family of Almeria, Alibech, and Orbellan, we can imagine a thorough contrast between Montezuma's three children and these three. These diagrams, I believe, begin to have the appeal of chess games. The possibilities for attack, defense, move and countermove are fascinating. The diagrams may also suggest the structural variation in Restoration plays, which, when described in terms of love and honor (or some similar pair), all seem the same.

Three pairs are involved in Settle's *The Empress of Morocco:*

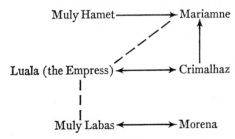

Though this situation seems neat, it is not. The confused relationships of the play are not exposed in the diagram because of another weakness. As drawn, the diagram cannot indicate time. There is no way to show how pairs form, develop, dissolve—or even whether any of these processes take place. Crimalhaz, for instance, develops his attraction to Mariamne late in the play, but his adultery with the Empress has begun before the play opens. The diagram is static, though the plays are not. This limitation can be remedied, as can most of the others, with additional notes.

Perhaps the most involved set of triangles in the betterknown plays appears in *Aureng-Zebe* (see diagram on page 123). Once again, *Aureng-Zebe* does not begin with these relationships fully developed. The diagram represents the situation at its most complex. The possible tensions are apparent, and Dryden makes full use of the vocabulary of role and status pertaining to these relationships.

Matched pairs may occur without their being interwoven into triangular or more complex relations. Crowne's *The Destruc-*

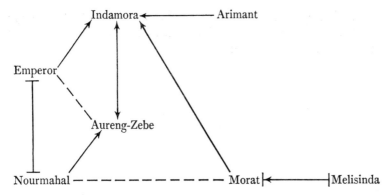

tion of Jerusalem, for instance, pairs two couples for mutual illumination, without mixing them:

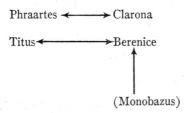

The fact that the two couples are mutually in love does not mean that the play is an idyll. There are barriers to both loves, and the barrier between Phraartes and Clarona is not present at their first meeting. One of the tensions affecting the Titus-Berenice affair is recognized with parenthetical reference to Monobazus, a relatively unimportant character.

Davenant's *The Seige of Rhodes* is even less complex:

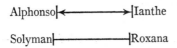

Here the lucidity of the diagram is matched by that of the play. The two couples are contrasts of Christian and pagan, and of spontaneous love (and honor) and political plotting (and hypocrisy). We are called upon to admire the one couple and disdain the other.

123

While we think of only one couple at the real center of Dryden's *All for Love,* the relationships when sketched out can be seen to be more elaborate:

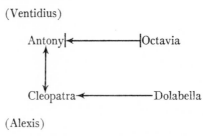

In this instance the advisors (in parentheses) seem an illuminating addition. The balance of the forces acting on the protagonists is the basic element in the harmony of structure created by Dryden's craftsmanship.

Two couples are important to Lee's *Sophonisba,* and a brief diagram would look like this:

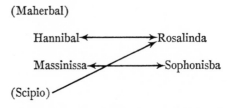

But the plot is such that more figures need to appear, if only to represent more accurately the tangle of affairs presented in the total play:

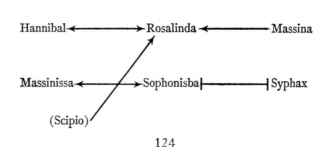

The second diagram is less easy to read at a glance, but more accurately represents the play.

Finally, to illustrate more fully the variety of patterns created by Restoration playwrights, more diagrams are shown below. The over-all effect of reviewing these is, perhaps, a reinforcement of the notion that these plays are highly "formal"; that is, the characters exist in a world of geometry more apparent than our own. The relationships are balanced, and even the dynamics of their lives seem formulaic, as though they obeyed the most precise of the laws of physics. Restoration plays are like seventeenth- and eighteenth-century dancing: geometric, rhythmically changing, beautifully organized when seen from above.

Here is Otway's *Alcibiades* (1675):

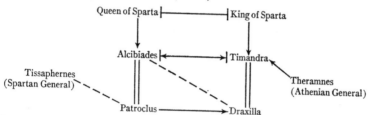

In this diagram, the parallel lines represent friendship.

Here is Dryden's play *The Spanish Fryar* (1681), and the diagram suggests that the play is misnamed—that the central figure is Leonora:

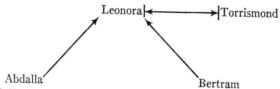

The following is an interesting pattern of relationships in Ambrose Philips' *The Distressed Mother* (1712):

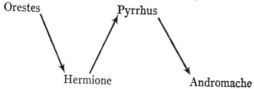

And, last, Orrery's *Mustapha:*

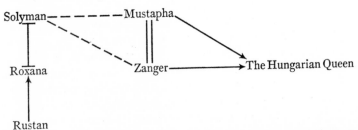

As has been mentioned, these diagrams are limited by being static and by their inability to show emphasis. To these limits might be added the fact that they cannot show anything about poetic or verbal skill; they cannot reveal artistry. In some ways, a simplified sketch of Sophocles' *Oedipus* and Dryden's and Lee's *Oedipus* might look the same, and that similarity would be very partial as a comparison of the plays. Nevertheless, the similarity is there, and we may too easily overlook it by focusing on the poetry of the plays or the genius of the artists. The diagrams are a modest tool in the study of these plays, and they can be helpful and illuminating in attempting to understand the matter and the manner of the plays.[45]

3

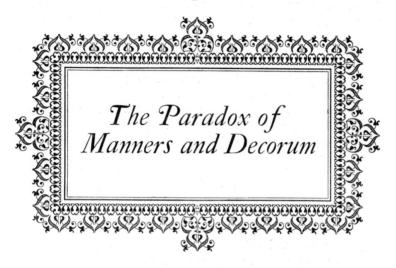

The Paradox of Manners and Decorum

T he terms *manners* and *decorum* have become constricted in meaning over the centuries and are now confined to narrow popular usage. Both are limited almost entirely to etiquette. The term "comedy of manners" was pejorative, or at least condescending, in its connotations until the work of Thomas Fujimura; and decorum, even as a literary concept, is still spoken of as a remnant of an older and less enlightened critical framework.[1] What I would like to argue in this brief chapter is that the related concepts of manners and decorum are fundamental to Restoration drama, and that both concepts are more intelligent and more understandable as human values than we sometimes give them credit for being. Both concepts are, in addition, as alive today as they were in 1670, although the contexts in which we consciously apply them have changed remarkably.

Hobbes contemptuously dismissed matters of etiquette as "small morals." What he understood *manners* to mean had to do with larger matters, matters of ethos. The best capsule summary of this larger view of manners is provided by Dryden:

> The manners in a poem are understood to be those inclinations, whether natural or acquired, which move and carry us to actions, good, bad, or indifferent, in a play; or which incline the persons to such or such actions. . . .
>
> The manners arise from many causes; and are either distinguished by complexion, as choleric and phlegmatic, or by the differences of age or sex, of climates, or quality of the persons, or their present condition: they are likewise to be gathered from the several virtues, vices, or passions, and many other commonplaces, which a poet must be supposed to have learned from natural philosophy, ethics, and history; of all which whosoever is ignorant, does not deserve the name of poet.[2]

Dryden is unquestionably speaking of the essentials of human character, and not of the superficial signs of social convention. As Fujimura has noted, to apply a definition like this to the phrase "comedy of manners" changes the meaning of the phrase drastically and, in fact, revitalizes it to make it more accurately applicable to English comedy of 1660 to 1700.[3]

Dryden's use of such terms as *choleric* and *phlegmatic* recalls the Jonsonian definition of humours—a concept more sophisticated than it is sometimes thought to be—and Dryden is somewhat ambivalent about the humours. On the one hand, he says that character is not simply a question of ruling passions: "From the manners, the characters of persons are derived; for indeed the characters are no other than the inclinations, as they appear in the several persons of the poem; a character being thus defined, that which distinguishes one man from another. . . . A character, or that which distinguishes one man from all others, cannot be supposed to consist of one particular virtue, or vice, or passion only; but 'tis a composition of qualities which are not contrary to one another in the same person." But a few lines later he adds that although character is a complex thing, "yet it is still to be observed that one virtue, vice, and passion ought to be shown in every man, as predominant over all the rest; as covetousness in Crassus, love of his country in Brutus; and the same in characters which are feigned."[4]

If I understand him correctly, Dryden is arguing that no matter how many motives and characteristics make up a man's ethos, all men have a predominant characteristic—at least this should be true of all men who appear in plays and poems. But the existence of a predominant characteristic does not preclude complexity of human character, and a playwright is theoretically justified—that is, he is supported by aesthetic theory—when he produces either type characters that are nearly personifications of dominant characteristics, or subtle psychological portraits that reveal the complexities of human character. This is a very flexible doctrine, and playwrights of the Restoration capitalized on its flexibility to write many kinds of plays. The central point here, however, is that there is an underlying assumption that human character is not uniform, unitary, or homogeneous, but that it is a farrago of motives, features, passions.

Five years before Dryden, René Rapin had said much the same thing about manners in the process of explicating Aristotle. Aristotle, Rapin says, "calls the manners the cause of the action, for it is from these that a man begins to act." Further: "The sovereign rule for treating of manners is to copy them after nature, and above all to study well the heart of man to know how to distinguish all its motions."[5] Manners, then, are related to motive, and motive to character, to feelings, and to the heart. Manners involve what is within a man, not what is without; manners deal with reality, not appearance. Hobbes had these distinctions in mind when he made manners the *raison d'être* of poetry (*belles lettres*): "The subject of a Poem is the manners of men, not natural causes; manners presented, not dictated; and manners feigned, as the name of Poesy imports, not found in men" (see note 25, Chapter 2, above). But if these theoreticians understood the task of poetry to be the depiction of manners in this subtly psychological sense, why then do the plays seem so stereotyped in characterization?

I believe the answer to this lies in a tacit paradox about the transactions of art in Restoration aesthetics. On the one hand,

129

the artists believed that man was a complicated creature, and on the other hand, they believed that man came to knowledge and truth by means of reason. Reason was understood to simplify, to clarify by finding the essential, "simple" core. Reason is a faculty which reduces complexity to essential simplicity and thus seems at odds with character in its complexity. The audience for a work of art naturally applies its reason. The artist, in order to help the audience understand, will also use his reason in the creation and ordering of his work of art. There are thus antagonistic assumptions involved in the concept of manners: the assumption that manners are multifaceted and subject to change, and the assumption that reason is necessary in the portrayal and understanding of manners.

To illustrate: John Dennis, in his *Remarks on Prince Arthur*, gives four qualities which are essential to the manners of characters in an epic poem: they are to be *good*, to be *like*, to be *convenient*, and to be *equal*. Taking these odd terms in order: "The Manners . . . are Poetically *Good*, when they are well mark'd; that is, when the Discourse and the Actions of the Persons which are introduc'd, make us clearly and distinctly see their Inclinations and their Affections, such as they are, and make us judge by the Goodness or the Pravity of those Inclinations, what good or what evil Resolutions they are certain to take." The quality of *likeness* refers to historical characters: "When a Poet introduces any such notorious Person, he is to paint him with the very same Qualities, which he is known to have had, or to have." The character should be recognizable. "The third Quality of the Manners, is their *Convenience*: They ought to be agreeable to the Age, the Sex, the Climate, the Rank, the Condition of the Person that has them." And, lastly, *equality*: "The Manners are to be constant and consistent. Every Person is so clearly to be shown at his first appearance, that he may afterwards assume no resolution, which may deceive the Expectation which he gave of himself at first." Characters who have these four qualities help to make the "Narration delightfull."[6]

All four qualities are useful, I think we would agree, in cre-

130

ating characters who are intelligible, recognizable, and coherent. They need not be types in any pejorative sense. Dennis does not limit the range of characters to be treated; he asks only that a character act according to motives which suit his ethos. But it seems fair to say, also, that characters with these qualities are more consistent than human nature typically is. The characteristic of *equality*, for instance, rules out spontaneous and irrational behavior, behavior which, while human (that is, possible) is not natural (that is, according to general laws of human nature). Following his definition of equality, Dennis explains: "Nature, for the most part, is uniform and regular, and maintains a constant course."

This last reference to uniform nature links the discussion of manners to the matter of what Dr. Johnson called "general nature."[7] Dennis argues, as did many of his contemporaries and many critics later in the eighteenth century, that the poet's task is not to number the streaks of the tulip: "In order to the giving this best Likeness, a Poet is not so much to consult Nature in any particular Person, which is but a Copy, and an imperfect Copy of Universal Nature; he is to examine that Universal Nature, which is always perfect, and to consult the Original Idea's of things, which in a Sovereign manner are beautifull."[8] One of the most important impulses moving the Restoration artist away from complexity and particularity in characterization, and moving him toward simplicity and generality, is the impulse to get at a profounder truth in character than is available in any particular ethos. The artist, if he wished to convey the truth and to be faithful to nature (*natura naturans*), must seek the universally significant, not the uniquely true.

The idea of general truth has roots as far in the past as Plato —as is evident in Dennis' reference to "Idea's"—and is not uniquely applicable to drama. But if we recognize that the desire to get at universal nature is not the same thing as believing that individual human beings are stereotypes, we might avoid an irresponsible error about the plays and their characterizations.

Characters were explicitly chosen for their significance. Characters are significant signs, carriers of general truths about hu-

131

man nature and human intercourse. If we were to ask Dryden if he thought there ever was such a man as Almanzor, I believe he would be astonished at the question but would answer that he did not know—or care, particularly. Almanzor was not created to be a portrait, or what Dennis calls a "Copy," of any particular hero; Almanzor carries qualities of heroism in his character, in his *manners*, and that is what is important. When Dryden defends Almanzor from attack, he does so by showing how Almanzor's heroic actions are paralleled in heroic literature, especially in the characters of Rinaldo and Achilles.[9]

In *The Intellectual Design of John Dryden's Heroic Plays*, Anne Barbeau has argued that the plays are purposefully designed to be intellectually challenging and stimulating, as opposed to being sensitive or sensual, and that as a result Dryden often created characters to be coherent rather than moving: "For Dryden, a character is successful if he is thoroughly intelligible and consistent, attributes undoubtedly suitable for a play of ideas." The intelligible characters are "manageable vehicles for the exposition of points of view." Barbeau's argument is often convincing; and, if we add to it, or temper it, with the recognition that Dryden, in critical theory and in practice, was also evidently concerned with creating a "lively" entertainment, we can see in her argument still another reason for the complexities of human life to be simplified in the plays. As she very perceptively notes, the complexity of the characters is not in the individuals but in their interrelationships.[10]

The tension of types was discussed in some detail in Chapter 2, but we can add that the clash and friction between characters, as distinguished from internal, idiosyncratic turmoil, creates a special kind of dramatic structure. If a character represents an idea or a group of ideas in a nearly allegorical way, then there is going to be no drama, no tension, no action, no movement, until he comes in contact with another individual who represents other ideas. Consequently, plays with this type of characterization are of necessity situation dramas. Everything depends on the situation, on who meets whom, at what time, and under what obligations. Eric Rothstein quotes Miss Sharon Saros as saying that characters at times appear "so many ping pong balls rebounding off suddenly materializing walls of circumstance."[11] But we notice immediately that reliance upon situation is not a disadvantage to the Restoration dramatist. His desire to create plays which are emotional and serial is satisfied by just such situational necessity. To look at this differently, it might be argued that situation drama, because it is a kind of drama which depends on predictable ("good," "convenient," and "equal") characters, contributes to the simplification of human complexity in Restoration drama.

Such characters are demanded by situation drama because more complex, more flexible (or less "equal") characters are unpredictable, adaptable, and therefore less threatened by situations, even unexpected ones. If Almanzor were capable of self-effacement, for instance, his confrontation with Almahide's father would present no suspense at all. It is because we know he cannot be humble that we are excited by the situation of confrontation. These distinctions are relative, not absolute, of course. Versatile and complex characters produce wonderful excitement in difficult situations—it is just that the excitement is not predictable, and suspense is ambivalent. In Restoration plays, ambivalence is not valued; predictability ("equality") is.

We have thus accumulated the following contributors to simplification: the desire to produce serial drama, the desire for rational intelligibility, the desire to imitate a rational universe, and delight in the combat of ideas.

The fundamental problem facing any artist who wishes to portray man's inner condition is the problem of how to do so in such a way as to be intelligible. There are two parts to this problem: first, how to bring what is within, without, and, second, how to make what has been brought without, intelligible. A psychiatrist might argue that everything a man does or says reveals something about him, and perhaps that is so, but that revelation is only step one. Step two is finding a way to turn the revelation into communication. The way to do the first, to bring out, the Restoration agreed, is through manners: "The Persons . . . ought to have Manners: that is, their Discourse and their Actions ought to discover their Inclinations and their Affections, and what Resolutions they are certain to take."[12] The way to do the second, to make intelligible, is to apply the principles of decorum. These principles make the manners coherent. Rapin describes both steps (manners and decorum) in these lines: "The poet represents the minds of men by their manners, and the most general rule for painting the manners is to exhibit every person in his proper character: a slave, with base thoughts and servile inclinations; a prince, with a liberal heart and air of majesty."[13]

Rapin's reference to "every person in his proper character" calls to mind the familiar literary use of decorum to create rather rigid character types. When applied by Rymer and Dennis, for instance, decorum and "proper character" become formalized descriptions of the correct actions, dress, speech, and psyche of every character, depending on his social station. But the concept of decorum can be applied more widely, as I have already suggested, and it occurs in its universal form in such phrases as the Marquis of Halifax's remark that "nothing is *truly fine* but what is *fit*."[14] Fitness is a criterion which can be applied, and was applied, to every aspect of life. There was conceived to be an appropriate mode for every occasion of action, of dress, of speech. There was conceived to be an appropriate manner of political activity and of home decoration and of landscaping. Moreover, comparative judgments, value judgments, are facilitated when there is a sense of decorum. The hierarchy which decorum implies makes sense of our remarks when we speak of what is "truly fine."[15]

Decorum can be understood mechanically, and a result is the "unnatural" regulation of human behavior which we associate with Thomas Rymer. On the other hand, decorum can be understood as the equivalent of verisimilitude (in which a character acts in such a way as to satisfy our sense of how he should or does act) and that fine "hitting off" of character which we admire in descriptive and narrative art. E. H. Gombrich has written that "there is no neutral naturalism. The artist, no less than the writer, needs a vocabulary before he can embark on a 'copy'

134

of reality."[16] What Gombrich is implying, and what I wish to make explicit, is that there must be a decorum in order for communication to take place between artist and audience. There must be a vocabulary which they share.

The trouble for us with Rymer's stiff little rules about who may kill whom is that they are not the rules which we apply. It is not that we do not have rules about who may kill whom; we most certainly do. However, we make our rules along lines different from Rymer's, and we are less concerned about servants and kings than we are about "nigger," "wop," or "Polack," or sexual explicitness, or political allegory. Only the slightest trace of decorum is necessary in order to wince at the story about the candidate for mayor of New York City who, in anticipation of his election, was said to have already picked out the linoleum for Gracie Mansion. Our decorum is different from Rymer's, but ours is every bit as pervasive and as profound to our daily and literary lives. Our responses to Restoration drama may derive less from the substance of the plays than from the violations of our conventions of decorum which we perceive in them. Restoration serious drama is, from our point of view, highly indecorous, though, ironically, decorum was one of the most cherished artistic ideals of that period.

The thoroughness with which concern for decorum permeated Restoration life can be illustrated not only in literary contexts but in daily life. Antoine de Courtin prepared, in France, *Rules of Civility* (1671), and his definition of civility is a definition of decorum and obviously involves all of a man's life. Civility, says Courtin, is "a science in instructing how to dispose all our words and actions in their proper and true places. And nothing can be said or done exactly, and with civility, without four circumstances be observed: First, That everyone behaves himself according to his age and condition. Secondly, That respect be preserv'd to the quality of the person with whom we converse. Thirdly, That we consider the time; And fourthly, the place where we are."[17] Although Courtin's description sounds mechanical—it sounds like a code of gestures, as in a duel, or a dance—the fact that *decisions* regarding behavior are involved,

135

links the description to the tradition which suggests that civility and decorum are uniquely human expressions and set man apart from the creatures which act solely by instinct and without conscious awareness of context.

Cicero, for instance, found one of man's unique capacities to be "that of discerning order, decency and a sense of proportion in words and deeds."[18] This is perhaps another way of saying that man alone has judgment and choice (free will). Fundamentally, it is the dignity of man that is expressed in decorous behavior, not slavery to artificial standards, although, like all forms of behavior, decorous behavior can be imitated by those who lack the freedom to choose how to direct their motives. We can teach a monkey to tip his hat. Courteous behavior may also conceal a motive which is evil; a man may smile and smile and so on. Nevertheless, only man can choose to be civil, and that choice is related to that most significant of choices, moral choice.

Thomas Tenison, later Archbishop of Canterbury, wrote in rebuttal to Hobbes's *Leviathan* that right reason, in its role as "the Law of Nature," "consisteth in the notice of that moral congruity or proportion which is betwixt the action (of mind, or tongue, or hand), and the object, considered relatively in their proper circumstances."[19] In Tenison's remarks appears the same vocabulary as has marked each of the passages just recently quoted: *proportion, action, relative, proper, circumstances.* This vocabulary suggests changing circumstances, shifting points of view, and *kinesis* rather than *stasis.* Decorum can be a matter of stasis, of fixed and immutable standards, only when an individual finds himself in one fixed circumstance. If the individual shifts his circumstances or has new circumstances impinge upon him, then his sense of decorum must also shift—subtly or suddenly, a little or a lot. Decorum can be understood as a set of rules only if we understand the set to include all the rules of human behavior under all conditions. Much more reasonably, decorum might be understood as a principle, unitary in nature, which prescribes fitness. Fitness, in turn, is related to, or is defined by, or is synonymous with, the truth. The man who perceives the truth of his circumstance and has, through education or experience, learned what is appropriate for him in that circumstance can act decorously.

Decorum is obviously not easily observed. It requires accuracy of perception, wisdom, and will. Restoration plays, comedy and serious drama alike, recognize these three parts (perception, wisdom, will) and show the variations of human behavior which result from partialism. In *The Indian Emperour*, Montezuma is paired with Cortez, pagan with Christian, and we can compare the men with respect to perception, wisdom, and will. We recognize Montezuma's lack of civilized polish, and we also recognize the artificiality of some Spanish behavior. The cultural differences contribute to differences in perception and in wisdom, and therefore to differences in decorum. The spontaneity and energy of the Mexican contrast with the urbanity and tradition of the Spaniard. In *The Orphan*, significant actions take place in the dark or in silence, and the resulting confusions, or lack of perceptions, lead to tragedy. It is not possible to act in a way which is fit when the circumstances are concealed. The Empress of Morocco is perceptive and has learned from experience the ways of the world, but she lacks the will to act decorously, except when those actions are selfishly useful.

Decorum is not, to summarize, a *corpus juris* of etiquette. Decorum is a condition of order achieved by proportioned relationships between object and context. The object may be an individual, a speech, a bit of clothing, a foreign policy, a marriage, a killing, a kiss. Everything occurs within a context, and thus everything is potentially decorous or indecorous.

The confusion of decorum with propriety is natural, but they are radically different. Propriety involves rules to which a person suits himself in action, word, and bearing. The rule is the crucial matter in propriety. In decorum, it is the truth that is crucial. The decorous act, or word, or man is so because proportion has been achieved, and any proportion can stand scrutiny and stress only if it is based upon the truth. A man

137

can behave with propriety if he knows which fork to use with his salad. A man can behave with decorum only if he knows himself and his situation.

It is not possible to illustrate a perfectly decorous man from Restoration drama because fractured decorum is the heart of comedy, and tragic figures, as everyone from Aristotle to Rapin has said, are flawed. I do not know a significant Restoration serious play in which the protagonist is perfect. What a decorous man would be like can be seen if we examine flawed characters and supply the missing or damaged part. Almanzor, for instance, knows himself well ("I alone am king of me"). He knows others less well, and his indecorous behavior—the attempted rape of Almahide, for example—is due to a failure to think in terms of his situation. More specifically, Almanzor fails when he does not think of other people. He must learn to think of others, his human context as it were, before we can accept him as a good man as well as an heroic one. The wildly ambitious men and women of some Restoration plays are indecorous in their inability to accept and adapt to their contexts. Ambition is a vice, after all, only in those whom circumstance has deprived of a natural way to advance. Ambition is decorous in a prince, but a vice in a prime minister (*The Empress of Morocco*), or a bastard (*Don Carlos*), or a woman (Lyndaraxa in *The Conquest of Granada*), or a soldier (Pierre in *Venice Preserv'd*). Aureng-Zebe is close to being a perfect man, and one of the signs of his perfection is his ability to accept his place in a kingdom where power is denied him by primogeniture. The brothers in *Mustapha*, too, control their rivalry in recognition of their situation. In contrast, the brothers in *The Orphan* attempt to manipulate their situation rather than to understand it, with tragic consequences. Villains may act with the appearance of decorum, but they cannot maintain this appearance for long because their behavior is not based upon the truth. Either they are concealing part of the situation or they are concealing part of themselves, and in either instance, sooner or later, the truth will out.[20]

Decorum was understood to be a fundamental artistic criterion, one which had to be filled before others could be met. In

Rapin's words, without decorum, "the other rules of poetry are false, it being the most solid foundation of that probability so essential to this art."[21] If the artist wishes to create the beautiful, he must achieve decorum, agrees Rapin's contemporary Jean-François Sarasin: "A thing cannot be called beautiful unless it has the order and magnitude which are suitable and proportionate to its nature."[22] If the artist wishes to create the sublime, he must be decorous. "Nothing is truly sublime that is not just and proper," says Dryden in his dedication of *The Spanish Fryar*.[23]

Decorum in drama was described often as a necessity if the form were to appeal to the intelligent and the thoughtful part of the audience. Presumably the proletariat could be amused with rude, indigestible fare, but the educated audience required food for thought. In 1674, Rymer wrote: "*Poetry* has no life, nor can it have any operation without *probability*: it may indeed amuse the People, but moves not the *Wise*, for whom alone (according to *Pythagoras*) it is ordain'd."[24] It is important to note that decorum, that is, probability or appropriateness, is not thought of as convention here, for even the vulgar appreciate convention and are at least amused by etiquette; but decorum is linked with intelligence and, I believe, the ability to understand nature. Nature is the standard by which probability is measured, and the wise man, who knows the truths of nature, is alone able to judge whether or not the artist has created probability. This summary is supported by an anonymous essay on *Hamlet* in 1736:

> Nature is the basis of all tragic performances, and no play that is unnatural, i.e., wherein the characters act inconsistently with themselves and in a manner repugnant to our natural ideas, can please at all. But a play may be natural and yet displease one set of people out of two, of which all audiences are composed. If a play be built upon low subjects, but yet carried on consistently, and has no merit but nature, it will please the vulgar, by which I mean all the unlearned and ill-educated (as for instance, *George Barnwell*, a piece calculated for the many), but it must be nauseous to the learned and to those of improved and exalted understandings.[25]

139

There is self-congratulatory smugness and class arrogance in this; but the basic contention is that intelligence is required to know the truth, or nature, and that the drama which imitates or conveys something of that truth will be appreciated only by the intelligent. We might note here, too, that a complaint against "low" words or actions or similar violations of decorum is not only a complaint against lapses of taste, but is, additionally, an objection to distortion of reality. Low words are for low subjects, and to use them for high subjects distorts the nature of the subject.

Decorum, in the Restoration and today, is a means of making truth apparent and communicable. Violations of decorum obscure the truth. A conscious violation of decorum is analogous to dissimulation and lying. Words reveal thoughts as behavior reveals character; if the words and behavior are fit, then the speech and the action are decorous. There is a wonderful inclusiveness about decorum, which may be one of the sources of the popularity of the doctrine.[26] Decorum does not rule out hatred, or jealousy, or envy, or delight. It requires that these emotions be expressed differently by different people under different circumstances. Dryden quotes Fresnoy on this subject in "A Parallel of Poetry and Painting" (1695): " 'In the passions,' says our author, 'we must have a very great regard to the quality of the persons who are actually possessed with them.' The joy of a monarch for the news of a victory must not be expressed like the ecstasy of a harlequin on the receipt of a letter from his mistress."[27] The question of whether this argument is psychologically sound, whether, in fact, delight differs from man to man depending upon his station, is never raised here because the focus is on the *expression* of that delight; but as far as I can tell, the Restoration did assume that there was a quantitative as well as a qualitative difference in the emotional responses of human beings which was directly related to status and role. The difference, in turn, was expressed through differences in diction and action.[28]

While decorum can be expressed in every aspect of life, in the drama the chief emphasis falls upon characterization (motive, behavior, personality), action, and diction. Decorum provides, as I have argued, a means for the coherent expression of personality. When decorum is violated, the character appears unnatural; it is not an exaggeration to say that he becomes a freak. Rymer accuses Beaumont and Fletcher of the creation of freaks in *The Maid's Tragedy*. "Did Hell ever give reception to such a Monster? or *Cerberus* ever wag his tayl at an impudence so *sacred?*" No lovers, declares Rymer, ever behaved like the King and Evadne: "Both the Kings behaviour and hers, uncircumstanc'd as we have them, are every way so harsh and against Nature, that every thing said by them strikes like a dagger to the souls of any reasonable *audience*."[29]

While Rymer's sensitivity to matters of decorum seems at times pathological, Dryden is always somewhat more interested in dramatic effectiveness than in anything else, and he, too, faults failures in decorum. Here he is speaking of the king in *The Maid's Tragedy*: "Fletcher . . . gives neither to Arbaces, nor to his King in the *Maid's Tragedy*, the qualities which are suitable to a monarch; though he may be excused a little in the latter, for the King there is not uppermost in the character; 'tis the lover of Evadne, who is King only in a second consideration."[30] To be effective, then, a character had to be decorous, and while the doctrine of decorum allowed, in sensitive hands like Dryden's, such subtleties as a proper behavior from a king carried away by love as distinguished from a king acting politically, there was nevertheless a standard for kingly behavior which distinguished the king, in any emotional condition, from lesser men. Beaumont and Fletcher together were criticised by Richard Flecknoe as "excellent in their kinde, but they often err'd against *Decorum*, seldom representing a valiant man without somewhat of the *Braggadoccio*, nor an honourable woman without somewhat of *Dol Common* in her."[31]

Even if the artist has completely imagined a character and has given him what Dennis calls "equality" (consistency), there is still the problem of timing, or matching the character and his circumstances. A kingly king is a comic figure in the wrong surroundings, and it is in comedy that we see the man and the circumstances grating against one another. Thomas Fuji-mura has even contended that the chief difference between Truewits, Witwouds and Witlesses is "their regard for decorum."[32] That seems oversimplified, but there is obvious truth in it, as Richard Steele recognized when, in the *Conscious Lovers* (1723), Myrtle mercilessly dissects Cimberton: "I own the man is not a natural; he has a very quick sense, though very slow understanding. He says indeed many things that want only the circumstances of time and place to be very just and agreeable" (II. i. 54–57). The comic irony of this turns on the airy "only the circumstances." The flaw is tossed off as an insignificant one, when Myrtle and Bevil Jr. and the rest of us all know that "the circumstances" are everything.

If the artist has created a consistent character and appropriate circumstances, the remaining major matter is diction, a topic so complex that it must be treated separately. Before turning to diction, I would like to review some of the difficulties created by a doctrine like decorum when it is given as much significance as it had in the Restoration. I am assuming still that what distinguishes our age from that one is our standards of decorum, and not the idea of decorum itself. What I am about to say can be said of today's theater as well, with appropriate changes in example.

First of all, decorum limits. As a doctrine shaping art, it is very flexible and very wide reaching, but it is nevertheless a doctrine which operates by limiting, not embracing. As Walter Jackson Bate has mentioned, decorum exposes the essential by exclusion, not by inclusion.[33] Decorum does not deny the fact that a king may fear spiders, bite his nails, prefer lamb to fish, and hate the archbishop. Decorum does mean that these matters are insignificant—they do not signify kingship. Decorum, as has been mentioned, simplifies and so acts as did seventeenth-century science by placing greater emphasis upon primary qualities. Decorum thus produces generalizations of great value, but at the same time creates a universe which is very nearly tasteless, odorless, smooth, and cold. This universe is especially dominant in the heroic world, populated as it is by men and women "above" most of us and unconscious of the niggling secondary qualities which so distract and delight ordinary men.

Still, we exaggerate the limitations imposed by decorum if we suggest that all kings, or all princesses, are the same. For example, I am not aware of criticism directed at the following women for breaking decorum, and yet they are all fully distinct personalities, and no reader of these plays would confuse them: Lee's Sophonisba; Settle's Empress of Morocco; Dryden's Cressida, Almahide, and Lyndaraxa; Crowne's Clarona; Otway's Belvidera. All these women are decorous as women of social standing, but at the same time there are villainesses and patient Griseldas here, active women and passive women. There is limitation in the doctrine of decorum which can falsify experience and human nature, but there is also enough room to make exciting characters of certain kinds.

Decorum also creates difficulties by looking backward rather than at the present or toward the future. A character, for instance, can be consistent ("equal") only in terms of past behavior. The term *consistent* cannot apply to novel behavior. It can be applied to adaptability, but only if the character has a history of being adaptable or has shown in some obvious way the potential for this sort of behavior. Surprise in character, the sudden discovery of strengths and weaknesses, is generally ruled out. Suspense in these plays is created by changes in situation, not changes in character. In another sense, decorum looks to other kinds of already established standards. That is, for a king to be kingly, he must act in a fashion certified as legitimate by other kings. It is true that each king may modify the pattern somewhat, permitting in that way some freedom for himself and simultaneously enlarging the boundaries which will confine kings who follow, but this room to innovate is restricted. The resources with which a character faces the future are limited to those available to him from the past—if he is to act decorously.

The relatively fixed nature of possible decorous behavior produces another characteristic of decorous drama—it begins to resemble ritual. Once the general limits of behavior are established, a playwright may find his fundamental creative act to

143

consist of choosing the characters and the situations in which they will be placed. A violently ambitious woman, a prince, a captive princess, a civil war—these become the stock pieces of Restoration dramatic construction. The stock pieces are so well recognized that they were parodied in *The Rehearsal*.[34] Furthermore, if the characters are already known—that is, if the limits of their possible behavior are matters of convention for playwright and audience alike—then so, too, must themes of the play be limited. Only so many stories can be told with limited characters within the confines of genre.

The conventions of Restoration decorum are so unlike our present ones that we are annoyingly aware of the formal and ritualistic nature of the plays. We find the plays predictable, not consistent. We find the characters stereotyped, not verisimilar. But I would argue that consistency and verisimilitude are functions of one's standard of decorum, and not absolutes. No one today would argue that our own comedy or serious drama is not highly ritualistic, even though we feel, or believe, or sense, or "know," that the characters are more "real" or convincing than those in earlier drama. Theater of the absurd, musical comedy, kitchen-sink plays, rock operas, well-made plays, the nude drama, and the living theater—the names alone suggest the decorums of our day and suggest character types, probable situations, probable responses, probable sets, probable costumes, probable plots. We can be surprised in the theater, and so could the Restoration audience, but surprise involves the risk that decorum will be shattered and that the audience will reject what they see as non-drama.

The audience of *Waiting for Godot* often responded at first, before we established a new decorum for such plays, with astonishment and anger. They felt they had been hoaxed and led to believe they were going to see a play when what they had seen was nothing at all—nothing happened.[35] Innovation baffles value judgments and forces nonritualized response from an audience. An audience witnessing something new, something which does not follow established patterns, is forced, without their will and thus violently forced, to respond without guidelines. Audiences hate that. Ritual is comforting and regular. No matter how catastrophic the event, ritual provides us with responses which enable us to cope. In fact, catastrophes are relatively easy to cope with because we have developed rituals for them—for death, for anguish, for losses, for natural calamities. But a new situation, a situation without a ritual, is a trial and at times a terror. A new situation requires that we respond (give outward signs) without guidelines. But if we do so respond, then we expose ourselves to scrutiny because only our *self* can be held responsible for the responsive behavior. If our response is judged appropriate by the judgment of those we value, then it is our real self—our intelligence, our taste, our judgment, our sense of discretion—which has been approved. But if our behavior is found faulty, then it is our real self which is flawed and faulty. The risk of responding without guidelines is therefore too great for most of us. There is too much to lose in being found faulty in response. We can all live with failures of ritual and decorum because these are failures, usually, of ignorance and lack of information, and can be repaired. We can learn the proper thing to say to a new widow, a new father, an old-timer, a half-wit, a girl cousin, an airline stewardess. But a failure of self is not easily repaired. The social situation without rules is dangerous to our "soul," and we protect ourselves by refusing to respond—by walking out of the theater or by accusing the situation of incoherence. It is the latter that we can document over and over again in the history of the arts.

In fact, this rejection of the new is one of the contingent difficulties with decorous drama. Drama which values decorum and which is supported by a critical literature in defense of its decorums is unable to cope with innovation in the theater. This will be discussed in greater detail in Chapter 5, but one illustrative example will indicate the nature of the situation. As the Restoration period closed, plays had begun to explore new possibilities for *dramatis personae*. In plays like *Venice Preserv'd* the central figures were no longer princes and queens, but were instead ordinary citizens. This innovation violated some of the most cherished decorums of the theater—tragedy and serious drama generally were to portray the fall of the great, not the misfortunes of the ordinary. How then was one to portray the anguish of an ordinary man? How was the audience to respond? Was it acceptable to feel pity for Jaffeir? In order to prompt pity for him, must the play be constructed differently from the way it would be to prompt pity for a king? If it is legitimate to write a play about Jaffeir which everyone will take seriously, was Aristotle wrong? Or, alternatively, was Aristotle right, and have we simply misunderstood him for centuries?

All of these problems arise with the appearance of new characters. All of these and more have arisen repeatedly from the Restoration until the present, with very few answers having reached consensus. Arthur Miller is grappling with the same critical problems as did George Lillo. The Restoration gives watershed evidence for a radical change in dramatic theory and practice in England and America. In the Restoration and early eighteenth century, playwrights began to explore new characters, although they did not in any significant way experiment with new situations, and the result was a critical chaos which has not yet been put in order. The closest we have come to ordering the chaos is to find labels for some of the problems. We do not know what it is, but we have a name for it—middle-class tragedy— or tragicomedy, or melodrama, or living theater, or any number of similar labels.

Decorum, then, seems to produce four interrelated difficulties: it limits, it looks backward, it tends to ritual, and it creates profound problems in aesthetic theory when something or someone new appears.

The Restoration valued decorum highly. Unlike the present moment, critics and dramatists in the Restoration explicitly recognized the central place of decorum in drama. If they are to be faulted, it is for their lack of recognition of the difficulties decorum imposes. The seventeenth-century passages which have been cited all have an obvious tone of approval. Decorum is spoken of as an ideal and as a positive value. Moreover, decorum does have the advantages that the period saw—coherence, clarity, consistency—but it tends also to produce stereotypes, rituals, and clichés. Restoration dramas are lucid, as the artists and the audiences wished them to be. Because they are lucid, Restoration plays are not suggestive, as we would like them to be.

The present study of Restoration drama stems from my conviction that manner, and not matter, is at the heart of our responses to these plays. There is no element of the manner of these plays more important than their diction, and it is to this that the next chapter turns. Perhaps the richest critical discussion of decorum and its influence in the Restoration centered on diction. Though it is true that even the thoughts of characters were held to standards of decorum, the speeches of the characters are their visible souls.[36] Speeches are the chief means of revealing a hero, since heroic action cannot be performed by unheroic actors. The actors cannot do heroic deeds onstage, but they can talk heroically. Speeches reveal internal tension; they reveal wisdom, and cowardice, and love. In Restoration drama, comic and serious, the speech is the thing.

147

4

Diction

I

In 1711, John Dennis wrote an essay in which he explored "Simplicity in Poetical Compositions." In this essay, prompted by Addison's *Spectator* No. 70, on *The Ballad of Chevy Chase*, Dennis quotes with approval a long passage from the French critic René Rapin and then translates it as follows:

> The Third Quality of the Diction is that it ought to be natural, without any manner of Affectation, according to the Rules of Decorum and of good Sense. Phrases that appear too much studied, a Style that is too florid, a Manner that is too nicely wrought, Things that are finely said, Terms that are too far fetch'd, and all Expressions that are windy and swell Us, are insupportable to the true Poetry. Only Simplicity can agree with it, provided that Simplicity be sustain'd by Nobility and by Greatness. But that is a Simplicity with which only great Souls are acquainted. 'Tis the Master-work of Poetry, and the Character of *Homer* and *Virgil*. The Ignorant look for what they call Wit and fine Thoughts, because they are ignorant. The fourth

Quality of the Diction is, that it be exalted and sonorous. For every thing that is vulgar in the Expression is below it. It requires Words which have nothing that is base and common in them, a Diction that is noble and magnificent, Expressions that are strong, and Colours that are lively, and daring and audacious Strokes.[1]

I have quoted this passage at length because it is an excellent summary of most of the ideals of diction as expressed by the Restoration critics. We note the idea of fitness, or naturalness, and ease, the avoidance of excess and every quality which seems artificial and studied. We note also elevation and vividness as prized qualities in diction.

Because Restoration serious drama involves noble characters in situations of stress which require dignity and courage, and in situations of affection or hatred which are especially intense because of the scope of soul possessed by the characters, the central quality required of diction in the plays is elevation. As Sir James Macdonald told Boswell in 1762, "for kings and heroes an elevation of language is necessary."[2] It is necessary because it is proper for them; elevated speech fits elevated characters. It is necessary also because they are speaking verse, not prose. Dryden, for instance, knew perfectly well that his characters were not speaking like the man on the street: "It is very clear to all who understand poetry that serious plays ought not to imitate conversation too nearly. If nothing were to be raised above that level, the foundation of poetry would be destroyed."[3] Poetry is not prose, and heroes are not ordinary men. These two propositions are easily enough stated, but difficult to act upon.

Then, too, the protagonists of serious drama need elevation of diction because their thoughts, ideas, and feelings, are elevated, and only elevated diction is suitable to carry this freight. The idea that words are related to thoughts is so obvious to most of us as to appear self-evident. In the *Rhetoric*, for example, Aristotle cautions against ambiguity, "unless, indeed, you really prefer to be ambiguous—as do those who have nothing to say, but pretend that they have something in mind."[4] But the consequences of this idea are not rigorously thought out in every age. If the right word indicates a right thought, does a wrong word indicate a wrong thought? The Restoration would have answered yes, without hesitation. By the end of the eighteenth century, the answer would have been, "Not necessarily." Dryden and Pope immortalized the unlucky would-be poets who made the mistake of writing and thereby giving concrete form to their pretensions. A witless man, the Restoration believed, spoke and wrote witlessly. A wit wrote and spoke wittily. A hero spoke heroically.

The doctrine of the proper word for the proper idea may seem reasonable and attractive enough, but the logical corollaries are not quite so attractive. The Restoration concern with "low" words, for instance, may appear to us one more instance of a classed society insisting on privilege and insisting that certain words are fit only for certain occasions and classes. But if words match ideas, then a low word is representative of a low thought, and there is no place for a low thought in an heroic play—at least no place in the mind or mouth of an heroic character. Low words are not to be identified solely with the vocabulary of the peasant or ruffian, but with the issue of shabby and ill-educated minds of any class.

Dr. Johnson objected to Lady Macbeth's employing the vocabulary of these lines:

> —Come thick night!
> And pall thee in the dunnest smoke of hell,
> That my keen knife see not the wound it makes;
> Nor heav'n peep through the blanket of the dark,
> To cry, Hold, hold!

Dr. Johnson objected to *dun*, to *knife*, and to *peep through the blanket*. Geoffrey Tillotson explains:

> In Johnson's time as well as in Shakespeare's, people spoke freely of knives, of dun horses and cows, and of blankets, and writers of prose were at liberty to follow suit. But for the climax of a tragedy—the murder of a king by a noble person—Shakespeare should, according to Johnson, have used words of a different status. The words that readers or spectators looked to find were

150

sword or *dagger, darkest,* and *cloak,* and they had been deliberately avoided by Shakespeare in preference to words so far insulting, it seemed, to decorum as to be words of the butcher, the ostler and the housewife.[5]

Tillotson goes on to show that Dr. Johnson is right about the meanness of the vocabulary, but that the meanness itself is fit for this occasion and this woman; in other words, Tillotson argues that in this instance low words are decorous. Once again, we need not agree with either critic in order to accept the basic notion that decorum is the crucial matter—the fitting together of word and context.

The presence in Restoration drama of bombast—high style without substance—was recognized at the time and correctly described in critical theory. Dryden noted that rant made every speaker sound the same: "no man can be distinguished from another."[6] In 1654, Georges de Scudéry wrote: "Every kind of perfect style has for near neighbor the faulty; indeed, it is very easy to pass from one to the other. The magnificent degenerates easily into the inflated and the swollen, the ordinary into the weak and sterile, and the low into the coarse and vulgar."[7] It appears that most Restoration critics would have agreed with Elder Olson's definition: "The true high style is simply that which is appropriate to the tragic character—one, that is, which manifests his dignity. It is not bombast."[8]

The theory of diction in Restoration drama is simply stated as requiring the suiting of speech, speaker, and situation. The level of diction should fit the speaker and his circumstances. This simple formulation was further qualified in two ways: the speech must be suitable to the genre, that is, to tragedy or to epic, and it must be suitable for poetry as distinct from prose. Over and over the critics and poets insisted upon suitability and proportion between words and ideas, words and the things the words represented. Here Dennis employs an organic metaphor: "Words are to Thought, what Flesh is to the human Soul; now Flesh encreasing to such a degree, imparts Comeliness, and perhaps Majesty; but swelling beyond it, it brings Deformity and

Impotence, and becomes a clog to the Mind."[9] Dennis' statement is dated 1695. René Rapin, quoting Demetrius Phalerius, had said much the same thing in 1674: "There must be . . . a proportion betwixt the words and the things; and nothing is more ridiculous than to handle a frivolous subject in a sublime style, for whatsoever is disproportionate is altogether false or at the least is trifling and childish."[10] Dryden recognized the trifling and childish nature of diction which was unsuited to the thought, and he feared that Restoration dramatists who imitated Shakespeare had failed to achieve Shakespeare's sense of proportion: "I fear . . . that we who ape his sounding words have nothing of his thought, but are all outside; there is not so much as a dwarf within our giant's clothes."[11] And, perhaps in the most famous exposition of this general theoretical position, Pope gives this famous summary in *An Essay on Criticism* (1711):

> *False Eloquence*, like the *Prismatic Glass*,
> Its gawdy Colours spreads on *ev'ry place*;
> The Face of Nature we no more Survey,
> All glares *alike*, without *Distinction* gay:
> But true *Expression*, like th' unchanging *Sun*,
> *Clears*, and *improves* whate'er it shines upon,
> It *gilds* all Objects, but it *alters* none.
> Expression is the *Dress* of *Thought*, and still
> Appears more *decent* as more *suitable*;
> A vile Conceit in pompous Words exprest,
> Is like a Clown in regal Purple drest;
> For diff'rent *Styles* with diff'rent *Subjects* sort,
> As several Garbs with Country, Town, and Court.
>
> (Ll. 311–23)

Whether this principle of decorum in diction is expressed in an organic or a mechanical figure (as in a figure of apparel), the import is the same—for a given character in given circumstances, only one kind of diction is appropriate. An organism grows one skin; a social situation demands one appropriate garb. A king whose speeches grow from his mind as an oak grows from an acorn is likely to speak in much the same way

152

as a king who carefully chooses his words to clothe his thought. And this brings us to the restrictions on dramatic diction imposed by the genre. Royalty make up the greater number of the important characters in Restoration serious plays; and although the ideal of decorum allows considerable variety in diction, limited only by character and circumstance, there is, in fact, very little variety in the plays. Because the characters are uniform, the diction is uniform. Because the circumstances appropriate to these characters are limited, diction is further limited.

Tragedy is a convention with its own decorum, and Restoration playwrights often adapted Shakespeare's work to their own times in the belief that he had offended against the decorum of tragedy. They reduced Shakespeare's metaphors in number, removed ambiguity, tightened the prosody, excised quibbles and puns and offensive words. As George Branam explains, "One of the reasons for the offensiveness of his language was the violation of the dignity of tragedy."[12] The epic, too, which was so often the explicit model for characters and situations in Restoration drama, demanded elevation and a consistency of tone: "That the epic should be clothed in noble, majestic, serious, and exalted language was almost a universal belief."[13]

In theory, then, the dramatist carried no responsibility which we would not want him to have. He was to match speaker, speech, and situation in a proportioned and verisimilar way according to the conventions of the genre. The practice of the drama reveals with wonderful lucidity how insufficient theoretical summaries are to the reality of the expectations of artist and audience. The theory looks flexible and potentially is flexible, but each of the key terms was so defined as to constrict the range of possibilities until the plays were homogeneous, and only the exceptional artist found a few moments of genius in variation upon theme.

The key terms are *speaker, speech, situation, verisimilar, convention,* and *genre.* Each of these critical concepts is redefined by each generation, and though the articulated theory is often indistinguishable from age to age, the practice is obviously in-

consistent. The Restoration audience and artist had an understanding of the key terms, but they left this understanding
unspoken. There was no need to articulate it—everyone understood. Everyone agreed what *proportion, character,* and *genre*
were. Passages like those quoted from Dennis, Rapin, Dryden,
and Pope were obviously meant to reaffirm what everyone already knew; moreover, each leaves the key terms undefined. A
bad poem, Pope, Shadwell, Blackmore, and Flecknoe agree, is
a poem which fails to manifest true eloquence. Without true
eloquence, a poem is like a clown in a king's attire, or vice versa.
But what is the proper dress for a king? *Regal* purple? I do not
wish to abuse Pope's simile, but to suggest how valid his assessment is, on the one hand (we all agree, even now, that a king
should be regal) and how empty of substance it is, on the other
(it is redundant). In essence, Restoration critical theory regarding diction said that a speech is decorous when the words
suitably convey the likely thoughts of a character in a specific
situation. Suitability is determined by comparing the words to
the standards of what is appropriate to a character in a given
situation.

Although the key terms are undefined, we can make some
reasoned inferences about their implications from the practice
of the plays. I have chosen to draw almost all of the illustrations
for this chapter from one play—Lee's *Lucius Junius Brutus*
(1681). This play is relatively easy of access to us in the Stroup
and Cooke edition of Lee's plays and in the edition prepared by
John Loftis for the Regents Restoration Drama series at the
University of Nebraska. The play represents a number of suitable characteristics: it is in blank verse and thus free of most of
the artificialities imposed by heroic couplet rhyme; it is from
the 1680's, a period of important dramatic work and one in
which the dramatist could rely upon contemporary political turmoil for extra powers if he wished—and Lee did.[14] Lastly, it is
a play which has a strong critical reputation for merit.[15] In
other words, it is not a helpless victim unfairly set out to cham-
pion the period.

In Act III of *Lucius Junius Brutus*, the play's lovers, Titus and Teraminta, meet and cling together in joy and in desperation. The first thing we might notice about their speeches is that we cannot distinguish man from woman:

> Thus let me rob the Fountains and the Groves,
> Thus gird me to thee with the fastest knot
> Of arms and Spirits that would clasp thee through;
> Cold as thou art, and wet with night's faln dews.
>
> . . . .
>
>   I give thee back thy joys,
> Thy boundless Love with pleasures running o're;
> Nay, as thou art, thus with thy trappings, come,
> Leap to my heart, and ride upon the pants,
> Triumphing thus, and now defie our Stars.
>
>   (III. iii. 50–53, 58–62)

There is nothing particular here in the vocabulary or tone to indicate sex. Indication of sex through diction is always difficult, no doubt, and especially so in what this period would have called the "softer" emotions of love, melancholy, pity, and sympathy. Nevertheless, here and elsewhere there is no significant difference in masculine and feminine vocabulary other than those differences imposed by subject matter. Similarities of the same sort exist when older and younger characters are compared, or when brothers and sisters, or even friends and enemies, are matched. Character, in the practice, as opposed to the theory, of choosing words for the drama does not seem to include such matters as sex or age. It does include class, which will be discussed below.

If physical character cannot be easily identified, perhaps the combination of character and situation can. For example:

> Not to remember you of his past Crimes,
> The black Ambition of his furious Queen,
> Who drove her Chariot through the Cyprian Street
> On such a damn'd Design, as might have turn'd

The Steeds of Day, and shock'd the starting Gods,
Blest as they are, with an uneasie moment:
Add yet to this, oh! add the horrid slaughter
Of all the Princes of the Roman Senate,
Invading Fundamental Right and Justice,
Breaking the ancient Customs, Statutes, Laws,
With positive pow'r, and Arbitrary Lust;
And those Affairs which were before dispatch'd
In public by the Fathers, now are forc'd
To his own Palace.

(II. i. 174–87)

This speech contains an allusion which might give a clue to that moment in Roman history which is referred to, but the general vocabulary is such that the speech might occur in any play involving Romans and a protest against tyranny. It is a narrative speech and, to an important extent, a speech determined by the nature of the rhetorical circumstances—the speaker is recalling to others past crimes in order to stir them to action (*anamnesis*). But the speech has no distinguishing characteristics; it can be placed in a probable situation (for example, before the Senate) but not assigned a specific speaker or occasion.

In a more intimate moment, intensely personal for the characters involved, the same diffuseness, the same tenuous link to place and time appears:

Now, by those Gods with which he menac'd me,
I Here put off all nature; since he turns me
Thus desperate to the World, I do renounce him:
And when we meet again he is my Fo.
All Blood, all Reverence, Fondness be forgot:
Like a grown Savage on the Common wild,
That runs at all, and cares not who begot him,
I'll meet my Lion Sire, and roar defiance,
As if he ne're had nurs'd me in his Den.

(III. i. 164–72)

In this speech it is easy to determine that a father has turned out his child who is here vowing defiance. But is there something in it that makes it distinct? Even if the play were constructed

156

with animal imagery of such power that this speech carried extra meaning against that figurative background, would we be able to determine the probable identity of the speaker from anything other than the child-father relationship? I do not think so. In this instance at least, the presence of figures of speech does not render the speech more distinctive. The *lion, den, savage, wild* construction is no more precise in its significance than is the allusion to tyrant and cruel queen in the preceding speech.

Ironically, it is those speeches intended to convey passion that are the least effective for us. It was for these speeches, more than for any other feature, that the plays were written, and yet the abstraction and the self-consciousness of the passionate speeches destroys their verisimilitude for us. Here Titus soliloquizes, imagining himself by the banks of a stream:

> ... if thy Passion will not be kept in,
> As in that glass of nature thou shalt view
> Thy swoln drown'd eyes with the inverted banks,
> The tops of Willows and their blossoms turn'd,
> With all the under Sky ten fathom down,
> Wish that the shaddow of the swimming Globe
> Were so indeed, that thou migh'st leap at Fate,
> And hurl thy Fortune headlong at the Stars:
> Nay, do not bear it, turn thy watry face
> To yond' misguided Orb, and ask the Gods
> For what bold Sin they doom the wretched Titus
> To such a loss as that of Teraminta?

(III. iii. 32–43)

This is a puzzling speech and needs to be read several times before the imagery is coherent, and yet the "metaphysical" image is not the result of Titus' passionate reaching after some means to communicate the nature of his feelings. Titus' cleverness with the image of his eyes reflected in the stream, which also reflects the surrounding scene, inverted, makes this moment seem artificial. Titus seems like an adolescent who is conscious of his melancholy and seeks a means to dramatize it. The cleverness, according to our conventions, is incompatible with spontaneous, and therefore genuine, emotion.

For contrast with the self-consciousness of Titus, we might choose the ring of truth which comes from the prose of the comic "Titus Oates" figure of the play, Vinditius. His asyntactic, proverbial, colloquial speech is the speech of comedy and of *Pilgrim's Progress* and gives one the impression of suddenly overhearing the real speech of the period.

> Come, Neighbours, rank your selves, plant your selves, set your selves in Order; the Gods are very angry, I'll say that for 'em: pough, pough, I begin to sweat already; and they'l find us work enough to day, I'll tell you that. And to say truth, I never lik'd Tarquin, before I saw the Mark in his forehead: for look you, Sirs, I am a true Commonwealths-man, and do not naturally love Kings, tho they be good; for why should any one man have more power than the People? Is he bigger, or wiser than the People? Has he more Guts, or more Brains than the people? What can he do for the People, that the People can't do for them selves? Can he make Corn grow in a Famine? can he give us Rain in Drought? or make our Pots boil, tho the Devil piss in the Fire?
>
> (II. i. 36–48)

I wonder if our sense of approval for this comic speech is not based on a naive convention of verisimilitude. We have, in some sense, inverted the canons of decorum which existed in 1680, and we now find what was low to be high. We accept the colloquial as genuine and reject the artful as artificial. In this instance, the colloquial prose seems to our ear to be genuine and spontaneous human expression. But if we were more discriminate—and this lack of discrimination is what I mean when I call our current conventions naive—we would note that Vinditius' speech is highly rhetorical and every bit as carefully crafted as Titus' stilted and self-pitying soliloquy.

Vinditius is speaking to a crowd of common people. His speech is therefore frank and direct. How do we know it is frank and direct? In large measure, we know this because he tells us it is: "to say truth . . ." Titus imagines the world turned upside down in the stream; Vinditius makes kings into bloated grotesques by taking abstraction (social stature) and rendering it physical: bigger? wiser? more guts? more brains? This comic amplifica-

158

tion is rhetorical, a conscious shaping of the prose, and not the spontaneous overflow of powerful feeling. The comic proverbs have the effect of diminishing the notion of kingship, and laughter at the impossibility of growing corn in a drought is transferred to the impossibility of monarchy—whether there is any actual connection between the ideas of king and corn or not. I think we are in some ways like the crowd Vinditius addresses; we will accept as genuine that which is merely colloquial.

To return to the point at hand, although theory emphasized suiting speech, speaker, and situation, the practice created a kind of uniformitarianism. Within the category of nobility, it is difficult to distinguish individual noblemen. Moreover, it is difficult to distinguish the circumstances in which they find themselves:

> Ah! See, Sir, see, against his will behold
> He does obey, tho he would choose to kneel
> An Age before you; see how he stands and trembles!
> Now, by my hopes of mercy, he's so lost
> His heart's so full, brimful of tenderness,
> The Sence of what you've done has strook him Speechless:
> Nor can he thank you now but with his tears.

(IV. i. 417–23)

A speech like this is portable. It can be placed in dozens of plays without changing a word. And this portability is possible because of the generalized nature of the vocabulary (*sir, obey, age, kneel, tremble, heart*) and because of the restricted number of plot situations which are possible within the limits placed by decorum on the behavior of nobility.

Eugene Waith has given, I believe, the best capsule summary of our difficulty with the diction of Restoration drama. He is speaking solely of Dryden's plays, but the judgment can be generalized: "The combination of explicitness and formality seems fatal. Tossed off informally, without benefit of similes, such comments might pass on the modern stage. If the meaning were entrusted more wholly to the figure of speech . . . they would pass for more interesting poetry."[16] Surely this is true, and yet it asks the Restoration playwrights to find a balance between poetry and informality which was not available to them. (Waith does not argue that it was.) On the one hand, the possibility of writing dialogue "informally" was precluded by two considerations. The first is represented in Dryden's flat assertion that "serious plays ought not to imitate conversation too nearly."[17] That is, these plays, are written in verse—they are poetry—and poetry is not informal. The second restriction on informal dialogue is the fact that common speech is what common people speak, and not what tragic figures speak. One might recall that when Ben Jonson proudly announced that his *dramatis personae* (unlike Shakespeare's) would show "deedes, and language, such as men doe vse," he was referring to "persons, such as *Comoedie* would chuse."[18] Lee and Otway were still a century away from Wordsworth's innovative suggestion that the "language really spoken by men" could be taken seriously.

The fact that the plays were poetic and that they were about nobility, then, restricted the Restoration playwrights. The restrictions they felt are not necessary in any absolute sense—Shakespeare managed to create great poetry and great men simultaneously—but the restrictions are necessary according to decorum. The restrictions held beyond 1700 and can be seen clearly in those plays of the eighteenth century which treat members of the middle class seriously. Because George Lillo, for example, had no aesthetic to help him create his play about merchants and their apprentices, he was forced to take the aesthetic which was available. The result is the terrible, pretentious, latinate diction of *The London Merchant* (1731). To dignify the merchant, Lillo makes him speak a "dignified" prose, even though it is a prose never spoken by any man, noble or ignoble. One example will illustrate: Thorowgood, the merchant, instructs his daughter Maria to prepare an evening's entertainment with a generous hand. She replies, "Sir, I have endeavored not to wrong your well-known generosity by an ill-timed parsimony" (I. ii. 6–7).

160

The theory of the decorum of diction is clearly at work also in comedy. The following is a brief example of what I have called "portable" dialogue: "Would I had daggers, darts, or poisoned arrows in my breast, so I could but remove the thoughts of him from thence!" (II. ii. 102–104). But these are the words of Mrs. Loveit, in Etherege's *The Man of Mode*, and, in that context, transparently comic. Bellinda says to her, "Fie, fie, your transports are too violent, my dear." They are too violent both in the sense that they exceed the cause (Dorimant's apparent fickleness) and in the sense that they are too violent for any character in comedy. Only tragic heroines can speak like this and be taken seriously because only in the tragic *situation* is this vocabulary suitable in the mouth of a protagonist. Loveit and other passionate ladies in Restoration comedy (such as Lady Wishfort in *The Way of the World*) often speak like tragic heroines, and when they do they make fools of themselves. Such speeches do not fit.

There is, then, a second major irony in Restoration serious dialogue. Although theory insisted on proportioning speech to speaker and to situation, the speeches actually produced seem to have no ties either to speaker or to situation. They are tied within the framework of the conventions of serious drama, but rarely so constructed that they seem expressly suited to only one play. Kenneth Muir, speaking of Dryden's *All for Love*, says that Dryden's poetry all too often does not grow out of the situation and thus cannot maintain the play as a poetic whole.[19] This is another recognition of the portability and the generalized level of diction in these plays.

To return for a moment to the alternatives mentioned by Waith for revitalizing dramatic diction—to abandon metaphor for the sake of the informality required by the modern stage (an impossibility in Restoration theory), or to entrust the meaning more wholly to metaphor and thus create "more interesting poetry." The latter possibility is more difficult to discuss, for any substantial discussion would in truth be a discussion of the general poetic fashions of the Restoration because it is obvious that the poetry of these plays is a reflection of the poetry of the age in nondramatic forms as well. The poets did not entrust meaning to figures of speech under most circumstances (as Waith recognizes) and thus they were unlikely to do so in drama. Restoration nondramatic poetry is memorable today when it is argumentative or satiric, or, to a lesser extent, when it is in the form of the great ode. We do not remember lyric poems of the Restoration as typical, and the absence of the lyric mode is apparent in the uniform tone of poetic drama. Put another way, if we followed our judgment of the nondramatic poems into the drama, we would expect the drama to be at its best in argument, satire, and, to a lesser extent, in epideictic celebration as practiced in the occasional ode.[20] In fact, this is our discovery. It is in comedy, in dialectics, and in narrative that the plays are effective for us. We admire the ironic and violent characters like Lyndaraxa, in *The Conquest of Granada*, whose eagle-sharp vision of power politics can be expressed with the same vigor we find in *Absalom and Achitophel*:

> I've seen
> This day, what 'tis to hope to be a Queen.
> Heav'n, how y'all watch'd each motion of her Eye:
> None could be seen while *Almahide* was by;
> Because she is to be her Majesty.
> Why wou'd I be a Queen! because my Face
> Wou'd wear the Title with a better grace.
> If I became it not, yet it wou'd be
> Part of your duty, then, to Flatter me.
> These are not half the Charms of being great:
> I wou'd be somewhat—that I know not yet:
> Yes; I avowe th'ambition of my Soul,
> To be that one, to live without controul:
> And that's another happiness to me
> To be so happy as but one can be.

(II, p. 17)

The narrative effects of Restoration diction were not always intended, at least not in theory. There was absolute agreement that a play was a thing of action, and not of words. Nevertheless, the persistent unwillingness to allow action to speak for

162

itself produced speeches which are narrative by way of commentary on action, present, past, or imagined. Here is Lucrece, after having confessed the rape:

> Ah Collatine! Oh Father! Junius Brutus!
> All that are kin to this dishonor'd blood,
> How will you view me now? Ah, how forgive me?
> Yet think not, Collatine, with my last tears,
> With these last sighs, these dying groans, I beg you
> I do Conjure my Love, my Lord, my Husband,
> Oh think me not consenting once in thought,
> Tho he in act possess'd his furious pleasure:
> For, oh, the name, the name of an Adultress!—
> But here I faint.
>
> (*Lucius Junius Brutus*, I. i. 391–400)

Lucrece speaks of herself in periphrasis ("this dishonor'd blood"), as though her actions were apart from her ("these last sighs, these dying groans"), and she explains her actions ("here I faint").

At times narrative is purposeful, as when a character recalls to another some episode from the past:

> Remember me; look on thy Father's suff'rings,
> What he has born for twenty rowling years.
>
> (II. i. 369–70)

Here the details of the past are not recounted, but the allusion is narrative and so is the tone. The audience, reading or listening, responds to such an invitation with expectations of storytelling.

On occasion the narrative is prefigurative, as when Titus, in a self-pitying scene, pictures himself in melancholy tableau:

> Choose then the gloomy'st place through all the Grove,
> Throw thy abandon'd body on the ground,
> With thy bare brest lye wedded to the Dew;
> Then, as thou drink'st the tears that trickle from thee:
> So stretch'd resolve to lye till death shall seize thee:
> Thy sorrowful head hung or'e some tumbling Stream,
> To rock thy griefs with melancholy sounds,

163

With broken murmers and redoubled groans,
To help the gurgling of the waters fall.

(III. iii. 22–30)

The narrative quality is underlined by the speaker's use of second person to describe himself. Language in this speech is its own justification. This is poetry, and not a form of action, as dialogue is primarily in drama.[21] The poetic interlude is a well established dramatic device, admittedly, and the point here is that it is a narrative moment when it occurs.

Restoration plays sometimes contain trials, moments in which one character sits in judgment on one or more others. These trials sometimes make use of the vocabulary of the courtroom, as in Act II of *All for Love*, when Antony indicts Cleopatra and provokes her response: "How shall I plead my cause, when you, my Judge / Already have condemn'd me?" But more often the scene is a matter of self-justification for past actions or defense against accusations of unfairness or cruelty. In a trial scene, narrative is the predominant mode. Here is the beginning of, as it were, a statement for the defense:

> *Brut.* Will you proceed?
> *Ter.*　My Lord, I will. Know then,
> After your Son, your Son that loves you more
> Than I love him, after our common Titus,
> The wealth o'th' World unless you rob 'em of it,
> Had long endur'd th' Assaults of the Rebellious,
> And still kept fix'd to what you had enjoyn'd him;
> I, as Fate order'd it, was sent from Tullia,
> With my death menac'd, ev'n before his eyes,
> Doom'd to be stab'd before him by the Priests,
> Unless he yielded not t'oppose the King,
> Consider, Sir; Oh make it your own Case.

(IV. i. 337–47)

This is, in addition, a repeated scene of the sort described in Chapter 2. We have already witnessed the moments being described by Teraminta and here experience the moment a second time with the variation which comes from the new circumstances.

164

Finally, narrative is produced in those imagined scenes, also described in Chapter 2, in which one character, for rhetorical effect, describes an exciting moment to another. Here Teraminta combines a description of events which have just taken place offstage with an imagined future moment. The hysterical exaggeration, which might be excused as the expression of terror, is made unpleasantly melodramatic here through abstraction and apparently self-conscious similes.

> No, let me fall again among the People,
> Let me be whooted like a common strumpet,
> Toss'd, as I was, and drag'd about the streets,
> The Bastard of a Tarquin, foil'd in Dirt,
> The cry of all those Bloodhounds that did hunt me
> Thus to the Goal of death, this happy end
> Of all my miseries, here to pant my last,
> To wash thy gashes with my Farewel tears,
> To murmur, sob, and lean my aking head
> Upon thy breast, thus like a Cradle Babe
> To suck thy wounds and bubble out my Soul.
>
> (V. i. 77–87)

When Teraminta delivers this speech, she seems to be describing emotion, rather than experiencing it. The speech rings false because it lacks charm as poetry—the final simile is disgusting, not touching—and because it does not have the sound of genuine distress. It falls between the chairs which Eugene Waith has offered as resting places for dramatic dialogue—the poetic and the colloquial. Both poetry and the colloquial are denied by this sort of generalization. The speech is filled with such generalizations as "the People," "like a common strumpet," "all those Bloodhounds," "this happy end," "miseries," "gashes," "tears." The speech is made up of plurals, not specifics; it is made up of types, not unique things. This typing is emphasized by periphrasis: "foil'd in Dirt," "Goal of death," "pant my last," "happy end." Not only is the speech descriptive rather than expressive, but it is descriptive of a generalized experience, and not a concrete and particular one. The speech is portable.

The point should be made again that the failure here would

have been regarded as a failure by anyone strictly interpreting according to the aesthetic conventions. Thomas Rymer had argued: "Many . . . of the Tragical Scenes in *Shakespear*, cry'd up for the *Action*, might do yet better without words: Words are a sort of heavy baggage, that were better out of the way, at the push of Action."[22] But could Lee have taken this advice with Teraminta? In order to do so, he would have had to show her dragged through the streets and through the crowds and to show her hooted and stoned. The spectacle was beyond the capacity of the Restoration theater—at least if it were to be done without losing the illusion of verisimilitude. In addition, as has been mentioned, some actions are better left unpresented if they cannot be presented effectively, because a flawed spectacle is indecorous and probably comic. As we all know, death onstage is difficult to perform convincingly.[23] An alternative to verisimilar action is affecting narrative as part of the dialogue, and that is what Lee has attempted.

Teraminta's self-consciousness is representative of a feature common in these plays. Restoration dramatists inherited a highly self-conscious and rhetorical dialogue from Caroline drama.[24] They found similar speeches in seventeenth-century French prose romance and in French drama. Whatever the source, this self-conscious dialogue makes Restoration characters seem to stand apart from themselves in a kind of rhetorical schizophrenia. They comment upon their feelings, actions, and intentions as though these feelings, actions, and intentions belonged to another individual separate and apart. We might recall Teraminta's "here I faint."

Sometimes this separation of speaker and self appears in powerful poetry. Brutus, for example, has an early soliloquy in which he looks back on his actions over the past twenty years and the roles he has been forced to play. (The speech is forty lines long *in toto*.)

> O, what but infinite Spirit, propt by Fate,
> For Empire's weight to turn on, could endure
> As thou hast done, the labours of an Age.

· · · · · · ·

166

To act deformity in thousand shapes,
To please the greater Monster of the two,
That cries, bring forth the Beast, and let him tumble:
With all variety of aping madness,
To bray, and bear more than the Asse's burden;
Sometimes to whoot and scream, like midnight Owls,
Then screw my Limbs like a distorted Satyr,
The World's Grimace, th'eternal Laughing-stock,
Of Town and Court, the Block, the Jest of Rome;
Yet all the while not to my dearest Friend,
To my own Children, nor my bosome Wife,
Disclose the weighty Secret of my Soul.

(I. i. 112–14, 118–29)

This is a narrative speech of the type required in drama to bring an audience up to date. The "you" Brutus addresses is himself, and the bitterness and vigor of his speech come in part from his having had to play these ugly roles and having had to keep secret his sanity and his concern for Rome. The poetry here, in addition, has sufficient interest by itself to make the moment dramatic, or emotionally affecting, even though narrative.

Brutus has the fact of his double identity and the force of his grotesque images in the poetry to give his soliloquy substance dramatically. But without such helps, rhetorical schizophrenia exposes a character's emptiness. He appears not to be manipulating appearance for a purpose, but instead to lack a mature personality to express. Dozens of Restoration characters appear immature and, if male, effeminate in their daydreaming and self-pity or self-aggrandizement. Typically, such characters are attempting to express tenderness in a poetry which does not sustain the lyric impulse. The result is not lyric poetry but tableau. In order to express tenderness, many dramatists turned from expression to description—in drama a form of narration. We are called on to imagine a tender scene, rather than hearing the tenderness or seeing it ourselves.

Act II ends with Titus speaking to Teraminta.

Yet we shall meet,
In spight of sighs we shall, at least in Heaven.

167

> Oh, Teraminta, once more to my heart,
> Once to my lips, and ever to my Soul.
> Thus the soft Mother, tho her Babe is dead,
> Will have the Darling on her bosom lay'd,
> Will talk, and rave, and with the Nurses strive,
> And fond it still, as if it were alive;
> Knows it must go, yet struggles with the Croud,
> And shrieks to see 'em wrap it in the Shroud.

This speech is expressive up to the point where the simile begins. The simile figure itself is surely legitimate in these circumstances, since comparison is an essential means of lyric expression. But Titus compares himself to a mother, a "soft" mother, who has just lost her child. The comparison is silly and suggests that Titus is either confused as to the nature of his feeling and seeks a general analogue for a vague inner sensation, or does not, in fact, love Teraminta so much as he feels self-pity (since pity is the point of the comparison). I think that none of these is the source of the image, but that Lee does what other dramatists do at such times—he relies upon a stock stimulus, a suffering mother, to produce the desired response, in this case pity for the lovers. The failure of this moment is the result of the inappropriateness of the simile to the situation.[25]

In the absence of the lyric voice, the dramatists turn to stock descriptions to produce rhetorical effects. This, in its turn, contributes further to the narrative quality of the drama and to the rhetorical schizophrenia. A character is not expressing himself at such moments. Instead, he is finding an analogue to his feeling, which he then holds up beside himself so that the audience may make a comparison. Here is Titus once again:

> My constant suff'rings are my only glory:
> What have I left besides? but ask Valerius,
> Ask these good men that have perform'd their duty,
> If all the while they whipt me like a Slave,
> If when the blood from every part ran down
> I gave one groan, or shed a Womans tear:
> I think, I swear, I think, O my Valerius,
> That I have born it well, and like a Roman.

> (V. i. 41–48)

168

Apart from the indecorousness of his discussing his own courage, we note once again the shift to narrative and the use of comparison and tableau for rhetorical effect ("like a Slave," "a Womans tear," "like a Roman").

The absence of spontaneity which is suggested by extensive artifice—ornate patterns of syntax, schemes, tropes—is recognized and warned against in classical rhetoric and in the rhetorical tradition which comes directly to the Restoration. Demetrius argues that the forceful style requires brevity and such devices, for example, as *asyndeton*, the absence of connectives.[26] Vigorous emotion is imitated in speech by fragmented syntax and exclamation. Quintilian influenced the French critic Lemaistre, who stated that "l'ostentation de l'art fait douter de la vérité."[27] Dryden, in the early *Essay of Dramatic Poesy*, criticized the frequent diatribes of French drama, noting that "short speeches and replies are more apt to move the passions and beget concernment in us" than are long declamations.[28] Saint-Evremond, in 1672, said much the same: "Neither have I any mighty opinion of the violence of that passion which is ingenious to express itself with great pomp and magnificence. The soul when it is sensibly touched does not afford the mind an opportunity to think intensely, much less to ramble and divert itself in the variety of its conceptions."[29] Dryden speaks of effect and Lemaistre of verisimilitude, but the point is the same. At the end of the century, Dennis added: "The Sentiments ought to be disorder'd in the violent Passions, and the Language ought to be bold and figurative; and the more violent the Passions are, the bolder may the Language be."[30]

Yet despite this critical consensus, the practice is almost uniformly for extended passionate exclamation in the form of description and narration. Theory held that fragmented syntax, exclamation, even incoherence and flights of bold imagination, were expressive, but in practice the playwrights distrusted any form of expression which was not articulate and crafted. As they were unwilling to trust meaning to gesture, they were unwilling to trust meaning to fragments. This distrust appears to break down to some extent with the move toward the pathetic and what

Eric Rothstein has called the "style of pathos." This style is "mimetic rather than conventional" and consists of fragments, gasps, and all forms of spastic interjection.[31] It is a style brilliantly mimicked in *The Tragedy of Tragedies* (1731):

Glum.	What do I hear?
King.	What do I see?
Glum.	Oh!
King.	Ah!
Glum.	Ah! Wretched Queen!
King.	Oh! Wretched King!
Glum.	Ah!
King.	Oh!

(II. viii. 13–14)

Yet I would argue that, even in the style of pathos, Restoration playwrights did not find fragments expressive. But they seem to have believed that many fragments combined might be expressive. That is, rather than rely upon implication and the spectacle of character so moved as to be inarticulate, playwrights piled exclamation, fragment, gasp, and interjection upon one another, as if to make up in numbers what was missing in syntax:

Scourg'd like a Bondman! ha! a beaten Slave!
But I deserve it all; yet here I fail:
The Image of this suff'ring quite unmans me;
Nor can I longer stop the gushing tears.
Oh Sir! O Brutus! must I call you Father,
Yet have no token of your tenderness?
No sign of mercy? what, not bate me that!
Can you resolve, O all th' extremity
Of cruel rigor! to behold me too?
To sit unmov'd, and see me whipt to death?
Where are your bowels now? Is this a Father?
Ah, Sir . . .

(*Lucius Junius Brutus*, IV. i. 534–45)

I believe Lee would have argued that this speech exemplifies the theory of decorous violent passion as described by the rhetorical tradition, but, in fact, the speech contains all the characteristics

170

which have been discussed in the preceding pages: rhetorical schizophrenia ("yet here I fail"), abstraction and periphrasis ("token of your tenderness"), and amplification of a sort that destroys all illusion of verisimilitude (*scourg'd, beaten, suff'ring, mercy, resolve, rigor, unmov'd*).

Rothstein is certainly correct in his isolation of the style of pathos and in his contention that the style is mimetic and a part of the tendency toward prose. I would only add that other tendencies in the language, as well the mimetic impulse, push towards prose. The narrative preference which has been described is perhaps, also, more fully realized in prose than in poetry. We speak prose, it is true, but we can go on at greater length in prose. Prose takes less for granted than poetry. It relies less upon implication. Prose is, in a very limited and discursive sense, clearer than poetry, less ambiguous. And in Restoration drama a question about meaning is certain to produce a lengthy, perhaps narrative, response:

> *Tib.*   What means my Brother?
> *Tit.*   O Tiberius, O!
> Dark as it seems, I tell thee that the Gods
> Look through a Day of Lightning on our City:
> The Heav'n's on Fire; and from the flaming Vault . . .
>   (*Lucius Junius Brutus*, IV. i. 143–46)

Only in theory could one find agreement with Richard Cumberland's perceptive recognition of the power of silence in the dramatic experience. In a late eighteenth-century essay on Rowe's *The Fair Penitent*, he writes: "I have . . . both generally and particularly observed upon the effects of dramatic silence. . . . What could Charalois have uttered to give him that interest in the hearts of his spectators which their own conclusions during his affecting silence have already impressed?"[32]

"Affecting silence" is not a feature of Restoration dramatic diction. The features which do mark that diction have not been examined in great detail except in terms of Shakespearean adaptation and prose comedy.[33] Dale Underwood, in his study of Sir George Etherege and other Restoration comedy, has provided

a valuable analysis of the qualities of comic language. He finds
the language both "metaphoric" and "nonmetaphoric." I want
to show that it is illuminating to trace the nonmetaphoric qualities in serious drama as well. Underwood says the nonmetaphoric quality stems from three aspects of the dramatic
language: it is " 'substantive' in nature," that is, nouns rather
than verbs carry meaning; it is nonsensuous; it is assertive and
indicative; and it is frequently marked by parallelism and balance describing highly schematic relationships. Characteristically, the language reveals a "continuous preoccupation with
the generalized and schematized level of experience."[34]

It is easy to illustrate these features in the serious drama and
thus to recognize, more clearly than before perhaps, precisely
what there is in the dramatic language to which we respond
unfavorably. Our aesthetic values, or at least those widely held,
are exactly the opposite of the three aspects Underwood describes. We admire language that is metaphoric, sensuous, verbal, implicit, suggestive, and elliptical. We prefer language that
deals with becoming rather than being, process rather than
product.

The substantive nature of Restoration dramatic diction is
striking, once it is isolated. This is the opening speech of *Lucius
Junius Brutus*. Titus is speaking to Teraminta and anticipating
their wedding night.

> O Teraminta, why this face of tears?
> Since first I saw thee, till this happy day,
> Thus hast thou past thy melancholly hours,
> Ev'n in the Court retir'd; stretch'd on a bed
> In some dark room, with all the Cortins drawn;
> Or in some Garden o're a Flowry bank
> Melting thy sorrows in the murmuring Stream;
> Or in some pathless Wilderness a musing,
> Plucking the mossy bark of some old Tree,
> Or poring, like a Sybil, on the Leaves:
> What, now the Priest should joyn us! O, ye Gods!
> What can you proffer me in vast exchange
> For this ensuing night? Not all the days

Of Crown[ed] Kings, of Conquering Generals,
Not all the expectation of hereafter,
With what bright Fame can give in th' other World
Should purchase thee this night one minute from me.

The substantive nature of this speech can be illustrated schematically by a list of nouns and their accompanying modifiers. In each instance, the noun is generic and the adjective something like a species. Each pair is a form of periphrasis described by John Arthos in his foundation study of eighteenth-century poetic diction:[35]

happy	day	some old	Tree
melancholly	hours	ensuing	night
some dark	room	Crowning	Kings
some	Garden	Conquering	Generals
Flowry	bank	bright	Fame
murmuring	Stream	other	World
mossy	bark		

The nouns are type nouns and lack almost all specificity. The adjectives which should "modify" the nouns in these instances have almost no modifying power or effect. A "Flowry bank" is more specific than "bank" alone, but only slightly. Certainly no image is formed by the periphrasis. Even "bright Fame" calls no image to mind. Many of the pairs are clichés ("murmuring stream," "mossy bark"). Strikingly, a few of the pairs emphasize generality by stressing the generic noun: "some room," "some Garden," "some Tree." Which room, or garden, or tree is irrelevant.

Apart from *dark* and *bright,* no adjectives engage our senses, and *bright* is metaphoric rather than sensual. Passages of this sort deal, as Underwood says, with the generalized level of experience and nature. At the same time, they reveal something of the unspoken philosophic framework which leads to generalization. Many adjectives are formed from verbs—*murmuring, ensuing, Conquering, Crowning*—making the passage appear active rather than descriptive. There are also participial adjectives—*melting, musing, plucking, poring*—adding to the false

173

sense of movement. Verbs, verbal adjectives, and a profusion of *-ing* endings give a sham vivacity to what is actually stasis and tableau. Titus says, "Since first I saw thee, . . ." and what follows is a description of something seen. It is a description of a tapestry or a painting.

Titus is not always so pathetic as these exemplary quotations have made him appear. In contrast to the speech just considered, his speech at the end of Act III is active, sensuous, figurative. Again he is speaking to Teraminta, and in this moment they are about to begin their wedding night after Titus has announced his willingness to betray his father. He is resigned and bitter as he speaks to his "dear bought prize":

> Come to my brests, thou Tempest-beaten Flower,
> Brim-full of Rain, and stick upon my heart.
> O short liv'd Rose! yet I some hours will wear thee:
> Yes, by the Gods, I'll smell thee till I languish,
> Rifle thy sweets, and run thee o're and o're,
> Fall like the Night upon thy folding beauties,
> And clasp thee dead: Then, like the Morning Sun,
> With a new heat kiss thee to life again,
> And make the pleasure equal to the pain.

The verbs are present tense and active—*come, stick, wear, smell, rifle, run, fall*. The language is metaphoric, and sometimes complexly so, as when simile joins metaphor: "Fall like the Night upon thy folding beauties." The image of the flower is maintained throughout, and the speech is sensual, even sexual, and intense.

There is no magic formula for poetry, and the contrast just described is by no means prescriptive. It is not true that substantive diction is less dramatic than verbal diction. It is not true that a specific word or statement is more poetic than a generalization, or an image than an abstraction. The distinction between these speeches is meant to illustrate the contrast, and the vividness of it, and not to make qualitative judgments about the nature of dramatic poetry. I prefer the "Tempest-beaten Flower" speech, but I believe that preference is in important measure cultural and temporal.

The effect of nonmetaphoric language is to produce dialogue which appears consciously elaborated, nondramatic (that is, narrative), abstract, and explicit. By way of brief review, elaboration seems to have been a correlative of the universal critical agreement that serious plays should be "elevated and lofty in character" and the language "heightened."[36] In the speech that follows, Titus uses one of the Restoration's most common images for a man cut loose from the control of reason; but, paradoxically, the speech is not the speech of a man without reason. It is too thoughtful and consciously rhetorical for that.

> Since I deliver'd thee that fatal Scrole,
> That Writing to the King, my heart rebell'd
> Against it self; my thoughts were up in arms
> All in a roar, like Seamen in a Storm,
> My Reason and my Faculties were wrack'd
> The Mast, the Rudder, and the Tackling gone;
> My Body, like the Hull of some lost Vessel,
> Beaten, and tumbled with my Rowling fears.
>
> (IV. i. 134–43)

As has been shown, the self-consciousness of this passage comes in part from the fact that Titus is not expressing himself but comparing himself to a tableau.[37] *Tatler* No. 47 (1709) contains an essay on "tragical passion," and there the fact of self-consciousness is recognized and criticized: "The way of common writers in this kind, is rather the description, than the expression of sorrow." In contrast, Steele cites the scene in *Henry IV* where Northumberland, learning of young Percy's death, does not stand mute, but is "still enough himself . . . to make a simile."[38]

The narrative elements in Restoration diction range from explicit storytelling, as when Lucrece recounts the rape ("Hear then, and tell it to the wondring World" [I. i. 361]), to commentary upon an action taking place before us ("I see his Father's mov'd: Behold a joy, / A watry comfort rising in his eyes" [IV. i. 388–89]). No matter what shape the narrative takes, it corrupts what we feel to be the essence of drama. Elder

Olson says, "The greater part, and the chief part, of playwriting has nothing to do with words." Rather, "a universal and absolute condition of drama is the possibility of its being *enacted*."[39] Narration in the form of dialogue is not action. The only chance for Restoration drama in our theater would come if, as George Steiner suggested about French classical drama, "we . . . learn to listen to these plays as we would to music; we must learn to be audience rather than spectator."[40] We might learn to listen to the plays as we would to a symphony, noting shapes, variations on familiar structures, motifs. We would be more passive than active. At least we might do this if we wished to make Restoration drama a theatrical experience once again.

The characters in Restoration serious drama live important and influential lives, lives which touch on matters of universal and atemporal concern. Consequently, they speak in abstractions more than most of us. Their creators might have chosen to make them speak in concrete universals. Perhaps that choice would have produced more sensuous, more figurative poetry. But their creators did not, and thus the scope of their thoughts and actions is represented in an appropriately universalized language. When a passage is effective, we see the figure on a vast scale, genuinely heroic and towering above us. When the passage fails as poetry or fails to match its context or its speaker, we see the figure as an outline, a specter and a type, unfixed in time and space, untouched by physical reality, and imperceivable through the senses in any precise or vivid way. Brutus addresses Tiberius before the Senators:

> I know thy Vanity, and blind Ambition;
> Thou dost associate with my Enemies:
> When I refus'd the Consul Collatine
> To be the King of Sacrifices; strait,
> As if thou had'st been sworn his bosom Fool,
> He nam'd thee for the Office: And since that,
> Since I refus'd thy madness that preferment,
> Because I would have none of Brutus Blood
> Pretend to be a King; thou hang'st thy head,
> Contriv'st to give thy Father new displeasure,

As if Imperial Toyl were not enough
To break my heart without thy disobedience.
But by the Majesty of Rome I swear. . . .

(III. i. 144–56)

The vocabulary—*Ambition, Enemies, Office, preferment, Blood, Imperial Toyl, Majesty*—is severely limited in its applicability. Only the greatest and most powerful men may speak to one another seriously with this vocabulary. I believe this particular example of elevated diction is successful, both in itself and as an expression of character and circumstance.

If we separate speaker and situation from the decorum of this diction, we can still speak of subject matter. While the subject matter of dramatic dialogue is often identical with that of the nondramatic genres, certain subjects or approaches to subjects seem ill suited for dramatization. Theoretical discussion, for example, tends to narrative if prolonged. The lines from *Lucius Junius Brutus* which follow might be compared with similar passages in Dryden's *Absalom and Achitophel*, written in the same year. Dryden's narrative poem touches on these topics and often makes the same points; but his context is narrative, and the discussions, if they come in the mouths of characters, are dramatic interludes in narrative setting. In what follows, Lee presents a narrative moment in drama. If we are engaged by the substance of the speech, we can call the moment an interlude; if we are not, we can call it a digression. Brutus is addressing the Senate, and the full speech, with one two-line interruption, is sixty-five lines long. Brutus accuses Collatine and his followers of being

Such as had rather bleed beneath a Tyrant
To become dreadful to the Populace,
To spread their Lusts and Dissolutness round,
Tho at the daily hazard of their lives;
Than live at peace in a Free Government,
Where every man is Master of his own,
Sole Lord at home, and Monarch of his House,
Where Rancor and Ambition are extinguish'd,
Where Universal peace extends her wings,

177

As if the Golden Age return'd, where all
The People do agree, and live secure,
The Nobles and the Princes lov'd and Reverenc'd,
The World in Triumph, and the Gods Ador'd.

(III. ii. 55–67)

We should note that this is a decorous and verisimilar speech for a senator before the senate. It is rhetorically crafted—as is exemplified by the climactic series at the conclusion—and full of familiar and reassuring values ("every man is Master of his own"). Like much political rhetoric, it is extremely abstract. This leads to the further conclusion that the political roles of these characters are an additional motive toward substantive and nonmetaphoric language.[41]

George Steiner has described what he calls the "poetry of the explicit" in seventeenth-century European drama. "In Shakespeare," he writes, "the words in their complex groupings accumulate meanings in excess of the actual statement. In Corneille as in Dryden, they signify exactly what they say, but they signify the whole of it."[42] K. G. Hamilton has qualified this somewhat, at least with regard to Dryden, by arguing that in Dryden's poetry many "words . . . tend to have repercussions *beyond* themselves, but not *within* themselves, and this power of association is both extended and controlled by the pattern of which the words are a part."[43] Dryden and his peers construct reverberations through allusion rather than trope and so appear explicit. "I am as tired as Sisyphus," for instance, is an expression that explicitly states tiredness, but achieves the implications of specificity through the allusion to the mythical and proverbial figure. The myth reverberates with its own rich associations and, the writer hopes, will act like a struck tuning fork to set up sympathetic vibration in the context.

When the poetry is without allusion, on the other hand, it is a pure form of the "poetry of the explicit." Teraminta here employs the rhetorical schizophrenia mentioned earlier and speaks of herself as though the speaking voice were someone else:

Swear, swear, my Lord, that you will never hate me,

178

> But to your death still cherish in your bosom
> The poor, the fond, the wretched Teraminta.
>
> (I. i. 57–59)

There is nothing here for the audience to do except to listen. The audience is not allowed to see, or to learn by implication or other form of indirection, that Teraminta is poor, fond, wretched. The audience is told these facts. It is told again in Titus' response to a speech by Brutus:

> Oh, let me fall as low as the Earth permits me,
> And thank the Gods for this most happy change,
> That you are now, altho to my confusion,
> That aw-ful, God-like, and Commanding Brutus
> Which I so oft have wish'd you.
>
> (I. i. 244–48)

The awe-struck exclamation can be powerfully affecting and obviously verisimilar. We all tend to exclaim the obvious in the face of the awesome: "My God, it's huge!" But that is the catch —explicit exclamation is verisimilar when it occurs in the presence of the awesome. If it occurs in the presence of anything less, it is ironic. I return here to an initial contention of this study—it is not the devices of this drama alone that create our responses, but it is the failure, according to our conventions, to match device and context, style and substance, or matter and manner. When we hear Teraminta say to Brutus, about Titus, "Do not upbraid his soft and melting temper / With what is past," it is not the explicitness of her description that is offensive (IV. i. 431–32). What is offensive is the qualities which Titus possesses. He *is* soft and melting, and those are not appropriate, not heroic, characteristics. We are offended by having his weakness brought to our attention. Teraminta has breached decorum in precisely the manner of someone who asks a cripple at a party, "What's the matter with your legs?"

Emerson Marks has seen this effect clearly. He points out that elevation of diction is not a weakness in the heroic plays. The weakness comes from the disproportion of the elevated diction to the other elements of the drama:

179

[Dryden's] Almanzors and Benzaydas, for all their lofty concernments, are in outward deportment actually at a lesser remove from the familiar than is compatible with the highly stylized mode of expression imposed on them by rhyme. The result is a total inconsistency, not infrequent in literary history, that invited the barbs of *The Rehearsal*. The valid objection, then as now, is not that kings and princesses in the real world never spoke like this, but that these particular kings and princesses of Dryden's imagined world *would* not have done so.[44]

D. R. M. Wilkinson, in *The Comedy of Habit*, argues, in addition, that the exaggeration of Restoration heroic diction implies disbelief in the heroic mode: "The exaggeration of moral ideals . . . of wicked ambitions and noble sentiments, implies almost total unbelief on the part of the writers in these things." They "could but substitute the spectacular gesture for the genuine experience."[45] I think that this interpretation is possible, but alternative explanations exist: the exaggeration implies either lack of poetic skill or a different decorum from our own.

The reverse of what Marks has outlined seems also true: that is, even when the characters can be distinguished one from another, or are given potential dynamics by virtue of their situation, the language often fails them. In the examples cited throughout this chapter, there are failures attributable to generalization, explicitness, and narrative. In Elder Olson's terms, "it is the almost constant use of common signs which accounts for the general flatness of the heroic drama." Characters seem "mere bundles of general traits and emotions—the abstract virtues in high degree."[46] Even the genuine hero appears unheroic if his vocabulary is limited to abstract nouns and vague adjectives, or if he is limited to narration at moments when lyricism is called for.

III

The Restoration play seems characteristically to fracture the decorum linking speaker and speech. As Marks points out, char-

acterization often seems insufficiently grand for the formal requirements of the heroic couplet or elevated blank verse. On the
other hand, Achilles himself might seem bombastic were he as
limited in diction and tone as the Restoration hero. And yet we
must keep in mind a consideration pointed out by Earl Miner
in writing about Dryden's handling of historical materials:
"The destinies of nations, and the place of personal tragedy or
achievement in them, the overcoming of impending disaster by
reasoned human action, and the faith in man's capacity to improve his civilization in the frame of its supporting values are
subjects no less charged with feeling now than three centuries
ago. It can only be our expectations of poetic expression that
have changed."[47] Our expectations of poetry have changed, and
this is no small matter because, as far as art is concerned, our
expectations are nearly everything. We might learn to appreciate the moral fervor of these plays, their sociopolitical stance,
and even their place in the development, and perhaps the death,
of the hero figure—we might do all of that and yet find them
artificial and distasteful.

Only drastic reconstruction of our expectations, our conventions of decorum, and our knowledge of the last three hundred
years' poetry would revitalize Restoration drama. Even if this
were desirable, it would be impossible. It has the same precious
futility as Almanzor's wish to take back the moment Almahide
became engaged to Boabdelin:

> Good Heav'n thy book of fate before me lay,
> But to tear out the journal of this day.
> Or, if the order of the world below
> Will not the gap of one whole day allow,
> Give me that Minute when she made her vow.
>
> .   .   .   .
>
> So small a link, if broke, th'eternal chain
> Would, like divided waters, joyn again.
> It wonnot be; the fugitive is gone:
> Prest by the crowd of following Minutes on:
> That precious Moment's out of Nature fled:

And in the heap of common rubbish layd,
Of things that once have been, and are decay'd.
(Conquest of Granada, Part I, Act III, p. 30)

What is possible and crucial is the recognition that it is our expectations that have changed, and not our moral or artistic integrity. There is a tone of moral superiority in much recent study of Restoration drama, a tone which is presumably justified by the "limitations" of Restoration art. There is no justification for this tone because art is not a progressive phenomenon. Moreover, the path of aesthetic superiority is a critical dead end because, whether or not we accept the notion that we have made progress in art since 1660, we can admit surely that progress itself would give us nothing of value when we turn back to the Restoration. We cannot better understand the art of that period by asserting the superiority of our own. (The superiority of our art is never the explicit justification of condescension to the Restoration. The explicit justifications are the period's sexual licence, its bombast, its limited themes, its reliance upon faddish French models.) Historical relativism, on the other hand, might produce some new understanding of the period. And that is all it can provide, as valuable as new understanding is. The Restoration may be the last remaining "age" (according to the standard historical divisions of English literature) in which the tired old slogans of historical relativism may retain some vigor. We need to get back "into" it as we have done in the Elizabethan and Victorian periods. We need sympathetic studies of the *Weltanschauung* and we need the "Restoration World Picture." None of these will make the indecorous decorous. All they might do is clarify the rules of the art as the Restoration understood them.

A study of the diction of the period and its decorum illuminates our ambivalence about the relationship between the style and the man. The French phrase *le style c'est l'homme même* can be quoted by friend and enemy alike—an elegant style reflects an elegant mind, and foolishness reflects foolishness. The relationship is, the phrase suggests, organic; Restoration and early eighteenth-century artists agreed. Uniformly they described an intimate, unshakable relationship of style and speaker. The most memorable examples are satiric, as when Dryden speaks of Shadwell's "issue":

> ... still thy fools shall stand in thy defence,
> And justifie their Author's want of sense.
> Let 'em be all by thy own model made
> Of dullness, and desire no foreign aid:
> That they to future ages may be known,
> Not Copies drawn, but Issue of thy own.
>
> (*Mac Flecknoe*, 155–60)

Or, earlier and more to home, Butler describes Hudibras' style, in a phrase which anticipates Pope's "vile Conceit in pompous Words exprest":

> His ordinary Rate of Speech
> In loftiness of sound was rich,
> A *Babylonish* dialect,
> Which learned Pedants much affect.
> It was a particolour'd dress
> Of patch'd and pyball'd Languages:
> 'Twas *English* cut on *Greek* and *Latin*,
> Like Fustian heretofore on Sattin.
>
> (I. 91–98)

The style and the man were a match, whether the metaphor for the relationship was organic or mechanical. While the distinction of metaphors for artistic creation has helpfully separated classic and romantic aesthetics, it may not, as was mentioned earlier, be altogether useful when examining a specific work of art. That is, when Pope says, *"True Wit* is *Nature* to Advantage drest,"* or "Expression is the *Dress* of *Thought,"* we recognize the image of clothing and the implication that words and their combinations are superficial—something to be put on or off over the reality, the body, which is thought. This is in clear contrast to the romantic notion as expressed, say, by Keats: "If Poetry comes not as naturally as the Leaves to a tree it had better not come at all."[48] Here expression is not superficial adornment, but something like skin—an inevitable, necessary growth matched flawlessly with the essence within. But if we look at a poem, as distinct from the theory, can we tell the difference between Keats and Pope on this mechanic-organic basis? If Pope has chosen the one word which is "fit" and Keats allows the word to grow from within, will they be different words? And if so, will the difference be the necessary consequence of the conception of the artistic process which the artist has? How can we tell the dancer from the dance?[49]

In any case, the theory that the style reflects the man has seemed to lend support to the notion that the bombast of the Restoration is the expression of little, and perhaps frightened, men, thoroughly unheroic, and conscious that they were caught up, for the first time in human history, with nearly unavoidable responsibility for what happens in the world, and, conversely, unable to look for help to the king (they put him there), or to God (who might not be there or might be the disinterested watchmaker), or to each other (if Hobbes was right). According to this approach, the bombast and heroic pretension of Restoration serious drama are the responsibility of playwrights who either failed to comprehend the nature of genuine tragedy and heroism or who consciously chose to ignore the genuine articles in favor of escapist melodrama.

But what would happen if we separated the question of responsibility from the question of the conventions of art, and did so for a moment in full awareness that the separation was false to reality, in which responsibility and conventions are part of an inseparable whole? Suppose that instead of assuming that there are only two parts to an artistic expression—artist and artifact—we assumed that there were three: the artist, the conventions of art, and the artifact. If there were three, then responsibility could be treated as a question separate from style or artistic expression. Those critics who wished to analyze the artists and their culture on the basis of their expressions could do so, while others pursued the nature of the conventions and their effects on the artist and the artifacts.[50]

In other words, I think it would be profitable for some criticism to proceed from the assumption that an artist who begins to create something from words is not free to choose any word, like any suit from a closet of all possible suits; nor is he bound by chemical necessity to choose only one word, like genetic replication in the nucleus of a cell. Instead, he expresses himself through the significant signs which are available to him and which are significant to him. The number of possible significant signs is limited by his education, intelligence, and fancy, and by the number of signs in the public stock, which, to be sure, may be increased if he creates new ones in his own works of art. The artist is neither an "innocent eye" nor an automaton. He is not bound to what has been said before, nor is he free to speak a wholly new language—at least not if he wishes to communicate.

My argument is nothing new, except, perhaps, as applied to Restoration serious drama.[51] I do not know whether Dryden and Lee and Otway were like us, but I think it is interesting to assume that they were. Furthermore, I assume that they wrote as they did because it seemed to them an appropriate way to write seriously about serious subjects. Looking at their diction is not looking directly at the men, but looking at historical conventions, which are interesting in themselves and illuminate our own conventions. Every artist deals with conventions, and every man lives with them. It is only the work of occasional genius (a redundant expression) which transcends the conventions of its age.

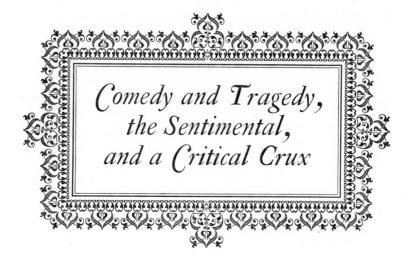

5

Comedy and Tragedy, the Sentimental, and a Critical Crux

I. COMEDY AND TRAGEDY

In the Restoration, theatrical fare changed quickly, with the companies changing their offerings every few days. Comedies followed tragedies on sequential evenings as the repertory companies competed for a very small audience. The audience was so small that it failed to support the two theaters which were chartered at the Restoration, and the companies were forced to merge. The United Company was the only theater for more than twelve years (1682–1695). Under these circumstances of audience size and theatrical variety, it is puzzling, even baffling, to compare Restoration comedy and tragedy. The bombast and posturing of the serious plays seem to belong in a different universe from that of the sexual Darwinism of the comedies. Rant and wit seem contrasting poles of rhetorical effect.

Alan Downer, in a history of the British drama (1950), describes the Restoration split: "The serious counterpart of Restoration comedy is so utterly different that it is difficult to believe they were intended for the same theatre and audiences."

Obviously the same theater and audience are involved, however, and Downer wonders at the phenomenon of "the same actor, the same audience, each apparently accepting and believing in a totally different concept of virtue, a totally different set of ethical values," as they change from comedy to tragedy and back again.[1] More recently, Anne Righter, in a survey of heroic tragedy, has said much the same thing: "In their attitudes and values, in all of their basic presuppositions, comedy like Etherege's *She Wou'd if She Cou'd* (1668) and a tragedy like Dryden's *Tyrannic Love* (1669) exist quite simply at opposite poles."[2] Both Downer and Righter go on to attempt to explain the coexistence of apparently irreconcilable genres in this era, as have other historians of the drama.

In a quick and visceral response to this split between comedy and tragedy, one might immediately suspect that the dichotomy is false. It does not seem likely that an audience, especially a homogeneous audience like that of most of the Restoration period, when so few people attended, would change its ethical standards from night to night—even if only two standards were involved, one for each genre. While not impossible, it seems untrue to our experience that the audience would, for example, systematically accept libertinism one night and piety and chastity the next. Certainly hypocrisy is possible for any audience, and so is intellectual and moral inconsistency. Imlac, in Dr. Johnson's *Rasselas*, wisely notes, "Inconsistencies cannot both be right; but, imputed to man they may both be true" (Chapter 8). Nevertheless, allowing for the profound differences in convention between comedy and tragedy, and allowing for hypocrisy and fuzzy thinking, and allowing for the human willingness to be entertained at the expense of coherence, it remains unlikely that two antithetical forms would exist simultaneously. If they are like other human products, the genres in this era should show similarities, together with their differences. This is, I think, the case. In what follows, I will assume the existence of considerable differences between the genres, differences which are superficial and differences which are subtly profound. But these differences have received due attention, and I would like to show some of the similarities which exist. The similarities exist together with the differences, and not rather than the differences.

The preceding chapter has offered some evidence that there is fundamental similarity between the nonmetaphoric language of comedy and the language of tragedy in this period. Once one begins to explore similarities of language, moreover, many begin to appear. The prose spoken by the comic protagonists is often, for instance, rhythmical and structurally balanced. Our ear picks up the rhythms created by parison and isocolon, which create effects similar to those achieved by balanced heroic couplets.

> She's the most passionate in her love and the most extravagant in her jealousy of any woman I ever heard of. (*The Man of Mode*, I. 172–73)

> It is our mutual interest to be so. It makes the women think the better of his understanding and judge more favorably of my reputation; it makes him pass upon some for a man of very good sense, and I upon others for a very civil person. (*The Man of Mode*, I. 399–402)

> Come, madam, in short, you see I am resolved to have a share in the estate, yours or your son's. If I cannot get you, I'll keep him, who is less coy you find. But if you would have your son again, you must take me too. Peace or war? Love or law? (*The Plain Dealer*, IV. i. 323–27)

> Then let 'em show their innocence by not understanding what they hear, or else show their discretion by not hearing what they would not be thought to understand. (*The Way of the World*, I. i. 475–78)

The verbal wit represented in these speeches is everywhere in the comedies and tragedies alike. The Restoration playwright and audience delighted in the neatly balanced or antithetical phrase, the rhythmical open and close of a sentence. We can find these wonderful, highly crafted sentences everywhere—in letters, in dispatches, in essays, in courtesy books, in prose fiction.

In comedy and tragedy alike, the language is marked by extensive use of simile. The simile is the most explicit of rhetorical figures; it calls attention to itself with *like* and *as* and, as it were, protects the artist from any accusation of distorting reality. The simile stops short of identifying A and B, which, according to some theories, would be a distortion of reality.[3] The simile appears in the serious plays, perhaps as a conscious echo of the epic simile, in those moments when vividness is sought:

> My hearts so plain,
> That men on every passing thought may look,
> Like fishes gliding in a Chrystal brook:
> When troubled most, it does the bottom show,
> 'Tis weedless all above; and rockless all below.[4]
> (*The Conquest of Granada*, Part I, Act IV, p. 35)

> I stand
> Like one that in a Desart seeks his way,
> Sees several Paths, yet doubting of the right,
> Stands in a maze, and fears to venture upon any.
> (Banks, *The Island Queens*, III, p. 33)

> Then like the Monarch o' the Winds, I'le go
> And loose my stormy Squadrons on the Foe,
> And when the mighty vapour's spent and done,
> The wasting *Roman* inundation gone,
> And not a Cloud in all the Heav'ns we see,
> I'le come a hot and pleasant Calm to thee.
> (*The Destruction of Jerusalem*, Part II, Act III, p. 34)

In comedy, simile appears as the foundation of one form of wit, most famously exemplified by Witwoud, in *The Way of The World*:

> *Mir.* You seem to be unattended, madam. You used to have the beau monde throng after you, and a flock of gay fine perukes hovering round you.
> *Wit.* Like moths about a candle. I had like to have lost my comparison for want of breath.
> *Mill.* Oh, I have denied myself airs today. I have walked as fast through the crowd—

189

Wit. As a favorite in disgrace, and with as few followers.
Mill. Dear Mr. Witwoud, truce with your similitudes; for I am sick of 'em—
Wit. As a physician of a good air. I cannot help it, madam, though 'tis against myself.

(II. i. 296–307)

From everything we can read, we gain the impression that comedy and tragedy alike catered to the pleasure which comes from hearing an apt, pointed, or poignant comparison.

The characters of comedy and tragedy are similar in a surprising number of ways. Most important, they are alike *flawed* characters. The tragic protagonist is by definition flawed, whether the definition comes from Aristotle, some intervening French or Italian critic, or French or English dramatic practice. All agree, also, that comic characters are imperfect creatures whose limitations, follies, and affectations make them fit objects for laughter. Dryden describes the comic-tragic parallel clearly: "The characters of comedy and tragedy . . . are never to be made perfect, but always to be drawn with some specks of frailty and deficience."[5]

The theoretical position is familiar to students of literary history, but its critical implications are not always obvious. If the playwrights consistently followed this precept and displayed flawed characters, then some specific plays may need to be reinterpreted. If Etherege followed the precept, then Dorimant cannot be understood to be a "hero" in the sense that his behavior was designed to be a model for sophistication and wit.[6] If Wycherley followed it, then Manly must be flawed in some fashion. If Congreve followed it, then Mirabell is flawed (or not comic).[7] If Dryden followed it, then Almanzor is flawed. And so, perhaps, are St. Catherine in *Tyrannick Love*, and Aureng-Zebe, and Jaffeir in *Venice Preserv'd*, and Mustapha. There are other alternatives, of course, including the possibility that some of these plays are not tragedies—for example, *Tyrannick Love*.

I have tried to avoid defining these plays according to their genre in the belief that definition requires a different approach from that which I wish to take, and I have used the term "se-

190

rious" to indicate those plays which are not primarily designed to provoke laughter. Nevertheless, even within the capacious category of "serious drama," it seems fair to say that most characters are flawed—St. Catherine, in this instance, excluded—at least to the extent that they are unable to bring about external or internal harmony. Even good men like Aureng-Zebe are marred by weaknesses and indecision. Jaffeir's intentions are obviously good, but that is not enough in the ambiguous universe Otway has constructed. Mustapha's selflessness is admirable, but it is not sufficient to heal the suffering of his brother and rival.

In comedy, as well, the flaws are present in most cases, minor characters and some women excepted. I believe the case has been made that Dorimant is a "deficient" man in the sense that he sometimes loses control of the situation ("I never was at such a loss before!" [V. i. 299]), and in the sense that his libertinism, his pursuit of the "heat of the business," is defeated, apparently, by Harriet. Dorimant's "flaws" are nothing, of course, when compared to Sir Fopling Flutter's, and there are obviously degrees of deficiency in various characters. Manly, too, has been convincingly shown to be a man of often blind moral vigor. Manly is able to see and witheringly condemn the "spaniels of the world" with their "decorums, supercilious forms, and slavish ceremonies," but he is himself willing to be something less than a man: "I rather choose to go where honest, downright barbarity is professed, where men devour one another like generous hungry lions and tigers, not like crocodiles" (*The Plain Dealer*, I. 616–19). Manly's statement of preference is certainly downright and honest, but those qualities do not make the preference attractive. Manly is blind to his own misjudgment of character and his own extremism, though it may be that he would believe extremism in the pursuit of virtue is no vice. In any case, Manly's flaws appear in his paradoxes—"generous tigers"—which may be ironic, but which nevertheless express an extreme, not an ideal.

Mirabell is uncomic, I think. Our laughter is never directed toward him in a sustained way, and the only mildly satiric mo-

ment involving him comes when Millamant calls him "sententious Mirabell" and accuses him of looking like Solomon at the
dividing of the child (II. i. 523). Mirabell is too stuffy to be
amusing, and most of the play's comedy takes place apart from
him.

Whatever the degree of flaw in comic and serious character,
there is an important implication about the audience and its
response when a play is constructed with flawed characters. The
audience to such a play is assumed to be educable, alert, critical,
distanced, vain, and itself flawed. Each of these characteristics
is necessary for a play with flawed characters to succeed in de-
lighting and instructing its audience. They must be educable because otherwise instruction could not take place. They must be
alert because judgment is constantly required in order to distinguish fools from knaves. The audience must be critical rather
than forgiving because forgiveness erases flaws or renders them
impotent. They must be distanced from the play because otherwise flaws are not comic. Intimacy, sympathy, empathy—all
change laughter from a corrective to a loving acknowledgment
of the human community. To laugh *with* someone is to acknowledge shared flaws of no permanent significance. No one laughs
in shame. Moreover, the audience is assumed to be vain, because if they were not—if they were humble or perhaps indifferent to their fellow man—then no laughter could act upon
them as a moral force. The humble man is not shamed by
laughter directed at him—see, for example, Christian in *Pilgrim's Progress*—only the vain man is. Lastly, and perhaps most
obviously, the audience must be assumed to be flawed, for otherwise there is no point in revealing the ridiculousness of folly. A
play that does so might delight a perfect audience, but it could
not instruct them.

This outline speaks only of comedy, but a parallel justification could be developed for tragedy. The tragic audience also
must be assumed to be flawed, critical, and so on, in order for
pity and fear to work upon them. A perfect audience would
destroy a tragedy as quickly as a perfect protagonist would. A
perfectly good audience would feel no fear, though they might

feel pity, and a perfectly evil audience might feel fear, but no pity. Beneath the bantering tone of many prologues to serious plays, is the expectation that the audience is going to watch the play sharply, critically, and with reason as well as emotion. The audience is self-possessed and well informed. The bantering tone says, in effect, "We all know what is good, just, cruel, and so on, and tonight a playwright, very much like yourselves, is going to show these emotions in action." The rhetorical gambit is obvious, but if there were no shared values, the assumption of them in the prologue would not save the play. Here are the opening lines of the Prologue to *Venice Preserv'd*:

> In these distracted times, when each man dreads
> The bloudy stratagems of busie heads;
> When we have fear'd three years we know not what,
> Till Witnesses begin to die o' th' rot,
> What made our Poet meddle with a Plot?
> Was't that he fansy'd, for the very sake
> And name of Plot, his trifling Play might take?
> For there's not in't one Inch-board Evidence,
> But 'tis, he says, to reason plain and sense,
> And that he thinks a plausible defence.

Otway gathers up the audience in a casual "we" and assumes that everyone is aware of the Popish Plot and that everyone, in addition, has a slightly Tory bias. He traps the audience into critical approval by suggesting that the play is acceptable to reason and therefore every reasonable man will find it pleases him. This leaves the audience, presumably, without recourse except to applaud or be thought irrational. Nevertheless, all this badinage and warm-up before the play assumes an audience literate, well informed, familiar with the conventions of the form they are about to see, and prejudiced in favor of reasonableness as a value.

All of this changes as the eighteenth century begins and progresses. The definitions of comedy and tragedy change and so, radically, does the assumed nature of the audience. The nature of the audience and the play are so intimately connected that cause-effect relationships are difficult to determine. The change which takes place about the turn of the century may be due to a change in audience, or it may be due to a change in dramatic literature, or it may be due to some combination of these. All three possibilities have been suggested. In any case, the Restoration audience for comedy and for tragedy is assumed to be the same. The audience had expectations for comedy which differed from their expectations for tragedy, but their attitude toward their role as audience would seem to have been constant.

The admirable characters of comedy and tragedy alike—characters to whom we give our general approval, even though they are flawed to one degree or another—are predominantly characterized by self-possession, *sprezzatura*,[8] or what the period called "ease." Almanzor has given the catch phrase to the heroic protagonists with his bold assertion, "I alone am king of me" (I. i. 206). The remark indicates an unwillingness to accept superior moral authority and also a blunt confidence in his own standards. Almanzor's frequent changes in allegiance are superficial in the sense that his fundamental allegiance to his word and to his sense of honor never changes. He shifts allegiance as he must in a world where most men are not true to their word and are not motivated by honor. As men break their word to him, violate the standards of honor which he cherishes, Almanzor feels that his ties to them are broken and he is free to make other arrangements. No matter whom he serves at the moment, Almanzor is typically self-possessed and confident. He knows his impulses, he knows his strength, and he knows what he believes. This gives him the "freedom" of which he boasts (I. i. 206–209).[9]

Dorimant possesses the same conviction, the same sense of self-confidence, the same bold assertiveness of manner which comes from self-confidence and moral superiority. The last may seem an odd quality to attribute to Dorimant, but Restoration rakes typically act from what they feel to be a moral stance more honest and thorough than those of their contemporaries. It is only with slight irony that Medley tells young Bellair, in

The Man of Mode, that Bellair's fiancée will not approve his friendship with Medley and Dorimant: " 'Tis not her interest you should keep company with men of sense, who will be talking reason" (I. 298–99). Dorimant could say, with Almanzor, "I alone am king of me." His more likely phrasing of the same idea, however, would be, "I am honest in my inclinations" (II. ii. 188).[10] The libertine and the epic hero pride themselves on honesty, on courage, on self-control. They differ drastically, on the other hand, in the degree of their willingness to use dissimulation, in their sexual mores, in their social sophistication, in their political significance, and in many other ways. At the same time, the general appearance of the Restoration protagonist is remarkably the same, no matter what the genre.

The serious and the comic protagonist are similarly affected by women with whom they fall in love. The admirable women in Restoration drama are the chief means of socialization of their men. We can again parallel *The Conquest of Granada* and *The Man of Mode*. Almahide and Harriet both bring their lovers into line with social modes, or, more accurately, into line with custom. Almanzor is brought, though not very smoothly, into an awareness of the necessity for art in his manner, and into an awareness of the limitations inherent in his fellow men, who are nevertheless of hitherto unsuspected importance to him.[11] Dorimant, too, is brought into line with custom—specifically, marriage—and brought to the modification of his otherwise wholly self-interested behavior.

That women typically redeem the protagonists may reveal the existence of two different kinds of plays: there are serious and comic plays of the sort just described, in which admirable, self-possessed protagonists are brought to custom by love; and there are plays in which the protagonists are not admirable because, or partly because, they lack self-possession—such plays as *All for Love*, or *Venice Preserv'd*, or *The Plain Dealer*. Plays like the last three are ambiguous in their moral meaning and have been the subjects of considerable critical discussion. Our response to each of these plays is different, but we can be aware that, in all the plays, the protagonists are acted upon as much as acting—they lack the powerful self-assurance which marks the rake and the hero alike. Nor do they exhibit the arrogance, boastfulness, smugness, and contempt which are shabby imitations of *sprezzatura* sometimes found in would-be rakes.

Antony is the shadow of an emperor as *All for Love* begins, and Cleopatra's role does not bring him to heroism, but to defeat, at least in public, social, and customary terms. Belvidera, in *Venice Preserv'd*, at first appears to act redemptively, to bring Jaffeir back from the brink of treason and murder, but her good intentions are inadequate for dealing with the ambiguities and confusions of their world. The act to save Venice is the same act that makes Jaffeir a traitor to his friend. Belvidera preserves a state controlled by faithless and weak men, "Where all agree to spoil the Publick Good, / And Villains fatten with the brave man's Labours" (I. 208–209). The women of *The Plain Dealer* play no redemptive role. Manly learns something about himself by overhearing how easily he has been deceived by Olivia, and at the end of the play he turns away from misanthropy and exile with the help of Fidelia, a figure from the green world of romance and altogether unsuited, in language, morality, and faithfulness, for the world of the play. Olivia prompts him to revenge, not to socially acceptable patterns, and Fidelia is a *deus ex machina* and a cause of change only in the same sense that lightning is a cause of fire—unpredictably and incoherently.

Generally, and significantly, the characters in Restoration drama can be measured against a spectrum of inner strengths and weaknesses. The weakest characters are "naturals," individuals unable to control themselves and suitable only for farce and sentimentality. At the other extreme are saints or near saints, such as St. Catherine or Cato, and absolute villains, such as the Empress of Morocco or Abdelazer. This spectrum is carefully calibrated, and characters exist along its whole length. Dorimant and Horner and Fainall are all rakes, but they are easily distinguished personalities. Aureng-Zebe, Mustapha, Alexander, and Brutus also can be distinguished one from another. The spectrum of strengths and weaknesses is the same for comedy and tragedy, and the man of courage and action is of chief importance to both.

196

Formally, comic and serious drama are also similar. Both are extremely episodic. The emotionally serial tragedy is matched by comedies with notoriously complex plots. The difficulty that generations have experienced with *The Way of the World* is exemplary, and we have evidence that the audience of the Restoration preferred plays with elaborate intrigue and skillfully timed plots and counterplots. The most famous example is Sir Samuel Tuke's adaptation of a Spanish play, *The Adventures of Five Hours*. Tuke's play was a large success, and Pepys, in 1663, described it as "the best, for the variety and the most excellent continuance of the plot to the very end, that I ever saw, or think I ever shall."[12] In countless comedies, the rake-hero has so many irons in the fire that he must exercise perfect control of the world around him or else all will collapse in damaging discoveries and revelations.

Thematically, Restoration drama treats every major theme which appears in other literature of the period; moreover, most themes appear in both comedy and tragedy—with different emphasis, to be sure. The themes of the Restoration have been isolated in terms of dichotomies, and the dichotomies are useful so long as we do not confuse them with choices. When art and nature, for instance, appear as contrasts, they do not appear necessarily as choices; one need not choose *either* art *or* nature. In fact, Restoration drama insists repeatedly that only a combination of the two makes a full man in a whole universe.

The clash of art and nature appears in Dryden's drama almost from the start—which is to say, in Restoration serious drama almost from the start. In *The Indian Emperour*, first acted in 1665, Dryden draws the contrast between Montezuma, the native ruler, and Cortez. Cortez, as the play opens, sees the difference between the Indian manners and his own. "All their Customs," he says, "are by Nature wrought, / But we, by Art, unteach what Nature taught" (I. i. 13–14). Almanzor, the noble savage, is thus not the first figure to contrast spontaneous morality with civilized dissimulation. Almanzor does form something of a parallel to Manly, in *The Plain Dealer*, however, in

197

that both learn the necessity for art in life, and the need sometimes to call a spade a garden implement.

The heroic protagonists are often transparent men, whose
feelings, loyalties, and ideologies lie out in the open for all to
see. They are either naive about the use of appearance or
morally unwilling to dissimulate. Zanger, in *Mustapha*, woos by
proclaiming, "I for sacrifice bring such a heart / As Nature
offers in disdain of Art" (III. iii. 380). Villains, on the other
hand, are consummate manipulators of appearance. In Otway's
Don Carlos, for instance, two villains plan to deceive the king
and inflame his jealousy:

> Watch every look, each quick, and subtle glance,
> Then we'l from all produce such Circumstance
> As shall the King's new Jealousie advance.
>
> (I. 202–204)

This sounds something like *Othello*, and it is. In both plays, the
issue is manipulation of appearances. Villains live by deception,
and in every play which has a villain, dissimulation, artifice, and
pretense of all sorts are present.

Comic villains, like Fainall, are also dissimulators, but comic
protagonists can be distinguished from tragic often by the protagonist's skill with dissimulation. In heroic and tragic drama
the protagonist is often without any experience with or inclination toward art. Dorimant, Mirabell, and Horner are masters of
deception, and the naive comic protagonist, like Parson Adams
or Tom Jones, is a development of the eighteenth century.

The use of art—that is, any form of skilled manipulation of
nature—does not distinguish good from evil. Nature also fails
to provide an automatic measure of a man. Almanzor is "as free
as Nature first made man" (I, p. 7). This freedom enables him
to follow his standard of honor with single-mindedness and sets
him apart from the vacillation and compromise of those around
him. But what happens when that freedom is applied to the
moral realm, or, more specifically, to sexuality? Here is Don
John of Otway's *Don Carlos*:

> How vainly would dull Moralists Impose

198

Limits on Love, whose Nature brooks no Laws:
Love is a God, and like a God should be
Inconstant: with unbounded liberty
Rove as he list.

(III. 1–5)

Or here is Dorimant, the man of mode, turning to nature for the analogy to his infidelity: "Constancy at my years? 'Tis not a virtue in season; you might as well expect the fruit the autumn ripens i' the spring" (II. ii. 179–81). Dorimant and Almanzor are perhaps being selective about what part of nature they refer to, but the term *nature*, at any rate, appears in the mouth of hero and villain alike as justification for his behavior.

Neither art nor nature is itself good or evil. Both are ambiguous, and the ambiguity of these central terms can produce exciting dialogue as the terms appear and reappear like Proteus in varied shapes. If there is a consensus in the period, it may be represented by the proviso scene in *The Way of the World*. There Mirabell and Millamant work out an arrangement which contains both art and nature—an arrangement in which he insists on giving nature its place in such matters as breeding: "I denounce against all strait-lacing, squeezing for a shape, till you mold my boy's head like a sugar loaf"; and she insists that art shall have its place before she will "by degrees dwindle into a wife." To avoid the "fulsomely familiar," she goes to the opposite extreme: "Let us never visit together, nor go to a play together. But let us be very strange and well-bred; let us be as strange as if we had been married a great while, and as well-bred as if we were not married at all."[13] (IV. 235–36, 184–87.) In each play, when this theme appears significantly, the characters must make their own amalgam without a prescribed formula; each compromise and combination of nature and art is made afresh.

Compromise is also necessary in the conflict of the individual and society which appears in Restoration drama. The weight of custom, law, convenience, and lethargy is sometimes felt in bizarre ways. For example, in *Aureng-Zebe* the Mogul laws prescribe the death of all sons who rival the firstborn. Sometimes the signs of social pressure are more familiar as exemplified by the sexual double standard.[14] In comedy and in tragedy, the aspirations and inclinations of the central figures must clash with the demands of society sooner or later because, fundamental to all of the major philosophic views of the period, is the notion that men are flawed and therefore unable to work together smoothly. Sometimes social responsibility is expressed as duty, to parent, to state, or to friend. Sometimes it is expressed as law or custom. Sometimes it is expressed in abstractions which embody social values: law, order, peace, right, calm, social status. Against all of these responsibilities the individual, comic or serious, attempts to realize his will in the world.

Unlike the contrast of art and nature, however, the Restoration plays suggest that when the individual and society clash, there is, and should be, a winner—society. Sometimes the cost of society's victory is great, as in *All for Love,* and sometimes it is small, as in *The Man of Mode,* when Dorimant moves to the country for a trial period before marriage. But, so far as I am aware, no Restoration play unequivocally asserts the right of the individual against that of society.[15] The nation had just undergone a period of individual freedom—represented by parliamentary secular government and antiepiscopal church governments—which had led, in the judgment of those in control when the Restoration was accomplished, to anarchy. Society exacts its price for order, harmony, and peace, but the alternatives to order, harmony, and peace are worse. This lesson from experience was dramatized in comedy and in tragedy.

The complex relationships of reason and the irrational in man form another theme which appears in both genres, sometimes tentatively and sometimes with an aphoristic clarity which suggests that to know the truth is to live by it. There is no handy and accurate way to summarize this set of relationships. There was no universal formula for the application of reason or the release of passion, and although the claims of reason are stated repeatedly and aggressively, the claims are more often battle cries than statements of fact. For example, in Rowe's *Tamer-*

lane, the protagonist loses his temper with the Sultan Bazajet
and is about to kill him, when another character pleads for
Bazajet's life on grounds of honor. Tamerlane relents, saying,
"Sultan be safe. Reason resumes her Empire" (IV. p. 53).
Tamerlane's statement is at once a periphrastic way of saying,
"I have agreed not to kill you"; an assertion of a widely held
belief, that reason should rule; and wishful thinking. No one in
the audience then or now would believe that this momentary
victory over passion, coupled with exclamatory assertion of
reason's pre-eminence, is a description of future behavior.
Tamerlane is saying that he wishes he could live by reason at
all times; almost everyone in the Restoration would have echoed
the sentiment.

The comic and the serious drama are like fun-house mirrors—
stretching, compressing, and bending the image of man as he
passes between and before them. We can recognize the creature
in the mirror, despite the distortion, and that part which we
recognize, those significant clues to identity, are found in both
comic and serious reflections. As has already been mentioned,
there is an amusing parallel between some comic ladies and the
tragic heroines. These comic ladies are characterized by passionate impatience and lack of self-control. They are quickly
driven to extremes and out of the empire of reason. Lady Wishfort, in *The Way of the World,* is "panting ripe" and forever
impatient, forever in a haste to "marry anything that resembled
a man." In a brilliant moment in the play, Wishfort has been in
a passion and "frowned a little too rashly" for her makeup.
"There are some cracks discernible in the white varnish," Foible
tells her. "Cracks, say'st thou? Why I am arrantly flayed; I
look like an old peeled wall." (III. i. 129–33.) The circumstances are wonderfully comic, but the image has *Dorian Grey*
connotations which can echo in serious plays as well. The cracks
which appear in the facade under strains of passion are often
the fragmentations of madness—madness provoked by despair,
loss, and anger. Phraartes sees Clarona die, in *The Destruction
of Jerusalem,* Part II, and erupts in a great cry:

Aloft!—I see her mounting to the Sun!—
The flaming Satyr towards her does roul,
His scorching Lust makes Summer at the Pole.
Let the hot Planet touch her if he dares!—
Touch her, and I will cut him into Stars,
And the bright chips into the Ocean throw!—
—Oh! my sick brain!—where is *Phraartes* now?
Gone from himself!—who shall his sense restore?
None, none, for his *Clarona* is no more!—

(V. pp. 54–55)

Phraartes approaches schizophrenia ("where is *Phraartes* now?"), and Lady Wishfort exemplifies the follies of artful appearance as a substitute for reality, but there is a common ground between them. Both show versions of what it is to lose the art—and it is art, not nature—which is control. The characters and their situations are so obviously different that this small common ground is all the more revealing of the substantial links joining the dramatic genres.

It does not matter which of the traditional pairs we employ in examining the drama—thought and feeling, reason and passion, mind and matter—all Restoration plays reveal the same fear of uncontrolled feeling. All of them reveal a fear of madness. All of them imagine the human creature as delicately balanced, easily swayed, easily deceived, easily hurt, and much too often corruptible. "When we come to particulars," Southerne has a character say in *The Fate of Capua*, " 'tis only to find fault: / Men are but men" (I, p. 15).

If we examine the drama for its positive values, we find the same unanimity—allowing always for differences in emphasis. Ben Ross Schneider, Jr., conducted a methodical analysis of Restoration comedy to find quantitative evidence for the values in the plays. The result of his analysis was the isolation of four points of ethical emphasis in comedy: liberality, courage, plain dealing, and love.[16] In terms of volume of emphasis, these four values receive the most attention. As we might expect, these four appear also in the serious plays. I will not pretend to the systematic and voluminous methods employed by Schneider; but

I am confident that the employment of such methods in the study of the serious drama would certify these four as prominent values, although liberality might be relatively insignificant compared to the others, and reasonableness, that is, the ability to act upon the recommendations of reason, would take the fourth prominent position.

Love has always been recognized as essential to serious drama, and that fact does not need elaboration. Courage is an obvious necessity for heroic figures, and therefore provides us with further evidence for the ambiguity of certain Restoration plays—for instances, *All for Love* and *Venice Preserv'd*—in which the central characters seem to accept some value, such as love, as superior to courage, or perhaps seem to lack courage. On the other hand, even in those instances, the characters have a clearly established background of courage and manliness, which unambiguously affirms the playwright's assumption of courage as a great virtue.

Plain speaking is perhaps less obvious as a value in the serious drama, but plain dealing, plain speaking, and honesty in all forms are obvious virtues in plays in which villainy is characterized by deception and all other forms of manipulation of appearance and reality. In some serious plays, such as Otway's *The Orphan*, plain speaking is the thematic core;[17] in others, it appears as a virtue exemplified in the hero and lacking in the villain, without ever becoming the focus of the play, or even receiving particular attention. Pulcheria, in Lee's *Theodosius* (1680), gives an exemplary innocent heroine's point of view: "I thought the meaning of all rational men / Should still be gather'd out of their Discourse" (II. 204–205). One example is perhaps sufficient to illustrate the general context of plain dealing in the serious plays. Orrery's *Mustapha* contains advice to a virtuous but naive Christian queen on the art of policy:

Love does but change the weather of your Brow;
Which should no more a constant meaning bear
Than th' outward face of Heav'n should still be clear.
The Great should in their Thrones mysterious be;
Dissembling is no worse than mystery.

203

Obscurity is that which terrour moves;
The gods most awful seem'd in shady Groves.
And our wise Prophet's Text a rev'rence bears
Where it is hard and needs Interpreters.
    Queen. I ever was without dissembling bred,
And in my open Brow my thoughts were read:
None but the guilty keep themselves unknown.

                                        (IV. i. 152–63)

The last line, "None but the guilty keep themselves unknown,"
is analogous to Tamerlane's exclamatory assertion of reason's
empire. It is a value unquestioned in most plays, yet almost impossible to practice.

Virginia Birdsall has examined the Restoration comedies from
a different perspective to discover in the plays elements of hostility, aggression, and manipulation of power in the sexual relationships, together with a consistent appreciation and acceptance of "animal vigor" in the admirable characters. The characters who delight us and whose triumphs we actively support,
says Birdsall, "are on the side of the instincts and of freedom,
life, and health."[18] Certainly these matters receive distinctive
treatment in comedy, but they are present in serious drama as
well.

In a way, the serious plays provide the other half of the comedies. By that I mean that the animal spirits which are appreciated in the comedy are matched in serious drama by an element of control. The tragedies do not deny vigor; they say
instead that vigor is not enough to give life meaning or coherence. Libertine values and unchecked libido characterize the villains of serious drama. Villains possess the sexual hostility and
aggression which Professor Birdsall has described in the protagonists of comedy. But in both genres, I believe, the sexual
aggressiveness is evil if unchecked. Dorimant is, of course, seen
as an evil man by representatives of the older generation in
The Man of Mode and by all of the women in the play. The only
characters who find his sexual athletics admirable are his male
peers—and not all of them, but only his rivals. Part of Dorimant's excitement for us and for the characters in the play is

204

his antisocial threat. He is, if allowed to pursue his "flesh and blood," a threat to the order of society; and the witty exchanges, as the play opens, between Dorimant, Medley, and the Shoemaker are reverberant as well as amusing. The Shoemaker is able—and Etherege is able—to criticize Dorimant by being ironic and therefore indirect: " 'Zbud, I think you men of quality will grow as unreasonable as the women: you would engross the sins o' the nation. Poor folks can no sooner be wicked but th' are railed at by their betters" (I. 253–56). A man of quality is defined in this speech as a man who is jealous of his vices, and no perceptive audience would miss the point.

The raging lust of Maximin, in *Tyrannick Love*, is nothing like Dorimant's urbane lechery, except that both men are obeying vital instincts. That core in both of them is identical, while the manner of artistic development of character and the context in which they appear are the difference. Neither one at this core is less antisocial than the other. Dorimant is brought into line by Harriet. Maximin is killed. Almanzor, in *The Conquest of Granada*, is brought into line by Almahide. His attempted rape of her, in Part II, is barbaric and instinctive. It illustrates the moral ambiguity of nature. We see the appetite brought under control in another important instance with Morat, in *Aureng-Zebe*. Indamora acts the redemptive woman to Morat's libertinism. Morat is a serious version of the comic figure whom Professor Birdsall describes. He is anxious for "Renown, and Fame, / And Pow'r, as uncontrol'd as is my will" (V, p. 68). He is a dangerous and destructive man throughout the play until Indamora has had an opportunity to argue with him and to bring him to see that his is a "Soul irregularly Great" and that *regularity* (pattern, order, harmony) comes through the imposition of law upon appetite. Morat does not abandon his love for her, but he does cease his villainy and dies asking his wife's forgiveness.

The contrast of Dorimant and Maximin is a false one. They are not comparable characters *in toto*, whatever their initial similarities. Maximin attempts to live by unchecked will.[19] Dorimant may attempt it, but he fails. Morat is a better parallel to Dorimant, and their stories are, in some measure, similar. Certainly we can understand how the same audience could watch both plays and comprehend the characterization without a dislocation of its ethical system. This is not to ignore the considerable differences between *The Man of Mode* and *Aureng-Zebe* in terms of intention, scale, social and political significance, and language. It is, rather, to assert that there is a substratum which is similar if not identical in the two plays.

Finally, comic and serious drama seem to share one unattractive feature—neither seems to have been exploratory or even curious about moral possibilities beyond the stylized and limited problems permitted by their conventions. Both comic and serious plays are affirmative and defensive of established values. They have been described as catering to a clique by means of the manners and fashions which they exhibit, but there is, in addition, a moral cliquishness about the plays. The audience is not provoked by these plays, but reassured. The audience leaves having been reinforced in its beliefs, beliefs which it brought to the theater. There is nothing unsettling.

This is not to say that instruction does not take place, but it takes place by affirmation. Instruction comes primarily through satire in the comedies, which is to say, through shame. Shame cannot be experienced unless one understands and feels that he has violated a standard, and normally playwrights assume that the audience knows the standards and that the playwright's task is to illustrate the violation. In serious drama, instruction comes through similar illustration and through fear—the serious analogue to shame.

D. R. M. Wilkinson and others in recent years have been very critical of the ethical values of Restoration comedy. Unlike nineteenth-century criticism, with its sexual hysteria, recent studies have faulted the comedy for its poverty of imagination, its repetitiousness, its class arrogance, and its insularity.[20] Perhaps the faults can be found in the serious plays as well. But Wilkinson mentions one especially provocative idea: "Societies in which Reason provides the first court of appeal tend to recognize Folly as the chief crime and to make Ridicule the commonest form of punishment."²¹ Ridicule is not the mode of the serious plays, even though reason is the first court of appeal. In fact, serious drama focuses upon vice, the product of corrupted will, and not upon folly, the product of corrupted reason. Reason, then, is a weak or even helpless remedy for the disease in serious drama, and yet reason is the faculty which is emphasized repeatedly. If reason is a means to happiness or peace, then, theoretically, only a fool is unhappy. Theoretically, discursive argument can serve as a major means of correction. Theoretically, logic is the rhetoric of moral imperative. Yet, quite obviously, in reality and in the plays, none of these theoretical assertions hold. *De facto*, reason is not sufficient, and only theory holds that it is. The fact is that a man in love is not necessarily affected by ridicule, though theory says he should be. The fact is that a prince who is his father's rival has no rational solution to his problem, though theory ignores or denies such Gordian knots.

Restoration serious drama trips over its own feet by offering an explicit moral premise which it denies by the action. Such plays as *Aureng-Zebe, Don Sebastian, Venice Preserv'd, The Orphan, All for Love, Lucius Junius Brutus, Theodosius, Tamerlane, The Mourning Bride, The Empress of Morocco,* and *Mustapha* do not concern themselves with folly—a lack of good sense, understanding, or foresight. Sometimes villains are fools in these plays, but the protagonists rarely are. The protagonists are courageous, and they are men and women of intelligence, and at times of even excessive thoughtfulness. Their ability to reason with their problems is legendary. While they are not fools, the emphasis upon reason would suggest that failure to follow its dictates is necessarily the radical source of human misfortune.

Serious and comic drama, then, shared an emphasis on reason and its crucial role in man's health and welfare. At that point the two forms part company, however, with comedy touching only lightly upon man's passionate nature and with serious plays giving passion all the attention they can manage. It may appear perverse to accuse the comedies of ignoring man's passionate nature, but I mean that while they rather flippantly picture man as a creature driven by sexual self-interest, which he either satisfies, sublimates, or represses, they have nothing much of interest to say about pity, benevolence, anxiety, hatred, friendship, loyalty, filial affection, and on and on. They draw man with one passion or at most two, the second usually being fear. The serious plays come much closer to illustrating the variety of human passions.

The analogies which I have suggested between comedy and serious plays end with the Restoration—I do not mean 1685 or 1700 or any fixed date, but that traditional place, that continuum, in which one set of isolatable patterns is replaced by another near the end of the seventeenth century. In their place appears a new set of analogies to accompany the new comedy and the new serious drama. Every element can again be paralleled, but the drama from 1700 to 1800 is not the present concern. A few illustrations may reveal something of the nature of the change from one era to the next, however, and give extra emphasis to the nature of Restoration thought and practice.

In the generalizations which follow, I do not mean to describe a wholesale, absolute change in manner. Plays similar to those of the Restoration continued to be written and performed throughout the eighteenth century. But there were notable changes. The protagonists of the new plays are not significantly flawed. Instead, they are essentially good men and women caught in misfortune. Their flaws, such as they are, are underplayed, or appear as temporary aberrations. Addison, in *Spectator* No. 39, cites approvingly Seneca's statement that a well-written tragedy is one which describes "a virtuous man struggling with misfortunes." This very non-Aristotelian definition can apply equally well to comedy or to tragedy. For instance, it applies to Addison's own tragedy, *Cato*, which shows "A brave man struggling in the storms of fate" (Prologue, l. 21) or to Steele's *The Conscious Lovers*, which hopes to "please by wit that scorns the aids of vice" (Prologue, l. 19).

In comic and serious plays in the new manner, the protagonists act as models for emulation rather than as patterns of be-

havior to be shunned.[22] The prologue to *Cato*, contributed by
Pope, begins:

> To wake the Soul by Tender Strokes of Art,
> To raise the Genius, and to mend the Heart,
> To make Mankind in conscious Virtue bold,
> Live o'er each Scene, and Be what they behold:
> For this the Tragic-Muse first trod the Stage.

Here is an amazing and genuinely radical statement couched in
tactful heroic couplets. The key phrase is *"Be* what they behold." Catharsis is gone, or at least diminished. The audience
might have pity, but not fear. *Hamartia* is gone. Emulation has
apparently replaced admiration, the emotion of respectful awe
which had been emphasized as one effect of tragedy by the seventeenth-century aestheticians in both England and France.
One might aspire to act like Cato, or his son Portius, but one
would not aspire to act like Oedipus or Macbeth or Achilles or
Antigone. Neither Achilles nor Almanzor is a paradigm of virtuous social behavior.

If the central figure in comedy is no longer significantly
flawed, then he is no longer foolish, and if he is not foolish then
he cannot be satirized or ridiculed, and without ridicule the op-
portunities for laughter are severely curtailed. Steele recognized
this chain of thought and faced it squarely. In the Preface to
The Conscious Lovers, he raises the question whether there can
be laughter if the characters are not ridiculous. His answer is
no. Rather than satire and exposure, Steele's play will operate
by "example and precept." "Anything that has its foundation in
happiness and success must be allowed to be the object of
comedy," Steele says, "and sure it must be an improvement of
it to introduce a joy too exquisite for laughter."

The eighteenth-century audience changed with, or was
changed by, the new fashion. The new audience was almost the
converse of the Restoration audience, which I described as edu-
catable, alert, critical, distanced, vain, and flawed. The eighteenth-century audience is assumed to be educated, alert,
sympathetic, benevolent, emotional, sensitive, and good at heart.

Delight and instruction are still part of the transaction between drama and audience, but in an altogether new manner.

Steele acknowledged that some people cried at performances of *The Conscious Lovers*, and he argued that this reaction ought not to be blamed until we better understand the relationship between head and heart. Moreover, "to be apt to give way to the impressions of humanity is the excellence of a right disposition and the natural working of a well-turned spirit." Tears thus become the outward sign of an inward condition which the audience is presumed already to possess. The older comedy had hoped to inspire or promote reason and good sense in the audience, not to tap funds of it already there. The new audience is already good, or very nearly so, and the new plays are expected to reinforce or excite that goodness.

Prose became the language of both comedy and tragedy in the eighteenth century, while thematically most of the earlier issues remained. Perhaps the most significant thematic change involves attitudes toward the country. In Restoration comedy, the country was a purgatory, desolate and barren of entertainment, fashion, and conversation. The country was lethargic, rude, tedious. In Restoration serious plays, the country appears only in the guise of the pastoral conventions or the country retreat of the Happy Man, both guises being direct descendants of classical models.[23]

Country folk remain bumpkins in the eighteenth century, but their rustic manners often only cover a sharp edge of honesty and spontaneous benevolence. Characters like Sir Willful Witwoud, in *The Way of the World*, are satiric naifs as well as clumsy churls. Belcour, in *The West Indian* (1771), is a man of feeling and a naif from an uncivilized world. The country family, the Hardcastles, in *She Stoops to Conquer* (1773), are out of date, unsophisticated, socially embarrassing, and considerably more attractive in the honest forthrightness of their emotions than the polished city folk. Eighteenth-century tragedies, on the other hand, remain primarily in the Restoration mode developed by Otway, Banks, and Southerne; and the country remains a pastoral ideal, impossible for a political man, and something to be spoken of wistfully as a place of paradisiacal loveliness and peace. In the Gothic and melodramatic plays, like John Home's *Douglas* (1756) and George Colman's *The Iron Chest* (1796), the country has little thematic importance and is primarily a backdrop—isolated, ancient, vaguely sinister.

The clash of passion and reason remains the life of eighteenth-century drama, comic and serious alike. George Barnwell, in *The London Merchant*, is seduced "when every passion with lawless anarchy prevailed and reason was in the raging tempest lost" (III. iv. 51–52). He gives clear expression to the entire era's understanding of the agony of a man who knows his flaw and is helpless nevertheless. "Oh, conscience," Barnwell exclaims, "feeble guide to virtue, who only shows us when we go astray but wants the power to stop us in our course!" (III. v. 27–29).

We find the comic analogue, as in Restoration comedy, in the hysterical, middle-aged women. Forty-five lines into George Colman's *The Jealous Wife* (1761), Major Oakly says to his wife: "I beg, my dear, that you would moderate your passion! Shew me the letter and I'll convince you of my innocence."

> *Mrs. Oakly.* Innocence! abominable! innocence! But I am not to be made such a fool: I am convinced of your perfidy, and very sure that—
>
> *Oakly.* 'Sdeath and fire! your passion hurries you out of your senses.

There seems to have been little change here in one hundred years. The ethical predisposition of the eighteenth century is profoundly different in its emphasis upon feeling and benevolence, but the tendency is still to treat passion in much the same way as in the Restoration.

II. THE SENTIMENTAL

The traditional turning point from Restoration to eighteenth century in the drama has not been 1700, but 1696, the date of

Colley Cibber's *Love's Last Shift*. This play marks, the tradition has it, the birth of sentimentality, a birth represented also by such things as Jeremy Collier's *Short View of the Immorality and Profaneness of the English Stage* (1698). Today few would admit to the sort of historical naiveté which dates a literary movement by the appearance of a single document, and yet the date 1696 stays with us in literary history.[24] The subject of sentimentality is further complicated by the doctrine of *sensibility* and by the popular use of *sentimental* as a synonym for tenderness—concepts which have elicited occasional careful studies, such as that by Erik Erämetsä of the word *sentimental*.[25]

The word *sentimental* is a coinage of the latter half of the eighteenth century, appearing for the first time in a dramatic context, according to Arthur Sherbo, in 1749 in the prologue to William Whitehead's *The Roman Father*.[26] The doctrines and literary techniques which mark the sentimental for us, however, developed earlier. Ernest Bernbaum argues that the mainspring of sentimentalism is "faith in the natural impulses of contemporary middle-class people," a faith which would not develop until English thought began to move away from the Christian and humanist view of man as essentially flawed.[27] That move took place with increasing momentum in the late seventeenth century. Arthur Sherbo disagrees with the notion that the middle class is necessarily involved, but agrees generally that sentimental plays reveal a belief in the "fundamental goodness of human nature."[28]

If fundamental goodness is essential to a definition of sentimentality, then we will have to keep two meanings of the word (as we have in fact been trying to do for most of this century)— one which is scholarly and one which is popular. The popular use of the word, a use extensive and vigorous, does not require that we examine the image of man in an episode or poem or painting before calling the work sentimental. In popular usage, for instance, in an undergraduate class, few would hesitate to label scenes in Otway's plays sentimental, and yet the labellers would not argue that Otway evidenced any faith in the fundamental goodness of man. In fact, I believe popular usage would apply "sentimental" to scenes in Shakespeare, and Sophocles, and Racine. The word probably would not be employed to describe any of the works of these playwrights when considered as wholes, but it is difficult to reserve a word for only those occasions when all of an object fills the qualifications. We do not, for instance, reserve the adjective *tragic* to whole plays and employ another term for a scene, a character, or a speech.

I would like to suggest a distinction between two terms—*sentimental* and *sensibility*—which might help us in literary history and literary criticism and yet not place us at odds with popular usage. I would like to suggest that *sensibility* be applied to an attitude toward life which developed in the mid- and late eighteenth century and which assumed innate human goodness and cherished a keenly developed moral sensitivity. *Sensibility* is not in popular usage, and neither are the ideas to which I refer. Ideas and term alike are historical phenomena. Sensibility is the mark of such works and characters as Sterne's Yorick, Henry Mackenzie's *The Man of Feeling*, Goethe's *The Sorrows of Young Werther*, and Faulkland in Sheridan's *The Rivals*. Sensibility is a *whole* approach to life and cannot be exercised genuinely in parts. An individual who is morally sensitive is so in most or all aspects of his life. The character who exemplifies candor, in the eighteenth-century sense of expecting the best of those whom one encounters, does so spontaneously, naturally. It is of course possible to feign an attitude of sensibility, but to do so requires attention to all aspects of life—the encounter with a bird, a young girl, a snuff box, a friend, a cloud, a chance remark at a party, and so on *ad libitum*. A creature of sensibility is a sensitive being who believes all men basically good.

Sentimental, on the other hand, should carry broader, less precise, and less historical meaning. It should apply equally well to a part and to a whole. *Sentimental* should apply to any moment when one is asked to respond with affection, or closely related feelings, in the absence of any other emotion or any thought. That is a difficult definition at first, but I hope not unclear. A scene might be sentimental, in this sense, without the

play being so. A character or a bit of dialogue might be sentimental. A dog might be sentimentally treated—or even a style
of architecture.[29]

We have associated sentimentality with tears through most
of the history of the term, but I believe that is confusing the
effect with the stimulus. Tears are the sentimental response to
drama as often as they are because we are spectators to distress
suffered by those for whom we feel affection. We can calmly
watch a villain suffer the same distress. We see those for whom
we feel affection in distress often, because that is the stuff of
drama. It is tedious to watch those for whom we feel affection
being happy. Happiness, while pleasant, is without tension,
without suspense, without drama. Tears, then, are not a necessary consequence of sentimentality, although they are the likely
response to a great many sentimental instances.

My proposed definition of sentimental excludes other emotions like anger, contempt, chagrin, gaiety, or lust because they
destroy affection. One cannot feel contempt and affection simultaneously, for example. The definition, at the same time, excludes *thought* because thought, too, can destroy affection.
Bonamy Dobrée may have been referring to this effect of thought
in his flat assertion that "the sentimental is that which takes the
immaterial to be the real (using the words in their most evident
sense), and ascribes more importance to the feeling, than to the
fact which is supposed to arouse the feeling." Dobrée's definition requires a value judgment. According to him, if the facts
warrant weeping, then weeping is not sentimental. If the object
warrants affection, then affection is not sentimental. As Dobrée
says, "thus sentimentality is only another name for falsity."[30]
I think Dobrée's definition could be a useful one, but it requires
an assessment of genuineness at each application; every correct
use would require the accurate assessment of the fact and the
feeling aroused by the fact. In other words, Dobrée's definition
could lead us to arguments about whether or not a scene was
"genuinely" sad or not, "genuinely" pitiful, "genuinely" terrifying. It seems to me that these are matters about which there
are no absolute standards and thus *sentimental* would be limited

to moments which we disliked, or found false. This limitation would result in one more addition to the vocabulary of subjective response. Certainly my definition is not objective in any absolute way, but it does not require an assessment of the value of the sentimental stimulus, and it carries no pejorative connotations.

Thought is excluded in my definition because thought is by its nature inimical to feeling. It is nearly impossible to think when laughing, lusting, hating, loving. In addition, rational inquiry often makes the object of our affection appear unworthy. Professor David French, a colleague, has suggested to me that the violent distaste which the sophisticated express for such sentimental objects as the collie Lassie or Shirley Temple movies stems chiefly from the distaste which we feel for ourselves for being so easily moved to affection. It is not Lassie that makes us angry; it is the lump that Lassie has created in our throats. *Sentimental* is a contemptuous and pejorative term, therefore, in part because we dislike, and even fear, the speed and lack of discrimination with which we can be moved to tender feelings by dogs, orphans, old class rings, flags, and our old home town.

My definition purposely allows for objects, as well as individuals or scenes, to be the occasion of sentimental moments. The "local affection" which Goldsmith manipulates in *The Deserted Village* is therefore sentimental, as are, for that matter, some references to "this scepter'd isle, / This earth of majesty, this seat of Mars, / This other Eden" in Shakespeare. Sterne's use of the souvenir is a manipulation of sentimentality, and so is the appearance of children in much of Restoration drama. These children are nameless, ageless, and sexless, both in the dialogue and in the *dramatis personae*, for two reasons: first, the company had to be free to employ whatever child actors and actresses it had available; and, second, they are *objects* in these plays, not characters.

The characteristics which Arthur Sherbo has carefully detailed for sentimental drama are thus still applicable within my definition, except for one—faith in the natural goodness (perhaps *potential* or *innate* goodness is more accurate) of man.

215

Sentimental moments, scenes, and plays, Sherbo shows, are characterized by the explicit presence of a moral (sentfrom) element, greater appeal to the emotions than to the intellect, eschewal of humor and bawdry, repetition and prolongation, frequent and prolonged appeals to pity.

Accepting my suggested definition would mean that we would be able to recognize that even Hobbes allows for sentimentality. He has no faith in man's innate goodness, but he does recognize pity: *"Grief* for the calamity of another is PITY, and arises from the imagination that the like calamity may befall himself, and therefore is called also COMPASSION, and in the phrase of this present time a FELLOW-FEELING."[31] Hobbes complicates the definition by ascribing the source of the "fellow-feeling" to self-interest. I am not confident about the source or the nature of the affection that is essential to sentimentalism, but will only match Hobbes's definition with another involving a less harsh judgment of man. Nicholas Rowe, in the dedication to *The Ambitious Step-Mother* (1700), hoped that the audience to his tragedy would be struck with terror in several parts of the play, "but always conclude and go away with pity; a sort of regret proceeding from good-nature which, though an uneasiness, is not altogether disagreeable to the person who feels it."

To repeat, pity is not the key to the definition of sentimental which I have offered. Affection (tenderness, fondness) is made the key instead in order to encompass the phenomenon of homesickness, the pleasure of seeing six-year-old girls in raw-pink chiffon tutus performing in their first dance recitals, the acceptance of a pet parakeet as a member of the family, and the countless other varieties of human behavior which would commonly be classified as sentimental. Pity, however, whether prompted by good nature or self-interest, is certainly the dominant sentimental emotion in Restoration drama.

Although the sentimental is pervasive in Restoration serious drama, there is little evidence of sensibility. The attitudes which form part of the genealogy of the man of feeling are present, but not the developed notion of a total attitude toward life, based on assumptions about the goodness of human nature and

216

on sensitivity to moral experience. What we find is automatic use of sentimental icons and sentimental vocabulary. Everywhere we find the act of comparison (which I argued in Chapter 4 takes the place of lyricism) involving a bankrupt stock of sentimental stimuli—children, orphans, widows, filial love, marital love, parental feelings. Everywhere the vocabulary of sentimentalism is couched in the rhetoric of exclamation, declamation, and hyperbole. All of the features of serious diction can be employed in the service of sentiment.

Characters, for example, who describe themselves and their responses, create portraits for our tender sympathy:

Oh, I am drown'd, I'me melted all to Pity!
(Banks, The Island Queens, I, p. 12)

Is there no filial duty to a parent?
No vertue in a Mothers tears, to stir
Obedience in a Son? then I will kneel,
Thus, like a Vassal, follow on my knees,
And never leave pursuing.
(Southerne, The Loyal Brother, III, p. 34)

In the Southerne quotation, the heavy use of the vocabulary of role is obvious and exemplifies a ubiquitous sentimental device. Role and sentiment are closely linked, and this is especially true of familial roles. Even bravery can be sentimental:

Was ever man thus wretched and durst live,
Yet will I not one tear to nature give,
Least Bankrupt like I lavish what's not mine,
Since all my stock of sorrow love is thine.
(Lee, Sophonisba, IV. 325–28)

It is courage that King Massinissa expresses here; yet the moment, one of confrontation with the body of his beloved friend Massina, is, I think, sentimental. It is made so partly by the sentimental object—the body of Massina which had been brought forth to the sound of trumpets and Scipio's question, "What means this mournful noise, whose Tragick sound, / With solemn horrour does my thoughts confound?" The moment is made sentimental also by the context. Massinissa is being sorely tested and tempted to give up Sophonisba to Scipio's wrath. And the moment is made sentimental partly by the language—explicit, hyperbolic, heart-warming.

The narrative moments in the serious plays are more often sentimental than anything else. Their function is primarily to move us, and, more specifically, to move our feelings of tenderness and affection for certain characters. In the following speech the narrative description appears together with a rhetorical paradox—a four-line simile followed by an exclamation that the speaker is unable to think:

> As when some dreadful Thunder-clap is nigh,
> The winged Fire shoots swiftly through the Skie,
> Strikes and Consumes e're scarce it does appear,
> And by the sudden ill, prevents the fear:
> Such is my state in this amazing wo;
> It leaves no pow'r to think, much less to do.
>
> (Dryden, *The Indian Emperour*, IV. iv. 95–100)

Otway has a genius for sentimental vignettes involving imagined scenes and narrative moments. In *Caius Marius* the final act involves a sack of Rome. We are shown a young boy who has just been orphaned (he witnesses his parents' death) and left to the care of his grandfather, who is too weak to fight or to flee. The tableau of the two would create a sentimental scene, but Otway goes on to have the boy describe his plans to protect them if the soldiers come:

> I'll fall upon my Knees and beg your Life.
> I am a very little harmless Boy;
> And when I cry, and talk, and hang about 'em,
> They'll pity sure my Tears, and grant me all.
>
> (V. 174–77)

This is an imagined scene, a narrative moment, full of explicit appeals to our affection ("very little harmless Boy"). The boy then has an opportunity to plead with Marius, and he does so:

> For my sake spare his Life. I have no Friend
> But him to guard my tender years from Wrongs.

London Merchant. The London Merchant in Beaumont's play is prohibited by a citizen because he knows, from the title, that it will be satiric and he does not wish to be abused again, as he so often is at the theater.

The hybrid nature of a tradesman's tragedy is reflected also, Goldsmith argues, in contemporary weeping comedy, which could not be comedy, he thinks, no matter what it were called: "Though we should give these Pieces another name, it will not mend their efficacy. It will continue a kind of *mulish* production, with all the defects of its opposite parents, and marked with sterility." This is the critical crux which Goldsmith has isolated. According to the accepted definitions of the genres, no such thing could exist as a weeping comedy or a tradesman's tragedy. These hybrid forms must be as fabulous as mermaids, or griffins, or satyrs.

What began to happen in the Restoration continued in the eighteenth century, until the definitions which formed the structure of contemporary aesthetics no longer applied to all of the art which was being produced. The new characters and new subjects and new methods of exposition were obviously there as experienced realities, but they were very hard to defend. The usual method of legitimization involved "improving" the traditional definitions, but the attempt to improve was flimsy and subject to such easy scorn as that of Goldsmith's essay. The eighteenth century lived with this ill-fitting combination of shopworn and beloved definition clumsily draped on the new body of art, and so, I think, do we. The mulish forms which Goldsmith condemned are still present, side by side with plays which exemplify the old definitions. Fielding's *Tom Thumb*, we recall, is a joke at the expense of the little man as the hero of tragedy. We also recall that in the same year as *Tom Thumb*, and with Fielding's wholehearted approval, Lillo produced *The London Merchant*. The critical crux has never been solved, although we continue to laugh with Fielding and weep with Lillo. A crisis in criticism occurs whenever genuine novelty appears, but the new "tragedies" forced a crisis of an unusual order. We feel so strongly about what has happened to tragedy that we discuss seriously the "death" of tragedy and the possibility of its resurrection and the shape this phoenix might take. Moreover, a student of literary history and criticism is aware in the course of this discussion, as he is often aware in other contexts, that the discussion employs the same vocabulary which was employed throughout our written past. Our discussion of tragedy still makes us use such terms as *pity, fear, hamartia, catharsis, fall, admiration*. This means that we cannot turn back to Restoration criticism and discover the causes of the change in drama because Restoration criticism resembles our own. For instance, Elder Olson wrote in 1966 of action in drama: "Nothing can really be called a play, in which the action is merely incidental to declamations, songs, dances, and so on, The action must be primary."[37] In 1692 Thomas Rymer wrote, "Words are a sort of heavy baggage, that were better out of the way, at the push of Action."[38] Here is critical agreement that action is the *primum mobile* of drama, and yet the plays which exemplify this quality for the eras these two critics represent are so different that, while we do not know how the Restoration might find our taste, we know certainly that we find its plays tedious, prolix, and either exhaustingly slow or static. And this is true despite its having affirmed the central value of action to all that is truly dramatic.

The practice of an art alone reveals the operative conventions of the artist and his audience. Moreover, it is only the conventions that can be determined with any certainty, while the "meanings" of the conventions for another culture are almost impossible to discover. If we were to ask Dryden what he thought he was doing in *The Indian Emperour*, he would say he was attempting a "just and lively image of human nature, representing its passions and humours, and the changes of fortune to which it is subject, for the delight and instruction of mankind."[39] We would applaud the definition as an admirably made statement of nearly universal truth and at the same time deny that this play was lively, passionate, humorous, changeable, or delightful. We would concede that it was just and instructive. And when this imagined dialogue was finished, we would be at a dead end. There is nowhere further to go with this sort of exchange. Dryden might pursue his definition and show how in practice he *was* lively and delightful, to which we would respond, "But that is *not* lively and delightful."

I have attempted in these chapters to suggest that we have reached the dead end of arguing with Dryden about delight and instruction. The argument has been exhausted of its informative potential and should be abandoned, together with the hysterical studies of Restoration adaptations of Shakespeare that come to the astonishing conclusion that Nahum Tate was not so great a dramatist as Shakespeare. Once we discovered that it was possible to examine Tate's play as Tate's play, and not as Shakespeare's, we began to learn new things about Restoration art.[40] I hope that by examining Restoration serious drama as another example of the variations that artists have worked upon theme and genre, and not as a series of failures to be either Elizabethan or twentieth-century, we can come closer to understanding what artistic conventions are and how they work. Even if we choose to use the artifacts of a culture to tell us about the culture and not the artifacts, we must still begin with the artifacts. There is no need to retreat to the old "new criticism" in such a statement. Careful examination of *The Conquest of Granada*, say, need not foolishly exclude whatever external or internal material seems to be useful. What does seem foolish is to read *The Conquest of Granada*, respond with distaste, and conclude that Dryden was incompetent as a serious dramatist. The only evidence for that conclusion is our own distaste.

Notes

NOTES TO PREFACE

1. "Of Heroic Plays" was prefixed to the first edition of *The Conquest of Granada*. It is included in the collection *Of Dramatic Poesy and Other Critical Essays*, ed. by George Watson, 2 vols. (London, J. M. Dent, 1962), I, 157; cited hereafter as *Critical Essays*.

2. *Ideas of Greatness: Heroic Drama in England* (New York, Barnes and Noble, 1971), 266.

3. *The Well-Tempered Critic* (Bloomington, Indiana University Press, 1963), 100.

4. *Imagination and Power: A Study of Poetry on Public Themes* (New York, Oxford University Press, 1971), 39.

5. *Science and the Modern World* (New York, Macmillan, 1925), 24.

NOTES TO CHAPTER 1

1. *Restoration Drama, 1660–1700* (4th ed., 1952), 88; issued as Vol. I of *A History of English Drama, 1660–1900*, 6 vols. (Cambridge, England, Cambridge University Press, 1952–59).

2. *The English Heroic Play* (New York, Columbia University Press, 1903), 110.

3. *The Language of Tragedy* (New York, Columbia University Press, 1947), 164.

4. *The Court Wits of the Restoration* (Princeton, Princeton University Press, 1948), 143.

226

5. *A Preface to Restoration Drama* (Boston, Houghton Mifflin, 1965), 67.

6. "Heroic Tragedy," in *Restoration Theatre*, ed. by John R. Brown and Bernard Harris, Stratford-upon-Avon Studies 6 (London, Edward Arnold, 1965), 135.

7. *English Comic Drama, 1700–1750* (1929; rpt. New York, Russell and Russell, 1963), 7.

8. The crucial studies which changed our points of view include: Thomas H. Fujimura, *The Restoration Comedy of Wit* (Princeton, Princeton University Press, 1952); Dale Underwood, *Etherege and the Seventeenth-Century Comedy of Manners* (New Haven, Yale University Press, 1957); Norman N. Holland, *The First Modern Comedies* (Cambridge, Massachusetts, Harvard University Press, 1959).

9. The courtiers are described at some length in John Harold Wilson's *Court Wits of the Restoration.*

10. *Preface to Restoration Drama*, 49.

11. *Of Dramatic Poesy: An Essay*, in *Critical Essays*, I, 87.

12. "Of Heroic Plays," in *Critical Essays*, I, 161.

13. *The English Heroic Play*, 193–94.

14. Chase may be cited as one important authority for our century: "Love and honor were theoretically the subjects of heroic plays . . ." (*ibid.*, 35).

15. "Of Heroic Plays," in *Critical Essays*, I, 158.

16. For two examples see George C. Sherburn, "Heroic Plays and Tragedies," in *A Literary History of England*, ed. by Albert C. Baugh et al. (New York, Appleton-Century-Crofts, 1948), 748–61; and "Heroic Drama," in *A Handbook to Literature*, ed. by W. F. Thrall, A. Hibbard, and C. Hugh Holman (New York, Odyssey, 1960).

17. *The English Heroic Play*, 35, 148–49.

18. This is true, for instance, of Cecil V. Deane's *Dramatic Theory and the Rhymed Heroic Play* (1931; rpt. New York, Barnes and Noble, 1967); Clarence C. Green's *The Neo-Classic Theory of Tragedy in England During the Eighteenth Century* (1934; rpt. New York, Benjamin Blom, 1966); and, more recently, Eugene Waith's *Ideas of Greatness*.

19. These two theories were first described in "English Tragic Theory in the Late Seventeenth Century," *English Literary History*, Vol. XXIX, No. 3 (September, 1962), 306–23. For further treatment, see Rothstein's *Restoration Tragedy* (Madison, University of Wisconsin Press, 1967).

20. *Dryden: A Study in Heroic Characterization* (Baton Rouge, Louisiana State University Press, 1965), 21.

21. *Dryden's Heroic Drama* (Princeton, Princeton University Press, 1965), 95.

22. *Dryden's Major Plays* (London, Oliver and Boyd), 2, 18.

23. *Ibid.*, 38.

24. B. J. Pendlebury is somewhat more cynical: "The setting is remote in time and place, merely that it may be vaguely picturesque and impressive, with no attempt at local or historical colouring." *Dryden's Heroic Plays: A Study of the Origins* (1923; rpt. New York, Russell and Russell, 1967), 93.

25. What the period meant by the epic (heroic) has been elaborately and carefully detailed by H. T. Swedenberg, Jr., in *The Theory of the Epic in England, 1650–1800*, University of California Publications in English 15 (Berkeley, 1944).

26. All quotations from Dryden's poetry, when possible, are from the California edition of *The Works of John Dryden* (Berkeley, University of California Press, 1956–), begun under the joint general editorship of Edward Niles Hooker and H. T. Swedenberg, Jr., and continued by Swedenberg. The published volumes (I–III) of the poems cover the years 1649 to 1692. All other quotations are from *The Poems and Fables of John Dryden*, ed. by James Kinsley (London, Oxford University Press, 1962).

27. For instance, when inappropriateness is sought in *The Beggar's Opera*, Gay often juxtaposes the lyric and pastoral impulse with the laissez faire economics and precarious lives of the thieves and thief takers:

> If any wench Venus's girdle wear,
>   Though she be never so ugly,
> Lilies and roses will quickly appear,
>   And her face look wondrous smugly.
> Beneath the left ear so fit but a cord
>   (A rope so charming a zone is!),
> The youth in his cart hath the air of a lord,
>   And we cry, "There dies an Adonis!"

(Air III)

28. *Art and Illusion: A Study in the Psychology of Pictorial Representation*, Bollingen Series XXXV.5 (New York, Pantheon Books, for the Bollingen Foundation, 1960), 87.

29. *Ibid.*, 217.

30. The windshield is first mentioned as Willy first appears, adding to the other details which illustrate his fatigue, approaching senility, and confusion of time. Arthur Miller, *Death of a Salesman* (New York, Viking, 1949), 14.

31. Anthony Levi points out that for St. Augustine the passions are neither good nor evil, since "moral qualities are predicable only of acts of will." *French Moralists: The Theory of the Passions, 1585 to 1649* (Oxford, Clarendon Press, 1964), 21.

32. The distinction between energy and order provides the thematic structure of Martin Price's admirable book *To the Palace of Wisdom: Studies in Order and Energy from Dryden to Blake* (New York, Doubleday, 1964).

33. Reprinted in *The Continental Model*, ed. by Scott Elledge and Donald Schier (Minneapolis, Carleton College and University of Minnesota Press, 1960), 85.

34. "There is a great difference between mind and body, inasmuch as body is by nature always divisible, and the mind is entirely indivisible." Meditation VI, *Meditations on the First Philosophy*, in *The Philosophical Works of Descartes*, ed. and trans. by Elizabeth S. Haldane and G. R. T. Ross, 2 vols. (1911–12; rpt. London, Cambridge University Press, 1967), I, 196. The pineal gland as connecting link is described in Article 31 of the First Part of *The Passions of the Soul* (*ibid.*, 345–46).

35. *Of the Laws of Ecclesiastical Polity* (I. 7. 3), in *The Works of . . . Mr. Richard Hooker*, ed. by John Keble, 3 vols. (Oxford, at the University Press, 1836), I, 275–76.

36. *Leviathan* (I. 5, 6), in the edition of Herbert W. Schneider (Indianapolis, Bobbs-Merrill, 1958). Hobbes's place in seventeenth-century discussions of the

will is discussed by Basil Willey, in *The Seventeenth-Century Background* (New York, Columbia University Press, 1934), 110–15.

37. "Otway Preserved: Theme and Form in *Venice Preserv'd*," *Studies in Philology*, Vol. LV, No. 3 (July, 1958), 482. Hauser links this idea to Descartes' *Passions of the Soul*.

38. John D. Boyd calls voluntarism the pattern that "best describes the moral climate of the time." *The Function of Mimesis and Its Decline* (Cambridge, Massachusetts, Harvard University Press, 1968), 233.

39. *The Formation of English Neo-Classical Thought* (Princeton, Princeton University Press, 1967), 177.

40. *The Advancement and Reformation of Modern Poetry*, in *The Critical Works of John Dennis*, ed. by Edward Niles Hooker, 2 vols. (Baltimore, Johns Hopkins Press, 1939, 1943), I, 258–59.

41. Cecil Deane traces this characteristic to the French prose romance, in which "interminable discussions hamper the course of . . . action." *Dramatic Theory and the Rhymed Heroic Play*, 9.

42. *Four Stages of Renaissance Style* (Garden City, Doubleday, 1955), 259, 261.

43. The text used is *John Milton: Complete Poems and Major Prose*, ed. by Merritt Y. Hughes (New York, Odyssey, 1957).

44. The phrase is Ruskin's, and implies seeing or perceiving reality free from any predispositions or predilections whatsoever. "The whole technical power of painting depends on our recovery of what may be called the *innocence of the eye*; that is to say, of a sort of childish perception of these flat stains of colour, merely as such, without consciousness of what they signify,—as a blind man would see them if suddenly gifted with sight." *The Elements of Drawing*, in *The Works of John Ruskin*, ed. by E. T. Cook and Alexander Wedderburn, 39 vols. (London, George Allen, 1903–10), XV, 27.

45. *Critical Essays*, I, 222.

46. *Democracy in America* (I. 20), ed. by Phillips Bradley, 2 vols. (New York, Knopf, 1945), II, 85.

47. *Hamlet* was one of Shakespeare's most frequently revived plays in the Restoration (Rothstein, *Restoration Tragedy*, 52). See also Herbert W. Hill, *La Calprenède's Romances and the Restoration Drama*, University of Nevada Studies, Vol. II, No. 3 (1910), and Vol. III, No. 2 (1911); and Eugene Waith, *Ideas of Greatness*.

48. Hugh Trevor-Roper finds Clarendon to be a man interested in " 'secondary natural' causes" for the revolution of 1640, not the evolution of classes, economic forces, or ideas. "What he condemns," Roper writes, "is not 'whig' doctrine . . . but personal inadequacy." "Clarendon and the Practice of History," in *Milton and Clarendon* (Los Angeles, William Andrews Clark Memorial Library, 1965), 35, 37.

49. Exceptions to this rule might be those who hold a determinist doctrine of some sort or those who write of events from the Christian providential view alone.

50. Nevo's entire study is valuable to a discussion of this subject, but Cromwell receives special attention (pp. 74–144). *The Dial of Virtue: A Study of Poems on Affairs of State in the Seventeenth Century* (Princeton, Princeton University Press, 1963).

51. In Dryden's *Astrae Redux* (ll. 288–91) Charles is reminded that his birth was prefigured:

> That Star that at your Birth shone out so bright
> It stain'd the duller Suns Meridian light,
> Did once again its potent Fires renew
> Guiding our eyes to find and worship you.

52. "Thoughts on Various Subjects" (1711), in *The Prose Works of Jonathan Swift*, ed. by Herbert Davis, 14 vols. (Oxford, Basil Blackwell for the Shakespeare Head Press, 1939–1968), I, 244. The full statement is, "The Stoical Scheme of supplying our Wants, by lopping off our Desires; is like cutting off our feet when we want Shoes."

53. George Savile, First Marquis of Halifax, *The Lady's New-Year's Gift: or, Advice to a Daughter*, in *The Complete Works of George Savile, First Marquess of Halifax*, ed. by Walter Raleigh (Oxford, Clarendon Press, 1912), 26; hereafter cited as *Advice to a Daughter*.

54. All quotations from *De Officiis* are from the John Higginbotham translation, *Cicero on Moral Obligation* (Berkeley, University of California Press, 1967).

55. *Nicomachean Ethics* (III. 6), trans. by Martin Oswald (Indianapolis, Bobbs-Merrill, 1962).

56. *Nicomachean Ethics*, III. 7.

57. *De Officiis*, I. 32. 118. Eugene Waith has discussed the entire pattern of heroic choice in *The Herculean Hero* (London, Chatto and Windus, 1962). Rothstein describes the functions of the pastoral dream in *Restoration Tragedy* (pp. 113–20).

58. The central study of the retirement theme in the seventeenth and eighteenth centuries is Maren-Sofie Røstvig's two-volume work, *The Happy Man* (Oslo, Oslo University Press, 1954–1958).

59. This subject will be taken up at greater length in Chapter 4, but it is interesting to note here that this sort of speech is paralleled, and perhaps parodied, in Restoration comedy. Here, for example, is Loveit in *The Man of Mode*: "I could tear myself in pieces. Revenge, nothing but revenge can ease me. Plague, war, famine, fire, all that can bring universal ruin and misery on mankind ..." (II. ii. 264–67).

60. Dryden describes the effect of the Popish plot on the citizenry in a similar figure in *Absalom and Achitophel* (ll. 136–41):

> For, as when raging Fevers boyl the Blood,
> The standing Lake soon floats into a Flood;
> And every hostile Humour, which before
> Slept quiet in its Channels, bubbles o'r:
> So, several Factions from this first Ferment,
> Work up to Foam, and threat the Government.

61. *Hudibras*, ed. by John Wilders (Oxford, Clarendon Press, 1967).

62. Manly, in *The Plain Dealer*, is described as being particularly naive for the exactly converse peculiarity of temper: "he that distrusts most the world trusts most to himself and is but the more easily deceived because he thinks he can't be deceived" (IV. ii. 211–13).

63. *The Diary of Samuel Pepys*, ed. by Robert Latham and William Matthews, 7 vols. published (Berkeley, University of California Press, 1970–), II, 169.

64. This unusual vocabulary of familial role is discussed at length in section 2 of Chapter 2.

65. *The Works of the Learned Isaac Barrow*, ed. by John Tillotson, 2 vols. (London, Brabyson Aylmer, 1700), I, 1–6, 15.

66. *Leviathan*, I. 11.

67. Castiglione's *Book of the Courtier* is mentioned here as an example for the reason that the courtier is an early prototype of the Restoration hero, and many parallels in outlook and morality exist between courtier and hero. These include such matters as the threefold division of appetite, reason, and will (IV. 51). For the inner-outer relationship, such passages as these are typical:

> "It is true that, whether favored by the stars or by nature, some men are born endowed with such graces that they seem not to have been born, but to have been fashioned by the hands of some god, and adorned with every excellence of mind and body; even as there are many others so inept and uncouth that we cannot but think that nature brought them into the world out of spite and mockery. And just as the latter, for the most part, yield little fruit even with constant diligence and good care, so the former with little labor attain to the summit of the highest excellence" (I. 14).

Or:

> "Beauty springs from God and is like a circle, the center of which is goodness. And hence, as there can be no circle without a center, there can be no beauty without goodness. Thus, a wicked soul rarely inhabits a beautiful body, and for that reason outward beauty is a true sign of inner goodness" (IV. 57).

All quotations are from the translation by Charles S. Singleton (Garden City, Doubleday, 1959).

68. The best survey of the eclectic thought called "libertine" is the second chapter, "The Fertile Ground," of Dale Underwood's *Etherege and the Seventeenth-Century Comedy of Manners*.

69. *Leviathan*, I. 8, 13.

70. *Leviathan*, I. 13.

71. These values exist in Restoration comedy as well and will be discussed in Chapter 5.

72. By 1722 even mundane minds were touting the satisfactions of doing good. Bevil Jr., in *The Conscious Lovers*, speaks of that pleasure as a kind of "taste," providing a delight "incapable of satiety, disgust, or penitence" (II. ii. 277–78). For a completely skeptical analysis of the pleasures of doing good, see Paul E. Parnell's "The Sentimental Mask" (*Publications of the Modern Language Association*, Vol. LXXVIII, No. 5 [December, 1963], 529–35). The roots of these notions are traced in the classic article, "Suggestions Toward a Genealogy of the 'Man of Feeling'," by R. S. Crane (*English Literary History*, Vol. I, No. 3 [1934], 205–30). Crane quotes Isaac Barrow as saying in 1671, for example, "nothing indeed [carries] with it a more pure and savoury delight than beneficence" (p. 228).

73. Dryden's interest in such subjects is traced in detail in Philip Harth's *Contexts of Dryden's Thought* (Chicago, University of Chicago Press, 1968); and Sanford Budick's *Dryden and the Abyss of Light* (New Haven, Yale University Press, 1970).

74. *Thirty-Six Sermons and Discourses.* 2 vols. (London, Tonal Boyer, 1728), I, 310.

75. *Works of George Savile,* 5.

76. G. R. Cragg provides a general survey of Restoration religious thought in *From Puritanism to the Age of Reason* (Cambridge, England, Cambridge University Press, 1950). Cragg notes that there was a vigorous attempt within the Church of England at the Restoration to moderate the intensity of religious feeling (p. 10), and such Cambridge Platonists as Benjamin Whichcote cast doubt on faith maintained with fervor: "The more false any one is in his religion, the more fierce and furious in maintaining it; the more mistaken, the more imposing" (quoted by Cragg, p. 41).

77. *Advice to a Daughter,* in *Works of George Savile,* 6.

78. All quotations from Shakespeare are from *The Complete Works of Shakespeare,* ed. by Hardin Craig (Chicago, Scott, Foresman, 1951).

79. *Leviathan,* I. 6.

80. *Leviathan,* I. 14.

NOTES TO CHAPTER 2

1. This is the center of the burlesque element of the play, but not the thematic center. Thematically, the play is more concerned with the "unnaturalness" of heroic drama and the thoughtless pursuit of novelty.

2. The quotations are from the essay, "Tragedy and Melodrama: Speculations on Generic Form," *Texas Quarterly,* Vol. III, No. 2 (1960), 38–39. A somewhat more extended discussion appears in *Tragedy and Melodrama: Versions of Experience* (Seattle, University of Washington Press, 1968), 10–13. The book-length study contends that tragedy arises, not from the death which is often involved, "but what goes wrong within life, the wrong that man does, the doubleness that forbids perfect choices" (p. 27).

3. *Critical Essays,* I, 25; Barbeau, *The Intellectual Design of John Dryden's Heroic Plays* (New Haven, Yale University Press, 1970), 144.

4. *Critical Essays,* I, 42.

5. *Dryden's Heroic Drama,* 75. For an example, see Muly Moluch, in Dryden's *Don Sebastian* (II. i. 347) or the Queen in his *Secret Love* (II. 284–86). Wylie Sypher calls this phenomenon "an examination of the self according to a logic of contradiction" (*Four Stages of Renaissance Style,* 293).

6. *Cavalier Drama* (New York, Modern Language Association, 1936), 61.

7. *Dryden's Heroic Plays,* 117.

8. *The English Heroic Play,* 103.

9. *The Language of Tragedy,* 186–87.

10. *The Advancement of Poetry,* in *Critical Works,* I, 258–59.

11. *The Usefulness of the Stage, ibid.,* 149. See also the quotation in Chapter 1, section 2, above, from *The Advancement of Poetry.*

Joshua Reynolds maintained this view much later, in the eighteenth century:

232

"I suspect that the rigid forms to be observed in tragedy, of admitting nothing that shall divert and recreate, is formed upon what we ought to like if we were endued with perfect wisdom and taste. But that is not the case. We are governed by our passions as well as our reason.

"Man is both a consistent and an inconsistent being. . . . The principles of art must conform to this capricious being." *Portraits by Sir Joshua Reynolds,* ed. by Frederick W. Hilles (New York, McGraw-Hill, 1952), 134–35.

12. *The Advancement of Poetry,* in *Critical Works,* I, 253, 258–59. François Hédelin, Abbé d'Aubignac, in *The Whole Art of the Stage* (1657), says we demand that all changes occur as the result of action, and not by the strength of "precepts and sentences" (Elledge and Schier (eds.), *The Continental Model,* 114).

13. *The Grounds of Criticism in Poetry,* in *Critical Works,* I, 337.

14. *Gulliver's Travels* (II. 3), *Prose Works,* XI, 88.

15. See esp. Hauser, "Otway Preserved," *Studies in Philology,* Vol. LV, No. 3 (July, 1958), 481–93; William H. McBurney, "Otway's Tragic Muse Debauched: Sensuality in *Venice Preserv'd,*" *Journal of English and Germanic Philology,* Vol. LVIII, No. 3 (July, 1959), 380–99; Derek W. Hughes, "A New Look at *Venice Preserv'd,*" *Studies in English Literature,* Vol. XI, No. 3 (Summer, 1971), 437–57; Bessie Proffitt, "Religious Symbolism in Otway's *Venice Preserv'd,*" *Papers on Language and Literature,* Vol. VII, No. 1 (Winter, 1971), 26–37.

16. *Tragedy and Melodrama,* 216.

17. These facts are cited by Brian Vickers in *Classical Rhetoric in English Poetry* (London, Macmillan, 1970), 16.

18. *Tragedy and the Theory of Drama* (Detroit, Wayne State University Press, 1961), 17.

19. *Dryden's Criticism* (Ithaca, Cornell University Press, 1970), 209.

20. *Divine Dialogues* (London, James Flesher, 1668), 13–14.

21. An interesting perspective on the full impact of this impulse can be obtained from later adaptations of Shakespeare. See Chapter 2, "Language," in George C. Branam's *Eighteenth-Century Adaptations of Shakespearean Tragedy* (Berkeley, University of California Press, 1956).

22. *The First Modern Comedies,* 15–16.

23. *The Herculean Hero,* 173.

24. *The Language of Tragedy,* 189. For instance, Jaffeir says to Belvidera:

> What means thy dreadfull story?
> Death, and to morrow? broken limbs and bowels?
> Insulted o'r by a vile butchering Villain?
> By all my fears I shall start out to madness,
> With barely guessing, if the truth's hid longer.

> (IV. 458–62)

25. For one pre-Restoration instance, Hobbes, in his "Answer to Davenant's Preface to *Gondibert*" (1650), distinguishes poetry (the material out of which drama is made) from history: "The subject of a Poem is the manners of men, not natural causes; *manners presented, not dictated*; and manners feigned, as the name of Poesy imports, not found in men" (my italics; reprinted in Joel E. Spingarn's three-volume *Critical Essays of the Seventeenth Century,* first

published by the Clarendon Press [1908–1909; rpt. Bloomington, Indiana University Press, 1957], II, 56). The root source is Aristotle's *Poetics* (II. 1), where the assertion that the "objects of imitation are men in action" is made immediately for poetry.

26. "A Parallel of Poetry and Painting" (1695), in *Critical Essays*, II, 201. This topic has recently been explored by Gerard G. LeCoat, "Comparative Aspects of the Theory of Expression in the Baroque Age," *Eighteenth-Century Studies*, Vol. V, No. 2 (Winter, 1971), 207–23.

27. *Restoration Tragedy*, 163.

28. Lavinia does not stop here, either. She describes at length the sufferings she would willingly undergo to remain faithful:

> Oh! bid me leap (rather then go to *Sylla*)
> From off the Battlements of any Tow'r,
> Or walk in Thievish ways, or bid me lurk
> Where Serpents are: chain me with roaring Bears;
> Or hide me nightly in a Charnell-house
> O're-cover'd quite with Dead mens rattling Bones,
> With reeky Shanks, and yellow chapless Sculls:
> Or bid me go into a new-made Grave,
> And hide me with a Dead man in his Shrowd:
> Things that to hear but told have made me tremble.

(IV. 505–14)

Compare *Venice Preserv'd*, I. 360–69.

29. Stroup and Cooke (eds.), *Works of Nathaniel Lee*, I, 4.

30. *Dryden's Poetry* (Bloomington, Indiana University Press, 1967), 48.

31. Unfortunately, despite the importance of the terms *status* and *role,* sociologists have not achieved consensus on their meanings. William R. Catton, Jr., in "The Development of Sociological Thought" (*Handbook of Modern Sociology,* ed. by Robert E. L. Faris [Chicago, Rand McNally, 1964], 936–43), provides a helpful historical account of the semantic evolution of the terms. In addition, Catton offers a convincing argument for the use of four terms to describe the complex of ideas usually compressed into two or three: *position*—an individual's place in any specific social relationship (e.g., thirty-eight years old, father, plumber); *status*—an individual's rights, privileges, and perquisites as a result of his position; *role*—an individual's duties and obligations as a result of his position; *social rank*—the prestige accorded an individual as a result of his position and his performance in that position. To a nonspecialist like myself, these definitions seem efficient and effective, but because they have not been widely accepted, I have not made use of them in the present study.

32. Kingsley Davis, *Human Society* (New York, Macmillan, 1949), 84, 87.

33. *John Donne: The Anniversaries*, ed. by Frank Manley (Baltimore, Johns Hopkins Press, 1963).

34. Introduction to Kaufmann's edition of *All for Love* (San Francisco, Chandler, 1962), xv. This excellent essay is reprinted with revisions in *Dryden: A Collection of Critical Essays*, ed. by Bernard N. Schilling (Englewood Cliffs, New Jersey, Prentice-Hall, 1963).

Anne Ferry is less convinced that these roles represent substantial psychological or moral possibilities in Antony or tension in the play. Antony and others, she says, "seem absorbed by 'names' almost as independent entities." The characters seem to admit the "irrelevance of words to feelings," and dialogue becomes a matter of mere style. *Milton and the Miltonic Dryden* (Cambridge, Massachusetts, Harvard University Press, 1968), 202, 204–205. The whole of the chapter, "The World Well Lost," presents an important alternative analysis of the play.

David M. Vieth has provided an analysis of this scene in the introduction to his edition of *All for Love* (Lincoln, University of Nebraska Press, 1972), xxii.

35. Arthur Kirsch has drawn special attention to this division in Dryden's plays (*Dryden's Heroic Drama*, 93–96).

36. For example, see the brief discussions in Lowell J. Carr, *Analytical Sociology* (New York, Harper, 1955), 44–46 and n. 3; and John F. Cuber, *Sociology: A Synopsis of Principles* (New York, Appleton-Century, 1963), 301.

37. As translated in *Dramatic Essays of the Neoclassic Age*, ed. by Henry Hitch Adams and Baxter Hathaway (New York, Columbia University Press, 1950), 11–12.

38. *Remarks on a Book Entituled, Prince Arthur* (1696), *Critical Works*, I, 130–31. Dennis illustrates "pathetick *Episodes*" with a reference to Virgil: "In the tenth Book, we see a Son dying for his Father; in the ninth we have a Friend who dies for his Friend. And in the fourth, we find a Mistress who kills her self for her Lover: So that in that admirable Poet we have three Calamities occasion'd by three of the dearest Tyes, that ever were known to Man."

39. Compare this with Queen Mother Elizabeth's ironic response to Richard's request that she woo her daughter for him, in *Richard III* (IV. iv. 337–42).

40. Arthur Kirsch argues: "Aureng-Zebe is less the best of subjects than he is the best of sons, one of the first heralds of the paragons of filial devotion that abound in eighteenth-century plays." In an appended note, Kirsch gives a brief notice of the family relationships in the play. *Dryden's Heroic Drama*, 125–26 and n. 4.

41. *The Herculean Hero*, 199.

42. Arthur Sherbo, in *English Sentimental Drama* (East Lansing, Michigan State University Press, 1957), discusses the sentimental use of status in his third chapter, "Repetition and Prolongation." See pages 46 to 60 for his discussion and examples of the use of children in sentimental drama. It is also apposite to note that, as William H. McBurney has pointed out, Otway treats Jaffeir and Belvidera as lovers, not as a married couple, throughout most of the play ("Otway's Tragic Muse Debauched," *Journal of English and Germanic Philology*, Vol. LVIII, No. 3 [July, 1959], 392).

43. Arrowsmith, *The Reformation* (London, William Cademan, 1673); Sypher, *Four Stages of Renaissance Style*, 250. A similar view of the lack of inner motivation in Dryden's heroic figures is expressed by Zebouni (*Dryden: Heroic Characterization*, 26, 36–41).

44. Sypher, *Four Stages of Renaissance Style*, 261; Rymer, *The Tragedies of the Last Age* (1678), in *The Critical Works of Thomas Rymer*, ed. by Curt A. Zimansky (New Haven, Yale University Press, 1956), 72. *The Maid's Tragedy* as an important prototype of Restoration drama and the dialectical nature of that drama are discussed by Kirsch (*Dryden's Heroic Drama*, 69–74).

45. The diagrams may easily be applied to comedies also. The confusions of

The Way of the World are relieved to some extent by this diagram, which also makes evident Lady Wishfort's central position in the family:

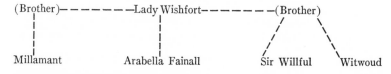

(Brother)— — — — — —Lady Wishfort— — — — —(Brother)

Millamant   Arabella Fainall   Sir Willful   Witwoud

NOTES TO CHAPTER 3

1. *The Restoration Comedy of Wit* was the first study which attempted to reveal the term *manners* as it was understood by the men of the Restoration.

2. "The Grounds of Criticism in Tragedy" (1679), in *Critical Essays*, I, 248.

3. *Restoration Comedy of Wit*, 6–7. Fujimura does not cite Dryden.

4. "Grounds of Criticism in Tragedy," in *Critical Essays*, I, 249–50.

5. *Reflections on Aristotle's Treatise of Poesy in General* (1674), in Elledge and Schier (eds.), *The Continental Model*, 284–85.

6. These passages are from *Remarks on Prince Arthur*, in *Critical Works*, I, 72–75 (my italics).

7. This famous passage is found in Chapter 10 of *Rasselas*. The relationship of the general to the particular has been redefined and illustrated in an important article by Howard D. Weinbrot, "The Reader, the General, and the Particular," *Eighteenth-Century Studies*, Vol. V, No. 1 (Fall, 1971), 80–96.

8. *Remarks on Prince Arthur*, in *Critical Works*, I, 73.

9. "Of Heroic Plays," in *Critical Essays*, I, 163–66.

10. *Intellectual Design of Dryden's Heroic Plays*, 148–49.

11. *Restoration Tragedy*, 159 and n. 12.

12. Dennis, *Remarks on Prince Arthur*, in *Critical Works*, I, 71.

13. *Reflections on Aristotle's Treatise of Poesy*, in Elledge and Schier (eds.), *The Continental Model*, 285.

14. *Advice to a Daughter*, in *Works of George Savile*, 26.

15. Rosemond Tuve has shown that decorum relies upon a hierarchy of values. See her *Elizabethan and Metaphysical Imagery* (Chicago, University of Chicago Press, 1947), 234.

16. *Art and Illusion*, 87.

17. Quoted in D. R. M. Wilkinson's *The Comedy of Habit* (Leiden, Universitaire Pers, 1964), 49. All of Part I of this interesting study is of value in coming to understand the concept of decorum in the Restoration milieu.

18. *De Officiis*, I. 4. 14.

19. Quoted by Michael Macklem, in *The Anatomy of the World: Relations Between Natural and Moral Law from Donne to Pope* (Minneapolis, University of Minnesota Press, 1958), 68.

20. For a comic analogue to this, see my article "Comic Worlds Within Worlds," *College English*, Vol. XXXII, No. 4 (January, 1971), 418–27.

21. *Reflections on Aristotle's Treatise of Poesy*, in Elledge and Schier (eds.), *The Continental Model*, 291. See also Tuve, *Elizabethan and Metaphysical Imagery*, 192. Decorum is the touchstone of all rules.

22. *Discourse on Tragedy* (1639), in Elledge and Schier (eds.), *The Continental Model*, 59.

236

23. *Critical Essays*, I, 277.

24. Preface to Rymer's translation of Rapin's *Reflections*, in *Critical Works of Rymer*, 8.

25. *Some Remarks on the Tragedy of* Hamlet, Prince of Denmark, in *Eighteenth-Century Critical Essays*, ed. by Scott Elledge, 2 vols. (Ithaca, Cornell University Press, 1961), I, 451.

26. Walter Jackson Bate, in *The Burden of the Past and the English Poet* (Cambridge, Massachusetts, Belknap Press of Harvard University Press, 1970), speaks of this effect, although he is interested in another aspect of decorum (pp. 17–20).

27. *Critical Essays*, II, 201. Dryden's essay is prefixed to his translation of C. A. du Fresnoy's *De arte graphica*.

28. This idea holds through the eighteenth century and appears, for instance, in the Preface to *The London Merchant* (1731).

29. *Tragedies of the Last Age*, in *Critical Works of Rymer*, 63.

30. "Grounds of Criticism in Tragedy," in *Critical Essays*, I, 251–52.

31. "A Short Discourse on the English Stage" (1664), in Spingarn (ed.), *Critical Essays of the Seventeenth Century*, II, 94.

32. *Restoration Comedy of Wit*, 24. It seems to me that Truewits are not only men of taste but also typically men of intelligence and worldly wisdom, as, for example, are Dorimant and Mirabell. Witwouds often possess wit, but they lack wisdom. Decorum is a sign of wisdom.

33. *The Burden of the Past*, 20.

34. D. R. M. Wilkinson and others have argued strenuously to establish the stereotypical nature of Restoration comedy as well. "The bewildering speed and surface complexity of Restoration comic dialogue is a cover to the dramatic poverty of playwrights who consistently employed stock assumptions, a stock manner and stock devices" (*The Comedy of Habit*, 114).

35. Perhaps this is obvious, but this phenomenon is easily illustrated in the plastic arts. The outrage which is prompted by violated decorums, ignored conventions, is passionate and predictable and appears with each innovation, whether successful or not. Often the innovation prompts the basic question, as when the startled witness to William de Kooning asks, "Is that art?"

36. Swedenberg, *Theory of the Epic*, 310.

NOTES TO CHAPTER 4

1. "Of Simplicity in Poetical Compositions" (1711, pub. 1721), *Critical Works*, II, 36. Rapin describes another quality of diction—"that it be harmonious, that it may maintain that great and majestick Air, with which Poetry is wont to adorn it self, and may express all the Force and the utmost Dignity of the great Things which it utters" (p. 37).

2. *Boswell's London Journal*, ed. by Frederick A. Pottle (New York, McGraw-Hill, 1950), 83.

3. "Of Heroic Plays," in *Critical Essays*, I, 157. Aristotle maintains that tragic diction should be elevated, "embellished with each kind of artistic adornment" (*Poetics*, VI. 2).

4. *Rhetoric*, III. 5, "Stylistic Purity."

5. *Augustan Poetic Diction* (London, University of London Press, 1964), 53.

6. "Grounds of Criticism in Tragedy," in *Critical Essays*, I, 255. Dryden explains bombast in this way: " 'Tis the Bristol-stone, which appears like a diamond; 'tis an extravagant thought, instead of a sublime one; 'tis roaring madness, instead of vehemence; and a sound of words, instead of sense" (*ibid.*, 259). Sarup Singh sees rhyme as the cause of rant and bombast (*The Theory of Drama in the Restoration Period* [Bombay, Orient Longmans, 1963], 119–20).

7. Preface to *Alaric, or Rome Defeated*, in Elledge and Schier (eds.), *The Continental Model*, 88. Scudéry's source is the "Ciceronian" handbook of rhetoric, *Ad Herennium* (see, for example, IV. x. 15–xi. 16).

8. *Tragedy and the Theory of Drama*, 258.

9. Preface to *The Court of Death*, in *Critical Works*, I, 44.

10. *Reflections on Aristotle's Treatise of Poesy*, in Elledge and Schier (eds.), *The Continental Model*, 289.

11. "Grounds of Criticism in Tragedy," in *Critical Essays*, I, 260.

12. Branam, *Eighteenth-Century Adaptations of Shakespearean Tragedy*, 90.

13. Swedenberg, *Theory of the Epic*, 335.

14. Some of the plays produced about 1680 were Dryden's and Lee's *Oedipus* (1678), Dryden's *Troilus and Cressida* (1679), Otway's *Caius Marius* (1680), Crowne's *The Misery of Civil-War* (1680), Lee's *Theodosius* (1680), Banks's *The Unhappy Favourite* (1681), and Otway's *Venice Preserv'd* (1682).

15. See John Loftis' balanced introduction to his edition of the play (Lincoln, University of Nebraska Press, 1967); and Stroup and Cooke, *Works of Nathaniel Lee*, II, 317–19.

16. *The Herculean Hero*, 172.

17. "Of Heroic Plays," in *Critical Essays*, I, 157.

18. Prologue, *Every Man in His Humour* (1616), in *Ben Jonson*, ed. by C. H. Herford and Percy Simpson, 11 vols. (Oxford, Clarendon Press, 1925–52), III, 303.

19. "The Imagery of *All for Love*," in Twentieth-Century Interpretations of *All for Love*, ed. by Bruce King (Englewood Cliffs, New Jersey, Prentice-Hall, 1968), 42; reprinted from *Proceedings of the Leeds Philosophical and Literary Society*, Vol. V (1940), 140–47.

20. Eric Rothstein says: "Directness, argumentative strength, moral generalization, and passionate appeal all characterize the style of the pathetic tragedy at its best" (*Restoration Tragedy*, 160).

21. Elder Olson argues that dialogue is dramatic only "when speeches become verbal actions, when dialogue . . . becomes interaction between the characters" (*Tragedy and the Theory of Drama*, 180). This position is too extreme if it is understood to exclude self-expression or reverie as action.

22. *A Short View of Tragedy*, in *Critical Works* of Rymer, 86.

23. Dryden has Lisideius say: "Dying is a thing which none but a Roman gladiator could naturally perform on the stage, when he did not imitate or represent, but naturally do it; and therefore it is better to omit the representation of it" (*Of Dramatic Poesy*, in *Critical Essays*, I, 51).

24. This feature of Caroline drama has been discussed by Alfred Harbage in *Cavalier Drama* (p. 37) and by Arthur Kirsch in *Dryden's Heroic Drama* (p. 30).

25. For a famous version of this, see Jaffeir's "tame lamb to sacrifice" speech, in *Venice Preserv'd* (IV. i. 86–95). Otway does as Lee has done—he supplies an

image provocative of pity (a little lamb led bleating to slaughter) in the place of self-expression. For one discussion, see McBurney's criticism of the "verbal excess" in *Venice Preserv'd* ("Otway's Tragic Muse Debauched," *Journal of English and Germanic Philology*, Vol. LVIII, No. 3 [July, 1959], 398).

26. Demetrius is quoted in Vickers, *Classical Rhetoric in English Poetry*, 96.

27. Lemaistre is quoted in Peter France, *Racine's Rhetoric* (Oxford, Clarendon Press, 1965), 39.

28. *Critical Essays*, I, 60.

29. "On the Characters of Tragedies" (1672), in Elledge and Schier (eds.), *The Continental Model*, 150.

30. *Remarks on Prince Arthur*, in *Critical Works*, I, 135.

31. *Restoration Tragedy*, 167–69.

32. *The Observer*, No. 77 (1785), in Elledge (ed.), *Eighteenth-Century Critical Essays*, II, 950.

33. See Chapter 2 of Branam's *Eighteenth-Century Adaptations of Shakespearean Tragedy* and the introduction to *Five Restoration Adaptations of Shakespeare*, ed. by Christopher Spencer (Urbana, University of Illinois Press, 1965).

34. *Etherege and the Seventeenth-Century Comedy of Manners*, 94–95. The complete discussion takes up all of Chapter 6, "The Comic Language."

35. *The Language of Natural Description in Eighteenth-Century Poetry* (Ann Arbor, University of Michigan Press, 1949), x.

36. Prior, *The Language of Tragedy*, 155.

37. Prior writes: "In the heroic plays, barring certain figurative words such as flame and fire which are common equivalents for love, the greatest number of the images are, generally speaking, built on an explicit pattern including even occasional 'as when' similes of the epic style" (*ibid.*, 170).

38. *The Tatler*, ed. by George A. Aitken, 4 vols. (London, Duckworth, 1898–99), I, 385–86.

39. *Tragedy and the Theory of Drama*, 9.

40. *The Death of Tragedy* (London, Faber and Faber, n.d. [1961]), 60.

41. The phrase "Monarch of his House" and others like it are certainly metaphors, but moribund if not dead in this context. It is possible to revitalize them, and Dryden and Racine, for example, occasionally do so. See France, *Racine's Rhetoric*, 66–71.

42. *The Death of Tragedy*, 70.

43. *John Dryden and the Poetry of Statement*, first American ed. (East Lansing, Michigan State University Press, 1969), 61.

44. *The Poetics of Reason* (New York, Random House, 1968), 71.

45. *The Comedy of Habit*, 24.

46. *Tragedy and the Theory of Drama*, 107.

47. *Dryden's Poetry*, 35.

48. Letter to John Taylor, February 27, 1818, in *The Letters of John Keats*, ed. by Hyder Edward Rollins, 2 vols. (Cambridge, Massachusetts, Harvard University Press, 1958), I, 238–39.

49. There are important psychological and aesthetic differences between the mechanical and organic views of reality and art, and I do not mean to minimize them. Instead, I wish to suggest that both views, on this issue at least, come very close to suggesting that there is only *one* right word in each context, no matter

whether it got there by choice or by growth. For an exposition of the differences between the two views, one might read Paul Fussell's *The Rhetorical World of Augustan Humanism* (Oxford, Clarendon Press, 1965).

50. Gombrich, *Art and Illusion*, 10 and *passim*.

51. A classic discussion of the limits and benefits of historical relativism is Chapter 4 of René Wellek's and Austin Warren's *Theory of Literature*, third ed. (New York, Harcourt, 1956).

NOTES TO CHAPTER 5

1. *The British Drama* (New York, Appleton-Century, 1950), 215.

2. "Heroic Tragedy," in Brown and Harris (eds.), *Restoration Theatre*, 141.

3. Hobbes lists the use of metaphors as one of the four abuses of language. It is wrong, he says, to use words "in other senses than that they are ordained for—and thereby deceive others" (*Leviathan*, I. 4). Locke, in *An Essay Concerning Human Understanding* (1700), admitted metaphors in some circumstances, but never in discourses which "pretend to inform or instruct." "All the art of rhetoric, besides order and clearness; all the artificial and figurative application of words eloquence hath invented, are for nothing else but to insinuate wrong ideas, move the passions, and thereby mislead the judgment; and so indeed are perfect cheats" (III. 10. 34). The edition is that of Alexander C. Fraser, in two volumes (Oxford, Clarendon Press, 1894).

4. Almanzor's simile reveals that inappropriateness discussed in the preceding chapter. If he were to stop with the comparison to the brook, the simile would be trite but harmless. Expansion of the simile into metaphor, in lines 46 and 47, takes the speech out of drama and turns it to narrative. The last two lines describe a brook, not Almanzor, and are therefore dramatically irrelevant.

5. "Parallel of Poetry and Painting," in *Critical Essays*, II, 184.

6. This has been persuasively argued by Charles O. McDonald, in "Restoration Comedy as Drama of Satire; An Investigation into Seventeenth Century Aesthetics," *Studies in Philology*, Vol. LXI, No. 3 (July, 1964), 522–44.

7. For a reading of *The Way of the World* as "an insufferably dull play," see A. N. Kaul, *The Action of English Comedy* (New Haven, Yale University Press, 1970), 101–103. A recent statement in the controversy surrounding Manly is made by Ben Ross Schneider, Jr., in *The Ethos of Restoration Comedy* (Urbana, University of Illinois Press, 1971), 97–100.

8. Schneider discusses this quality, in *The Ethos of Restoration Comedy* (p. 26). The term is important to Castiglione's *The Courtier* (I. 26, p. 43).

9. Aureng-Zebe is rarely flurried, even superficially: "Aureng-Zebe, by no strong passion swayed, / Except his Love, more temp'rate is, and weigh'd" (I. i).

10. For the libertine, as Underwood shows, nature—that is, man's spontaneous inclinations—was identified with freedom and pleasure and opposed by all manner of custom, including law (*Etherege and the Seventeenth-Century Comedy of Manners*, 13–14).

11. See John Winterbottom, "The Development of the Hero in Dryden's Tragedies," *Journal of English and Germanic Philology*, Vol. LII, No. 2 (April, 1953), 161–73; Zebouni, *Dryden: Heroic Characterization*, 37; Waith, *The Herculean Hero*, 151, 201. Waith finds Almanzor "not so much disciplined as he is educated towards a larger vision" (p. 161). Rothstein disagrees with the

notion of development in Dryden's characters (*Restoration Tragedy*, 56–57 and n. 7).

12. January 8, 1663. In February, 1669, after another performance, Pepys wrote, "We are well pleased with seeing it." Quoted in Helen McAfee's *Pepys on the Restoration Stage* (New Haven, Yale University Press, 1916), 192–94.

13. I was first made aware of the art-nature contrast in this scene by J. W. Corder's unpublished Ph.D. dissertation, "The Restoration Way of the World: A Study of Restoration Comedy" (University of Oklahoma, 1958).

14. The freight of custom is often contrasted with a hedonistic nature by libertines and villains. Nourmahal, in *Aureng-Zebe* (IV, p. 51), gives a graphic example:

> Custom our Native Royalty does awe;
> Promiscuous Love is Nature's general Law:
> For whosoever the first Lovers were,
> Brother and Sister made the second Pair.

15. The implications of *The Country Wife* are not clear to me in this regard. As I read the play, Wycherley has, in fact, shown us a man successfully avoiding the standard morality, and we are asked to allow his antisocial behavior to go unpunished because of the foolishness of those whom he deceives. Horner, then, is a social scourge while, ironically, being antisocial.

16. *The Ethos of Restoration Comedy*, 22.

17. See my essay, "The Coherence of *The Orphan*," *Texas Studies in Literature and Language*, Vol. XI, No. 2 (Summer, 1969), 931–43.

18. *Wild Civility: The English Comic Spirit on the Restoration Stage* (Bloomington, Indiana University Press, 1970), 21, 88–89, 147, and *passim*.

19. Horner, in *The Country Wife*, also attempts to live by unchecked will, and Horner is successful. He does not fit the pattern I am describing.

20. Wilkinson, *The Comedy of Habit*, 57, 67, and *passim*. Kaul echoes this judgment in *The Action of English Comedy*: "The bulk of Restoration comedy involves little beyond a flat exemplification of a value system or a philosophy which, in its turn, rests on a set of remarkably uncomplicated and unexamined assumptions" (p. 90).

21. *The Comedy of Habit*, 65.

22. Ernest Bernbaum makes this distinction in *The Drama of Sensibility* (Boston, Ginn, 1915), 78. For a more recent discussion, see Robert D. Stock, *Samuel Johnson and Neoclassical Dramatic Theory* (Lincoln, University of Nebraska Press, 1973), especially Chapter 2.

23. Rothstein, *Restoration Tragedy*, 113–20.

24. See, for example, B. R. Fone, "Colley Cibber's *Love's Last Shift* and Sentimental Comedy," *Restoration and Eighteenth-Century Theatre Research*, Vol. VII, No. 1 (1968), 33–43. The standard history of the shift to sentimental drama remains Bernbaum's *The Drama of Sensibility*.

25. *A Study of the Word "Sentimental" and of Other Linguistic Characteristics of Eighteenth Century Sentimentalism in England, Annales* of the Academia Scientiarum Fennica, Series B, Vol. LXXIV (Helsinki, 1951).

26. *English Sentimental Drama*, 2. Erämetsä finds *sentimentally* used in 1746 and *sentimental* used by Samuel Richardson in 1748 (*A Study of the Word "Sentimental,"* 18).

27. *The Drama of Sensibility*, 2.

28. *English Sentimental Drama*, 25.

29. When reading eighteenth-century writings, we must remain aware that the word *sentimental* carries there the meanings "full of sound judgments, opinions," and "highly moral, sententious," as well as, later in the century, connoting emotion. But, in present-day usage, I am suggesting that scholars adopt a less recondite definition.

30. *Restoration Tragedy*, 92. For a critical examination of the idea of *excess* as the key to definitions of sentimentality, see the review essay by Brian Wilkie, "What Is Sentimentality?" *College English*, Vol. XXVIII, No. 8 (May, 1967), 564–75.

31. *Leviathan*, I. 6.

32. Preface to *Don Carlos*, in *Works of Thomas Otway*, I, 174.

33. All of the quotations are from the dedication of *The London Merchant*. As a point of comparison, here is Dryden's definition of tragedy (a loose translation of Aristotle), from "The Grounds of Criticism in Tragedy": " 'Tis an imitation of one entire, great, and probable action; not told, but represented; which, by moving in us fear and pity, is conducive to the purging of those two passions in our minds" (*Critical Essays*, I, 243).

34. "Tragedy and the Common Man" appeared first in the New York *Times*, February 27, 1949, section 2.

35. "Popular" here is not pejorative or condescending. I wish to suggest only that we do not, as a culture, share a single definition of tragedy. There have been many exciting attempts at definition, each with many followers, but there has been no consensus.

36. All quotations are from *Collected Works of Oliver Goldsmith*, ed. by Arthur Friedman, 5 vols. (Oxford, Clarendon Press, 1966), III, 209–13.

37. *Tragedy and the Theory of Drama*, 28.

38. *A Short View of Tragedy*, in *Critical Works of Rymer*, 86.

39. *Of Dramatic Poesy*, in *Critical Essays*, I, 25.

40. For examples of the refreshing possibilities of this approach, see Christopher Spencer, "A Word for Tate's *King Lear*," *Studies in English Literature*, Vol. III, No. 2 (Spring, 1963), 241–51; and James Black, "The Influence of Hobbes on Nahum Tate's *King Lear*," *ibid.*, Vol. VII, No. 3 (Summer, 1967), 377–85.

Index

The paper on which this book is printed bears the watermark of the University of Oklahoma Press and has an effective life of at least three hundred years.